Digital Rights Management

NAB EXECUTIVE TECHNOLOGY BRIEFINGS SERIES

A series developed jointly between Focal Press and National Association of Broadcasters

The NAB Executive Technology Briefing Series consist of titles addressing current and future industry technologies, authored by experienced and well-known professionals, often industry consultants, for managers and investors in the industry. Readers should have an introductory to an intermediate level of knowledge of the technology. The primary goals of each title in the series are as follows:

- Provide the reader with a working knowledge of the topic. Each title clearly explains the technology discussed, the end-result providing the reader with a general technical understanding to adequately converse with industry engineers and other technology professionals.

- Discusses the impact (past, present and future) that the technology had/has/will have on the industry. This includes-but not limited to: financial implications, human resource implications, how the technology will change the industry, competitive considerations, advertising/marketing considerations, legal/legislative ramifications.

- Identify investment opportunities in the industry. Each title outlines not only areas of opportunity but also the risks that may be involved.

NAB EXECUTIVE TECHNOLOGY BRIEFINGS

Digital Rights Management

Joan Van Tassel

AMSTERDAM • BOSTON • HEIDELBERG • LONDON
NEW YORK • OXFORD • PARIS • SAN DIEGO
SAN FRANCISCO • SINGAPORE • SYDNEY • TOKYO

Focal Press Is an Imprint of Elsevier

Acquisitions Editor:	Angelina Ward
Project Manager:	Paul Gottehrer
Marketing Manager	Christine Degon Veroulis
Assistant Editor:	Rachel Epstein
Cover Design:	Frances Baca Design
Interior Design:	Frances Baca Design
Composition and Illustration:	Umbrella Graphics
Indexer:	Borrego Publishing (borregopublishing.com)

Focal Press is an imprint of Elsevier
30 Corporate Drive, Suite 400, Burlington, MA 01803, USA
Linacre House, Jordan Hill, Oxford OX2 8DP, UK

Recognizing the importance of preserving what has been written, Elsevier prints its books on acid-free paper whenever possible.

Library of Congress Cataloging-in-Publication Data
Application submitted

British Library Cataloguing-in-Publication Data
A catalogue record for this book is available from the British Library.

ISBN 13: 978-0-240-80722-5
ISBN 10: 0-240-80722-7

For information on all Focal Press publications
visit our website at www.books.elsevier.com

Printed in the United States of America

06 07 08 09 10   10 9 8 7 6 5 4 3 2 1

Printed in the United States of America

005.8
v28d

Contents

*Dedicated to
my mentors, with thanks and love:*

*Lucille Newton-Van Tassel
James Bromley
Mary Murphy
and Clancy Imislund*

Acknowledgments

There are always many people to thank for the ideas and support that make it possible to spend four years writing a book. I would like to begin with the people at PricewaterhouseCoopers, who have always treated me so well. Peter Winkler manages to be both gracious and demanding, always requiring the best possible work. Laura School is an excellent editor and a pleasure to work with. Former consultants Blake White and John Stubbs are both expert at content protection and monetization business issues. There's a reason they have advised clients at the highest level – they are brilliant and focused.

Richard Doherty, founder and CEO of Envisioneering is a friend, colleague and employer. We manage these multiple roles without too much difficulty, although Carolyn Doherty's calm is always a blessing. Rick is so well-connected and knowledgeable that always rely on him to point me in the right direction to solve a particularly knotty problem. A gifted writer himself, he also imposes the highest standards on the work I've done for him; but I always see him placing the same demands on himself. He is, quite simply, a wonderful human being.

Harry Jessell has provided opportunities to delve into the guts of television technology. I ask myself, how do I keep meeting these professionally demanding men, but I am much the better for it. Harry is a journalist's journalist – I never want to have a conversation with him until I have gathered the facts and have a pretty good grasp on the story. He has teamed up with Kathy Haley to launch www.tvnewsday.com, which will cover the business of television. They're a great combination and I think this enterprise could become a powerhouse in the industry.

Jane Kagon, Director of the UCLA Extension School Entertainment Studies and Performing Arts program, has allowed me to teach classes that focus on some part of work I am doing. By teaching, I learn myself, and Jane and UCLA Extension School have provided a laboratory for everyone to explore the cutting edge of the world of entertainment in the heart of its capitol. The school's contributions to the industry and students are nothing short of immense.

I met Mark Cuban before he was the Mark Cuban, and yes, he was always charismatic, controversial, entertaining, handsome, and dazzlingly intelligent. But it's his ideas that really count. I believe his influence on entertainment are and will continue to be profound. I once said to him that I hoped someday he would head a studio and I think he will. I hope so. He has a vision of the future and he expresses it in a clear and direct manner that points the way to maximum benefit for the entertainment industry and its customers. This book quotes him directly, but it also reflects the influence he has had on my thinking about digital rights management. Thank you, Mark.

I've also learned a great deal by attending industry conferences and events put on by iHollywood Forums, headed by Michael and Zahava Stroud, and Victor Harwood's Digital Hollywood. The events they put together with Hollywood insiders discussing such a rapidly-evolving industry have become important ways for people at all levels in the industry to learn about the state of the art. The events are well-thought out and well-attended, and I'm grateful to them for the opportunities I've had to hear from a range of high-level people in a short periods of time.

A particularly useful conference that was very helpful in the writing of this book was the 2004 DRM Conference and Expo, put on by JupiterMedia. It was an intense week for both presenters and attendees, and its specific focus brought out industry people who do not normally attend such shows. I was able to learn about the approaches, strategies, and experiments that the studios and labels were considering for adoption, and it added a great deal to the book.

Many experts guided me through the complex technologies that make up DRM. Raj Samtani, director of sales and marketing at ContentGuard, Carter Laren, senior security architect at Cryptography Research, and Reed Stager, vice president of corporate licensing, marketing, and public policy for Digimarc Corp. have all taken the time to help me understand their parcel of the DRM landscape.

Finally, James Bromley and Steve Rose have always given me the benefit of their expertise about industry technologies. They both taught me about the digital revolution back when most people thought digital referred to fingers. I learned the basics at the Annenberg School for Communication at the University of Southern California from my dissertation chair, Peter Clark, and then-Assistant Dean, Susan Evans. To all these people who gave me a peak over the horizon at a future that, unbeknownst to me at the time, was rushing full-speed ahead aimed directly at all of us, thank you.

Author Biography

Joan Van Tassel is a journalist, researcher, and author who specializes in the effects of digital technologies on the business of entertainment and media. She has written five books on these topics, and received the National Cable Center Book Award for contributions to the cable telecommunications industry, and the Kraszna-Kraus Award for excellence in the writing of a technical book. She was an award-winning documentary filmmaker before completing her doctorate in new media at the Annenberg School for Communication at the University of Southern California, giving her an extensive background in both professional and academic arenas. Joan continues to produce documentary works and to write about entertainment and media technologies. She also teaches at the UCLA Extension School in the Entertainment Studies and Performing Arts program.

1 Industry Overview

In a sense, rights management has always been part of the entertainment business landscape. After all, the first principle of the media and entertainment business is that content owners have to get their wares into the hands, or ears, or in front of the eyeballs of consumers to make money.

Paying to see or hear entertainment is a centuries-old practice that continues into the electronic world. Until now. Today, millions of people are freeloading copyrighted music and movies from Internet peer-to-peer networks without paying the creators, producers, marketers, or distributors of them. This free-for-all is just the most recent in a cascade of events that have steadily increased the risks of distributing their high-value material for content owners.

Protecting the Mouse from the mouse

In late 2004, Peter Lee, vice president of business development for the Walt Disney Company, delivered the keynote speech to a packed audience at the *Digital Rights Management Strategies* conference in Los Angeles, hosted by Jupiter Research. Disney is known to experiment with cutting edge digital rights management (DRM) systems and to test a wide array of entertainment technologies. But, like most entertainment giants, the company rarely discusses its strategies and tactics concerning DRM publicly. So an eager Hollywood audience awaited Peter Lee.

He did not disappoint. Laying out an unusually detailed presentation of a studio's approach to DRM, Lee articulated a vision of the near future that puts DRM at the center of the company's consumer strategy—and more. Lee described the range of activities in which DRM potentially plays a role: studios in the U.S., Europe, and Asia; theme parks and other destination parks; cruise lines; the ABC television and radio networks; online properties; and, finally, physical goods properties, such as home video products. The company is even using DRM in the enterprise as a way of tracking and protecting sensitive corporate communications and documents.

"As we look at content protection and DRM, we see that it impacts us in diverse units across a variety of global boundaries," Lee noted. "Broadly, we approach DRM as a way for us, for rights holders, to manage the terms and conditions of digital content delivery."

Disney is responding to the ways that digital delivery changes how consumers do things. As consumers receive high value content over broadband connections, they have started to alter their habits. Take the purchase of music: "When we look at consumers today, we are seeing how they are embracing the new digital technologies," said Lee. "Everyone knows how popular iPod is. But this business model was enabled through rights management that allowed content producers and distributors to make music available, not just as albums and collections, but as individual songs. And it's not just rental. There's purchase by download to own, download to burn, download to playback on a variety of devices. And there are creative options centered on subscription as well."

Lee's point was that the ability to manage the terms and conditions gives rights holders the confidence they need to distribute their content in a networked environment. And DRM is the primary mechanism they are using to manage those T's and C's.

The presence of DRM gave impetus to a Disney experiment called Moviebeam. It's a movie service that was initially launched in Salt Lake City; Spokane, Wash.; and Jacksonville, Fla. Consumers pay $6.99 a month to get a set-top box (STB) with a hard drive that is pre-loaded with 100 movies. In addition, the company attaches its signal in an unused portion of a broadcast signal, sending ten new movies a week to the STB. Customers use a remote to scan the library, watch trailers, and select films. At launch, first run movies cost $3.99 and catalog features $2.49, with a 24-hour viewing window. Billing information goes out over a phone line connected to the STB.

Disney is comfortable releasing its properties over Moviebeam because it is DRM-protected, using proprietary technology. However, the company doesn't just rely on a single DRM technology. Disney embeds special identifiers in its motion pictures, including digital watermarks and Digital Object Identifiers (DOI). Apart from movies, the company marks its television programming with the broadcast flag in the signals of its broadcast content and will use digital watermarking to track over-the-air ads to aid the ad reconciliation and payment process.

These are just the static, unchanging methods of copy protection Disney uses. But the company also experiments with systems that have "extensible rules" that change over the life cycle of the content. For example, a DRM system might display one price for a motion picture when it is classified as first-run, and then lower the price after a specified date when it becomes part of the catalog inventory.

> Disney plays an active role in the rights standardization process. The company is involved in the ongoing work of the Advanced Access Content System (AACS), SmartRight, the Digital Transmission Content Protection group, Content Protection Technologies Working Group, and many others.

According to Lee, while consumers like the simple traditional business models that they are familiar with—rental, purchase, and subscription—there are going to be new models. "There is no one single answer as to how DRM will roll out in the future," he said. "It is still a new technology, one that we are embracing and experimenting with in many different areas. We don't know yet what they are going to be or how they will work. Our approach as we address the challenges of the new ways to deliver content is to ask ourselves how we can use DRM to reach customers with new value models that let them obtain and utilize digital content."

Disney is not alone in its preoccupation with DRM. Every large entertainment company in the world is actively seeking to understand how to conduct business in the digital world. Entertainment may not be the most technology-friendly of industries, but it is one of the most technology-aware. After all, it came into existence via the fortuitous juxtaposition of performing and technology, and its growth spurts usually come on waves of advances in production and distribution methods and machinery.

Copy Protection and Monetization—the Old-Fashioned Way

In the good old days, the principal device to control the terms and conditions for viewing movies was the box office. All things considered, the box office is a marvel of promotion, product information, content security and monetization. It is an appealing, efficient mechanism that ensures that people who see a performance or a movie actually pay for it. Only the most persistent and devious 12-year olds are able to circumvent the box office and nearby ticket takers. So tied was it to revenue in its early days, its very name became synonymous with income from entertainment: a movie's b.o., or box office.

To begin with, the box office is attractive, decorated and lit in accordance with the overall themed environment of the theater itself. It also provides considerable metadata: It tells customers a movie's start time, running time, location, and cost. The box office is the velvet glove hiding the iron fist that moves customers from the critical point where they take out their wallets to the place where they take their seat.

(DRM) technologies have not yet reached the elegant effectiveness of the box office. Little attention has been paid to their attractiveness; indeed, they appear to be created in a manner to repel consumers. However, they must do a job the box office never had to do—protecting the content in transit. In a theater, the audience comes to the content; over a digital network, the content comes to the audience.

Moreover, the context of that delivery is the consumer's home. Almost everyone expects to exercise control over their homes and its contents. So, when intellectual property in the form of downloaded music, programs, and movies comes into the house, it cannot be surprising that people expect to control it as they see fit.

The need for transport protection is the one of the defining properties of DRM systems. So is the requirement for on-going protection, even as the content resides in the most intimate of environments, the home.

The other elements of the entertainment selling proposition that were previously handled by the physical box office—attracting an audience, providing information about the content, creating business models and monetizing them—can be handled in many ways in the digital world. Each of these functions may be tied to DRM, and may even be incorporated into it. And in some DRM products, they are. But if there were no network transport or expectation of control in the domestic context, there would be little need for DRM systems at all.

Content Is King!

In testimony on worldwide piracy before the House Government Reform Committee on September 23, 2004, John G. Malcolm, Motion Picture Association of America senior vice president and director of worldwide anti-piracy operations, said the copyright industries employ "3.5 percent of the American workforce and have created jobs at a rate more than three times faster than the rest of the economy" and "earn more money abroad than automobiles, airplanes and agriculture." He said that the movie industry has a "surplus trade balance with every single country in the world, and no other American industry can make that claim."

In 1999, the IIPA estimated that content owners' losses due to piracy reached $8.3 billion. In 2004, the Motion Picture Association of America estimates that the movie business alone lost $3.5 billion. In 2001, the sales of music CDs dropped 8% from the previous year. A casual search of the Internet will reveal the availability for download of popular film titles through such peer-to-peer programs as Morpheus, KaZaA and others even before they are released in theaters. One can get almost any music track from these same sites, and it's as easy as downloading music ever was during Napster's heyday.

Content Is Big Business

Content is central to the economic health of national and regional economies, as well as some of the world's largest corporations. A recent study by the International Intellectual Property Alliance (IIPA) estimates that the copyright industries; filmed entertainment, music, books, magazines, newspapers, computer and software contributed $791.2 billion, or about 7.75%, to the U.S. 2001 gross domestic product.

Content providers have always viewed piracy as a serious problem, but in the last few years, use of unlicensed content has undergone explosive growth and threatens to undermine the very foundations of both traditional businesses and electronic commerce. One for heightened concern on the part of content owners is the increased level of consumer access to high-speed Internet connections in countries around the world, as shown in Table 1.1. Prior to the advent of the Internet, pirates who engaged in wholesale infringements of copyrighted works served mostly local or regional markets. There were some limited exceptions, such as optical media pirates in Asia and Central Europe who managed to serve global markets.

However, with broadband connections to the Internet, pirates offering and distributing infringing product can now reach any part of the world with great ease, no matter where they are located. Borders and distances no longer matter. Content providers are trying to act before piracy spins irretrievably out of control. But how? The options they see are:

- **Do nothing.** Accept the concept that "content on the Internet should be free," and earn revenue from other sources, such as advertising;

- **Fight back.** Establish new legal and regulatory environments to defeat electronic piracy, such as international treaties and convention with stronger protections for IP; make unauthorized copying, circumvention of copy protection

REGION	2002	2003	2004	2005	2006	2007	2003-07 CAGR
United States	54.3	39.4	27.3	21.4	13.1	12.1	22.3
EMEA	66.7	50.0	46.7	31.8	27.6	21.6	35.1
Asia Pacific	46.7	48.1	35.0	29.6	22.9	16.3	29.9
Latin America	70.0	76.5	66.7	40.0	28.6	22.2	45.3
Canada	64.7	39.3	33.3	26.9	13.6	13.3	24.9
Tota	55.7	46.2	36.8	28.2	21.2	16.9	29.4

TABLE 1.1 *Broadband household growth (%)*
(Sources: Datamonitor, eMarketer, NUA, PricewaterhouseCoopers LLP, Wilkofsky Gruen Associates[1])

devices, and electronic distribution illegal – provide for strong and consistent enforcement once the laws and regulations are in place;

- **Protect and monetize the content.** Utilize technology to establish strong copy protection in all consumer electronic devices – or utilize an ever stronger deterrent generally known as Digital Rights Management (DRM) that allows content owners to specify the level of security and the business rules for access to content and tracks content usage.

The ultimate solution may include some elements of any or all these options. However, it is incumbent on the content producers and distributors to focus on the consumer and provide a package they perceive as a "good deal" that provides choice, convenience, ease-of-use, and fairness.

The Internet is rapidly becoming ubiquitous, yet content providers have been largely unsuccessful in their commercial exploitation of this promising medium. Largely, but not entirely, as we shall see shortly from the example of iTunes music downloading service.

---

1. PricewaterhouseCoopers, *Entertainment & Media Outlook: 2003-2007*. Most recent version, 2005-2009 available for purchase at:
http://www.pwc.com/extweb/industry.nsf/docid/6d3e2609d43ea77285257020007d1307.

Entertainment: A Risky Business

Risk is the potential for loss; in business, that usually means financial risk or the loss of money. The creation of entertainment products entails considerable risk partly because each product is unique and new. It's not like manufacturing a widget, then making a gazillion of them over the next five years, each one exactly like the first one.

Every song, motion picture, book, stage play is created anew. Every one requires a different location, costumes, makeup, props, and range of effects. Each production is undertaken by a one-time grouping of highly skilled people, both cast and crew.

Even after the product is created, marketing and distribution are also difficult. Fashion trends change swiftly. The audience is fickle and unforgiving. Increasingly consumers are difficult to reach en masse in order to communicate the essential elements of a unique product.

All these factors elevate the risks of distribution. In the past, the financial risks consisted of the cost of preparing prints of movies (or copies of books, tapes of programs, recordings on vinyl, etc.), and of transporting the physical goods to market. Many of the risks of distribution in motion pictures and music were shared or carried altogether by middlemen. And the final risks of sales performance: poor box office, were shared by exhibitors and mitigated by studio marketing machines and product exclusivity. In the record business, store owners bore the brunt of flops.

The Changing Risks of Distribution

Distribution costs can be significantly reduced by creating a digital master and distributing it over networks, but only by increasing the risks of piracy and unauthorized, uncompensated copying.

Yet even without creating digital masters and shipping them around the world, plenty of risks stem from distribution in the analog realm. For example, in the motion picture business, "camming," the illegal videotaping of a movie from the audience, is commonplace. Many of the VCDs sold in Asia stem from such camming, and the pirate rather than the studios reap the cost reductions of digital distribution.

Over the past few years, the music industry has served as the unhappy, unwilling, and unprofitable beta testing ground of the distribution dilemma for the entertainment industry as a whole. The small size of music files made them vulnerable to casual copying by users, even over slow 56K Internet connections. All the other industry segments are watching to see what will happen in the music industry.

Music Industry Sings the Blues

A decade ago, where was the intrepid prognosticator predicting that an entire industry would melt down because a generation of students wanted to have their music and burn it too?

The availability of free music via file sharing over peer-to-peer networks has significantly changed the economics of the music industry, although the exact negative economic impact has been hard to gauge. The industry is beset by other difficulties, including retail turmoil, competition from video games, and a paucity of breakout genres and hits. But there's nothing vague about the severity of the problems: In the US alone, annual music industry revenues declined by 8.1% in 2002, and experts agree that online piracy has been a primary cause.[2]

Peer-to-peer file sharing services have had an impact on the music business in unexpected ways, not just lower overall sales. In the past, music companies averaged out production costs by bundling together winning singles with loser tracks, allowing for a higher total album sale price. Through downloading the songs they like, customers now have an expectation that they will be able to receive only the single songs they want, which threatens a profit structure based on album sales.

The need to compete with free singles means that an online service can charge only a very low unit price for a track. This pricing poses a dilemma because it undermines the profitability of the industry unless it can vastly increase the legitimate sales of individual tracks, reduce production costs, or create an entirely new value proposition to cover its costs in the same way albums did. The labels fear that low-priced online sales will undercut profits to a greater extent than savings on production and distribution costs and sharing in ancillary revenue streams can make up for, especially when the loss of album sales is taken into account.   CONTINUED ▶

2. J Borland. *Music industry: Piracy is choking sales.* **News.com**, Apr 9, 2003. Available at: http://news.com.com/2100-1027-996205.html

CONTINUED ▶   The speed at which music was brought to its knees makes Hollywood execs tremble. "We may not be the smartest guys around," says Peter Chernin, president of News Corp. "But we'd have to be brain-dead to ignore what it did to those guys."[3]

Major music companies, the "labels," have moved against piracy on several fronts. In a nutshell, the industry's strategy is to make the cost of purchasing less than the cost of freeloading. To increase the costs to users of downloading music over peer-to-peer (P2P) services, the industry began taking them to court. The Recording Industry Association of America (RIAA) subpoenas to Internet service providers to reveal the names of peer-to-peer using subscribers have been highly publicized. After getting the names, the RIAA sued for damages or reached settlements with more than a few violators.

The industry has also released music on CDs that are protected by digital rights management (DRM) schemes, similar to the ones used on DVDs of motion pictures. On the whole, these technologies have been ineffective for music CDs as "crackers" have cracked the codes and put the music on the Net for P2P freeload.

Apple's Big Byte

The most successful strategy to date has been that of the iTunes service, a bright spot in an otherwise gloomy landscape. It's a relative success – sales are only a tiny fraction of all the music that is downloaded. But it has led the way for the industry as a whole to begin setting up online music sales efforts.

Making a rare public appearance, the company's director of marketing Peter Lowe, gave the keynote at the Music 2.0 conference. He said that Apple's first revolutionary step was to begin the process of creating an online music service from the point of view of the consumer. The company started with the question: What do consumers want? Through market research, Apple discovered that the answers were:

- Instant gratification
- Vast selection

---

3. Cover story. "Hollywood Heist." *Business Week Online.* Jul 4, 2003. Available at: http://www.businessweek.com/magazine/content/03_28/b3841001_mz001.htm

- Unlimited CD burning

- Unlimited portable players

- Unlimited computer use

- Free

The creators of the iTunes service also noted the presence of negatives to P2P file sharing. According to Lowe, it is unreliable, there is no cover art, and it is illegal.

However, until iTunes, consumers were unable to find legal alternatives to get music the way they wanted it. iTunes was born out of filling that consumer need.

"iTunes removes the negative aspects of illegal services, while making most of the features customers want available: broad personal rights and persistent presence. Our consumers can burn an unlimited number of CDs and move music to any number of portable players. They can play music on up to three computers and, while it's not free, 99 cents per song is widely perceived as a reasonable charge," explained Lowe.

The company made deals with the five major labels prior to launch, and has continued to build its library by adding than 200 independent labels. Currently, iTunes' library allows consumers to select from more than 500,000 songs. In March, 2004, the company announced that music fans had purchased and downloaded over 50 million songs from the iTunes Music Store. Users were downloading 2.5 million songs per week, an annual run rate of 130 million songs per year.

But it's important to keep that number in perspective. According to Big Champagne CEO Eric Garland, users freeload more than ten times that number of songs per month from illegal file sharing services. In other words, iTunes is a ray of light, but it's still a mighty thin ray. And although major entertainment companies are making progress towards dealing with the dilemma posed by digital distribution, there's still a long way to go, baby.

The Digital Dilemma

The new digital means of production and distribution hold many advantages for content creators, owners, and consumers. But there's a paradox — every exciting opportunity is linked with nerve-wracking perils, as shown in Table 1.2.

	THE GOOD NEWS	THE OTHER NEWS
New Digital Networks	**New opportunity:** Content owners can reach customers directly.	**New problem:** Everyone each customers directly – including pirates and other customers.
Ever-more Powerful Desktop Processing	**New opportunity:** Entertainment and media companies can produce and copy content for less money.	**New problem:** Everyone can produce and copy content for less money.
New Devices and Displays	**New opportunity:** New channels, products, and revenue streams.	**Traditional problem:** Undercut existing lines of business.
New Formats	**New opportunity:** Exciting new ways to tell Stories.	**Traditional problem:** Substantial investment with potential for expensive flops.

TABLE 1.2 *Content in the Networked World*

The Ticking Tech-Bomb

The notable trend so crucial to the future of the industry is that of ever-increasing bandwidth. Network architectures come and go. Wires are dug in and pulled out. Costs rise and fall. But bandwidth just increases and the speed of connections just goes up.

Even before it is a profitable distribution outlet, broadband is an excellent venue for media and entertainment companies to refine their business models and to test technological solutions in the evolving digital environment. Its capacity is big enough to allow experimentation with rich content, but not so large that it makes the transfer of high-value motion pictures truly convenient. And as thorny as the issues of intellectual property protection and piracy seem to be at the moment, they will only become more complex and difficult as time goes on and processing power and bandwidth increase.

We are less than a decade or so from the introduction of Internet2, which will bring fiber to the neighborhood, the curb, and the home in its wake. Internet2 already links major university research centers around the world, where computer scientists are busily engaged in developing the software and protocols that will manage it. At the same time, cable operators will upgrade to 40-gigabit per second or faster HFC (hybrid fiber coax) networks. Or even fiber to the home.

Downwire: New Devices, Displays and Formats

When a new delivery platform emerges, one prediction is sure: Everything downwire will change as well. Experience shows that new networks and network capabilities give birth to new devices, which in turn produce new formats as their offspring.

Devices and displays change how customers use content. Think TiVo, iPod, and Movielink. These technologies are even more dynamic than networks, and their deployment occurs in ever faster buy-to-goodbye cycles. Despite their relatively shorter life span, devices can be just as disruptive as networks. The potential effect of personal video recorders (PVR) on television's advertising revenue has been waking nightmare for free over-the-air TV companies, alleviated only by the slow up-take of the dratted (from the a industry perspective) devices.

Game consoles reproduce like rabbits with more genetic mutations than the flu virus. The latest multi-platform wonders come with DVD drives, hard drives, and Internet connectivity. Device convergence has found a home: Users can use consoles to play games, watch movies and videos, listen to music, send email and copy anything digital. Geeks are installing "mods," modified chips to bypass the limitations on the most popular boxes, and turning them into super-fast multipurpose computers for just under $300. It won't be long before solder-wielding 14-year olds are selling them at the local flea market for a few dollars over cost. If you're in doubt, check out http://www.modchip-sbox.com/: Its webpage starts with the following enticement:

> Free cheat codes for Playstation 2, PS2, PSOne, PSX, Playstation, Xbox cheat codes, GBA cheats codes, etc....ALL FOR FREE.

Attendant to the introduction of new devices and displays is a similar proliferation of content formats. Although it's a challenge for entertainment companies, every new format is a potential new release window and revenue stream.

Content Lifecycle

The view of content as having a life cycle emerged after Ted Turner's purchase of part of the MGM library. Now content has many lives: first as an initial product, then as an asset that can be reincarnated; repackaged, re-expressed, and repurposed and distributed, consumed, and experienced in multiple, co-existing forms in many venues and on a virtually unlimited number of displays and devices.

The implications of a content life cycle are enormous. A hit isn't just a single product, it is a franchise that may spawn many more profitable offerings. One reason why copy protection has dominated the discussion of digital distribution is that piracy of doesn't just have an impact on the first rendition of the hit. It may also threaten profits from the entire cascade of downstream releases.

High bandwidth to ubiquitous networks, displays, and devices, these are the elements of a communications revolution. Global reach and worldwide immediacy. Local affinity and neighborhood familiarity. Instantaneously. Simultaneously.

Few entertainment companies have moved to take advantage of the opportunities afforded by digital distribution because they believe that they must first deal with the problem of piracy. As Bonnie Jacobson, the Motion Picture Association of America's vice president of trade and federal affairs, testified before the House Commerce Subcommittee on Commerce, Trade, and Consumer Protection, "Internet piracy is the single biggest impediment to digital trade today."

Welcome to the Darknet

The Darknet, a term coined by a group of Microsoft employees, refers to the broadband network that people use to exchange desirable material. A great deal of the popular material that people want is copyrighted. Users call it file swapping; content owners call it piracy.

There is doubt that piracy causes substantial harm to copyright owners.[4]

- In 2001, the U.S. recording industry lost $4.2 billion to hard-goods piracy worldwide

- In 2001, the U.S. movie industry lost $3 billion to videocassette piracy

- In 2001, the U.S. entertainment software industry lost $1.9 billion due to piracy in just fourteen countries.

- In 2002, Viant estimated that between 400,000 to 600,000 pirate versions of movies were downloaded every day

- In April 2002, 1.1 billion files, the vast majority containing copyrighted works, were downloaded through the KaZaA peer-to-peer file trading network

---

4. D Chmielewski, *Online Film Piracy Cuts Into Industry Profit*, Mercury News, May 30, 2002.PricewaterhouseCoopers, Entertainment & Media Outlook: 2003-2007.
Most recent version, 2005-2009 available for purchase at:
http://www.pwc.com/extweb/industry.nsf/docid/6d3e2609d43ea77285257020007d1307

Unauthorized duplication of copyrighted works is particularly problematic because digital copying is something quite different from analog copying. Digital content is not pictures or sounds. It is composed of bits, zeros and ones, bits that give instructions to a display device on how to recreate the picture. Thus, digital copies are not really "copies", they are newly constituted originals, as perfect as the master from which they are re-created.

As digital files, entertainment products can be compressed and recompressed into smaller files, split into multiple files, broadcast to servers around the world in a few minutes, and downloaded by consumers with broadband service in a few hours.

The path of piracy is well-known. Motion pictures are captured from post-production facilities and studios, from "screeners," or viewing materials that go to marketers, publicists, reviewers, and awards committees. They may be copied via high quality equipment, such as telecine and telesync. "Cams" of movies can be shot by a handheld camera in a theater from under a patron's coat. "Rips" are copies stripped from DVDs by special hardware or protection-breaking software.

Once there is a digital copy, the material hits the Darknet. Music becomes available to the universe of Internet users on peer-to-peer services as soon as a copy is ripped and stored on someone's hard drive.

Movies may take several paths before showing up on a P2P service. Since movie files are so much larger, they begin their bootleg life as a re-compressed into VCD format. The VCD file may be split into several files and made available in Usenet news groups, via the Network News Transport Protocol (NNTP). Or the pirate may "distro" the file: place it on one or more servers where it can be downloaded through File Transport Protocol (FTP). Sometimes illegal movies are distributed with Hypertext Transport Protocol (HTTP) and placed on web sites, such as the now-shut down movies88.com. Finally, people can exchange files using the Direct Client-to-Client (DCC) protocol over the Internet Relay Chat (IRC) system.

P2P Access

Once copies of movies are on home hard drives, they can be accessed by others using peer-to-peer services. There are more than a hundred such P2P software clients and services available, but most are based on a few protocols:

- A pure P2P file sharing protocol, also used by Morpheus. Does not require a central server to store a director. Most broadband users can connect to about 1000 PC hosts that can share about 50 terabytes of stored information. CONTINUED ▶

CONTINUED ▶

- OpenNap was the protocol behind Napster. WinMX uses OpenNap.

- FastTrack is the protocol used by KaZaA and Grokster. When a user downloads material, the software can the content simultaneously from multiple sources and tie the streams together in the local machine, thus improving the download time.

DRM: the Digital Box Office Is Open for Business

Digital Rights Management (DRM) is the generic name for a range of technologies that prevent access to content without authorization. DRM satisfies two crucial needs of entertainment and media companies: saving money by preventing loss through piracy and making money by establishing a way for people to pay. DRM also makes consumers' rights explicit, although they may not like the specific terms and conditions.

The first step towards monetizing content is to protect it, to make it secure. Some experts argue that security is not a function of DRM at all, Rather, DRM means what it says – its job is to manage digital rights. In practice, however, security and DRM are often bundled together, both in discussion and in systems implementation. Even the most stringent security system must allow some form of companion DRM system that will enable business models to provide consumers access to the content.

The heart of DRM systems is to establish the conditions for playing or displaying the content. They identify content and specify the rights of both copyright owners and customers. They are integrated with security measures that enforce these terms. And they interact with payment mechanisms to provide authorization for consuming the content. In essence, they define the rules of engagement for commercial transactions involving intellectual property.

The information that DRM systems need to do all this can travel persistently with the content it protects and projects. Or it may reside in a database that is triggered by information that is forever embedded in the content. In this latter case, the content has an instruction set that "phones home" whenever the customer wants to view the material, transfer it to a new device, send it to another person, or slice and dice it. The message is actually a query to a DRM database, asking it to authorize or deny the requested action, according to the terms and conditions of the license.

DRM technologies can enable both old and new business models. But they will not bring piracy to a halt. Nor will they persuade customers to want or to buy content – indeed, they may well repel them. Making a sale requires an attractive customer proposition, followed up by easy, convenient ways to purchase and receive content – a thoughtful, thorough business model that well-thought out DRM techniques can protect and enable.

The new flexible business environment offers enormous opportunity for content owners can re-productize content that they already own. They can create customized packages to different customers at different price points. As companies' experience with DVDs is currently proving, these initiatives can bring in substantial revenue streams at a relatively small cost.

Despite concerns that online file swapping has created an environment where customers expect free content, many other examples from the entertainment and media world indicate that people will pay for digital content if they believe it has value.

- In less than thirteen years, BSkyB created a market for pay-TV in the UK, which generates annual Average Revenues Per User (ARPU) of US$548.

- The meteoric growth of the global DVD market indicates that customers will pay for digitized film content.

DRM and Beyond

This book looks at the one of the greatest challenge ever faced by the content-producing industries as a whole and the entertainment in particular: making money with digital distribution. It describes the business, technical, and legal contexts for digital content distribution and explores how the industry will use the Internet as a profitable channel for its content products.

Against this backdrop, this book goes beyond the use of DRM as simply a means to thwart piracy, and argues that it will be implemented it as a flexible platform for content owners to market and for consumers to enjoy digital content delivered on any media platform.

The book begins with an introduction to DRM and describes the conditions within the entertainment and media marketplaces that have driven companies to look at copy protection and DRM solutions to their current and anticipated business problems. Chapter 2 examines the legal backdrop to copyright protection and rights management, defining rights and royalties. Chapter 3 looks at the Content Revolution and how content is currently marketed, sold, and distributed as both hard goods and electronic files, completely change the business landscape for marketing, distributing, and delivering content.

Chapters 4 and 5 cover briefly the range of content protection and DRM technologies, what they are, what they do, how they work, and how they are put together into deployable systems. Chapter 6 presents entertainment and media business models and delineates how copy protection and DRM systems affect the ways companies formulate and act on them. It lays out the business strategies that industry executives are likely to adopt as they look at the new market place. Chapter 7 looks at copy protection and DRM systems from the multiple perspectives of the many stakeholders that are affected by them, including society as a whole.

Finally, Chapter 8 describes how we will all live with copy protection and DRM systems, some of us well and some of us, perhaps, not so well. It summarizes the remaining work to be done to develop such systems and offers points of view that emphasize alternatives to them.

The book is intended for anyone interested in the content industries, particularly commercially developed entertainment. It offers the reader a comprehensive view of secure digital content distribution, problems, solutions, accomplishments, and remaining barriers.

The next chapter is about intellectual property and copyright – both legal concepts with a long history. They also have a recent past and some future controversy, as the various participants in the creation, sales, distribution, and consumption struggle for their legal and

2 Intellectual Property and Copyright

This chapter will examine intellectual property (IP) and copyright, terms that acquire their meaning from the social, political, and legal contexts in which they arise. They necessarily entail a legal perspective because, as legal concepts and definitions, they result in legal processes, procedures, and consequences. However, legality itself is a function of political interaction and activities. And both politics and law reflect the social conditions from which they evolve. So while the legal aspects of IP and copyright are important, they are not among the most fundamental social rights; nor are they fixed or permanent. Moreover, as we shall see later, DRM systems may prevent consumers and the general public from the ability to exercise some of their fundamental social rights at all.

Jessica Litman characterizes copyright law as "arcane,"[1] which means little-understood, mysterious, and enigmatic. Entire books are written about each element of IP and copyright, and the exceptions to them. Some of the documents that establish the legal framework are book-length in themselves, containing a confusing array of wherefores, whereases, and hereinafters, with endless references to parenthetical clauses, such as "as specified in Section 107 1 (a) and 2 (d)."

No wonder that copyright has been a musty corner of the law, of little interest to any, save those who choose to enforce and exercise their copyrights. But no longer. Today, IP and copyright are the stock in trade of the Information Age, the building blocks of empire. If information is power, IP and copyright are the

---

1. J Litman. *Digital Copyright*, Prometheus Books:Amherst NY. 2001.

steppingstones to it, just as mineral rights and the industrial means of production were the keys to power in earlier times.

IP and copyright are the new "range wars." In the 19th century, there was a series of battles over the U.S. prairie between the farmers, who fenced in land to protect their fields and crops, and ranchers and cowboys, who drove cattle across the wide open range. The farmers put up barbed wire fences; the cowboys used wire cutters to pull them down. Violent confrontations are the stuff of Western movies, but they actually occurred in New Mexico and Wyoming. The song, *Don't Fence Me In*, is a cowboy lament that reflects that earlier era.

The cowboys lost. And as this chapter will document, the free range of information is also being lost. The first section places DRM systems at the heart of the battle, shows how the different stakeholders define the territory, and points out the potential conflicts between DRM and fundamental social rights such as free expression and freedom of the press.

From there, the chapter looks at definitions of IP and copyright, and summarizes the main points of the various documents, laws, court rulings, and international treaties that comprise the framework for digital rights management systems. It will cover some of the legislation and court decisions that are external to IP and copyright matters directly, but nevertheless influence how they are interpreted and handled. In a single chapter, it is not possible to present every aspect of copyright law nor to detail every twist of every loophole. Rather, it is written to provide a backdrop for the development of DRM systems and their development.

IP, Copyright and DRM

Digital Rights Management systems have come into being for many reasons, but primary among them is the ease of transport of digitally-available content over computer networks. Peer-to-peer file sharing and its effects on the music industry gave the entertainment and media industry a desperate incentive to drive the development of viable DRM systems. The assurance of relatively robust DRM to protect and monetize such content, could give owners the confidence to market their wares online, a shortcut to the worldwide reach of digital communications media and a method for content owners, licensees, and distributors to avoid the ravages of peer-to-peer sharing.

Or DRM could just become a despotic fiat issued by them. There are few limitations on how content owners package their products for sale. They can put them in shrink-wrapped plastic sleeves and containers. They can store them in a bank safe and require the presence of twenty armed guards accompanying each consumer. They can send content over the Internet in the clear. Or they can wrap it in a DRM technology and require consumers to pay, to provide information, to make a formal agreement to respect the terms of the agreement, or to stand on their heads and sing the Star-Spangled Banner before they can access the material. In short, the owners of a product can sell it pretty much under any conditions they want to specify as long as the actions they require are safe and legal.

The fear is that we will re-write our copyright laws and allow owners to lock up content for eons of time, perhaps forever, putting in jeopardy the greater good of free speech and a free press — all in the name of protecting the rights of huge companies to profit from their copyrights in *Don't Cha*, *Gilligan's Island*, *Star Wars*, and Mickey Mouse. DRM puts the power in the hands of content owners, backed up by an owned-and-operated justice system. Whatever the rights of consumers and the general public may be, they are rendered moot by the unfettered ability of owners to digitally lock up their products.

It is only after the content has been accessed from behind its DRM protection that the full panoply of public rights can play out. For example, the music labels did not wrap their CDs in any kind of DRM, so tracks leaked quickly and easily onto the Internet and streamed into millions of computers around the world. Movies, which were locked behind Macrovision, did not become available on the Net until the protection code was cracked and bandwidth increased to make it feasible to download the unlocked digital stream.

This protection means that researchers can't investigate motion pictures without paying for them. When prices are $20 or $25 per copy, conducting a large-scale research project can be expensive but within reach; if the price were higher, research could become impossible, since much of it is funded from the meager salaries of lowly-paid academics. Even more troubling is the high cost of scientific publications that are currently locked behind DRM and monetizing systems, already forming a barrier to independent research.

The social-political-legal environment of copyright always evolves, but until the dawn of the digital age, there was an implicit underlying balance of rights and interests that prevailed in discussions of copyright since the eighteenth century. Digital technologies are threatening to tear up that agreement, and DRM is yet a further challenge. Digital networks and DRM bring a tier of technology to the IP-copyright edifice that unsettles the previously stable social construction. What DRM means and how it could destabilize the traditional balance of rights depends on how the term "digital rights management" is parsed and understood, as shown in Table 2.1.

	DRM DIGITAL – RIGHTS MANAGEMENT	DRM DIGITAL RIGHTS – MANAGEMENT
Meaning	Digital content is not significantly different from other forms of content.	Digital content is different from other forms of content, exists in widely accessible networked environment, and owners thus require additional rights and protections.
Derivation of Rights	Tradition: IP and copyright have been defined in a process that began in the 16th century. Digital technology is a new means of managing them.	Situational: Digital technologies require a redefinition of copyright and new means of protecting it.
Interested Stakeholders	Computer industry, including hardware manufacturers, software developers, and service providers.

Consumer groups.

Some research and archiving groups, i.e., libraries. | Content creators, owners, licensees, and distributors. |
| **DRM Focus** | Use digital technology to protect and monetize content, based on traditional balance of IP rights between creators, owners, and society as a whole. | Use digital technology to protect and monetize content based on content owners', licensees', and distributor's rights. |
| **Concerns about DRM systems** | DRM systems may stifle the free flow of information, free expression, and technological innovation. Tracking consumer behavior may violate rights to privacy.

It may prove impossible to map DRM systems to conform to IP protection and legal copyrights, so that the public's rights cannot be protected. | DRM systems may not be effective enough to prevent piracy and other forms of illegal or unauthorized usage of content.

It may prove impossible to map DRM systems to conform to IP protection and legal copyrights, so that content cannot be protected. |

TABLE 2.1 *Parsing the Term "Digital Rights Management"*

	DRM DIGITAL – RIGHTS MANAGEMENT	DRM DIGITAL RIGHTS – MANAGEMENT
Destabilizing factors	Consumer and public rights, such as fair use, may not be amenable to translation into computer-operated DRM systems.	Gives control to content owners, licensees, and distributors, ignoring traditional rights of consumers and society as a whole. May conflict with rights of free expression, "free speech," and free press.

TABLE 2.1 *(Continued)*

IP: Not Internet Protocol

In the world of DRM, the acronym IP is more likely to stand for Intellectual Property, than it is for Internet Protocol, which appears commonly in another acronym, TCP/IP. Intellectual property describes the expressed creations of the human mind. In the United States, a circuit court defined it in 1847 as "the labors of the mind, productions and interests as much a man's own...as the wheat he cultivates."[2] IP rights are embedded in the Constitution in Article 1, Section 8, Clause 8, which says that Congress shall have the power to "promote the Progress of Science and useful Arts, by securing for limited Times to Authors and Inventors the exclusive Right to their respective Writings and Discoveries."

This clause in the Constitution reflects a careful balancing act between allowing authors to enjoy the benefits (financial and otherwise) through granting them exclusive rights to their creations and the social good of a free flow of ideas. There are two sides to the gold coin of the free flow of ideas.

The Founding Fathers mention that the purpose of awarding exclusivity to creators is to promote progress, by ensuring that they get rewards from their works. At the same time, one of the most important rights guaranteed by the Bill of Rights is that of free speech. How can there be free speech in the context of the ownership of arts, words, and inventions? This is where the phrase "by securing for a limited time" comes into play, so that after some limited time, as determined by Congress, IP enters the public domain.

2. Woodbury & Minot, *Rep. Cases Circuit Court of U.S.*, I. 56 (1847).

Intellectual property takes four forms: patents, trademarks, copyrights, and trade secrets. IP has a great deal in common with other kinds of property, such as real (land) property and chattel (physical goods). IP is an asset that can be bought, sold, rented, licensed, exchanged, given away, altered, or destroyed. The owner can prevent unauthorized transfer of rights to or use of the IP.

Although IP has some similarities with real property and chattel, it is not identical with them. IP is intangible, literally meaning that it cannot be touched or perceived. As a result, expression is a prerequisite for something to be pronounced as IP and to have copyrights enforced. Expression means putting words on paper, images on film, software and digital data on drives, discs or diskettes. As long as those words and images stay in the minds of their creators, they are not yet IP, and cannot be protected. They become IP and capable of being protected only when they are expressed.

This disconnection between the ideas in a work and their expression is sometimes called the fact/expression dichotomy. At the same time, IP is not the physical object in which the ideas are expressed. It is not the book; it is the words that are printed on the page. IP is not the physical film reels; it is the images that appear on the screen. IP is not the CD-ROM; it is the programming written to the CD. The poem is not the sine waves that our ears take in and translate to sound; it is the specific words that convey its meaning.

There is another crucial difference between IP and real and personal property. Billions of people can enjoy the ideas expressed in a newspaper, book, or magazine, the music of Celine Dion, or the films of Bernardo Bertolucci. You can benefit from reading a book without depriving me of the benefits I obtained from the intellectual property contained in it. John Perry Barlow calls this characteristic of IP, "unbounded IP," and he refers to the IP as the "wine" and their carriers and containers as the "bottles." [3]

By contrast, when it comes to physical goods, only a relatively few individuals can live in a mansion at the same time. If someone else buys it and moves in, the previous residents cannot stay in the house without the agreement of the new owner. Only one entity at a time can own or play a violin, wear a diamond ring, drive a car, or profit from a gold mine or an oil rig. All those who partake of a physical good must do so with the consent of the legal owner. Nor can a person easily make a copy of his or her home and give it to a friend or relative to live in it and enjoy it as you do without paying for it in the same way as you did the original

---

3 J P Barlow. *The Economy of Ideas: Selling Wine Without Bottles on the Global Net.* Posted at: http://homes.eff.org/~barlow/EconomyOfIdeas.html.

did. You must reassemble the means of construction and buy additional furnishings and possessions.

You can make a copy of a CD for far less than it cost to produce the original and give it to someone else, while still enjoying the copy that you still have in your possession. The copy of IP does not have to be digital. You can Xerox an article or even a book. You can copy a poem by hand. You can make an analog cassette tape of music or moving images.

These actions refer only to the physical expressions of the IP. Any number of people can both enjoy the poetry of e.e. cummings at the same time, anyplace on earth, savor the image of Lauren Bacall saying, "just put your lips together and blow," think about Martin Luther King's speeches, act on the ideas of Thomas Jefferson, or laugh at yesterday's Dave Barry comic. IP has always been infinitely share-able, long before the emergence of digital technologies.

These characteristics make IP difficult to protect. A look at the content protection landscape reveals a chaotic maze of rulings and a nasty thicket of lawsuits and countersuits. The commerce in trade secrets is largely hidden, often suspected but rarely proved, and costly to the businesses whose secrets are traded. Trademarks and copyrighted material are the most easily protected forms of IP, but the advent of digital reproduction and distribution over digital networks have made protection very difficult indeed.

One reason protection has become problematic is that digital technology unhinges the message from the messenger. Marshal McLuhan foresaw the digital age when he said 'the medium is the message.'[4] At its most physical, the message is an electronic blip that moves at the speed of light. Copyrighted material is no longer bound to a book, painting, a celluloid film strip, a CD-ROM, disc, or tape, so that the concept of expression becomes increasingly elusive.

Insofar as IP is protected at all, the protection occurs on a national basis, and varies considerably from one country to another, including what is protected, how well and how long it is protected, and the severity of the consequences for violating such protection. Until recently, nationally-based protection made sense. National boundaries were relatively impermeable. Communications infrastructure stopped at the border, and until as few as 15 years ago, the Soviet Union could control copying by putting Xerox machines under lock and key.

---

4. M McLuhan. *Understanding Media: The Extensions of Man.* McGraw-Hill:New York NY. 1964.

We all know that those days are long gone. The national footprint for copyright protection no longer seems so reasonable and useful as it once did. The Internet is a worldwide medium, transmitting messages from Seattle as easily to Moscow, Russia as to Moscow, Idaho. So it should come as no surprise that, as we shall see in a later section, there are many attempts to harmonize the various national laws into a more or less unified global legal copyright structure. And, more than most political enterprises, such international agreement would appear to be quite difficult to accomplish.

Copyright: How Creators Control Their IP

One researcher looks at copyright as originating in ancient Egypt where only priests and appointed scribes were allowed to create and access written works.[5] Copyright in the U.S. is built upon development of copyright in England. In1662, the Licensing Act controlled copying by granting the right to publish books to selected printers. The Statute of Anne, enacted by Parliament in 1710, established authors as owners of copyright and provided a fixed period of protection of 14 years, renewable for another 14 years if the author was alive upon expiration. The statute created a "public domain" by limiting terms of copyright and by ensuring that once a work was purchased, the copyright owner no longer had control over its use.

These principles were embedded in the U.S. Constitution, which gave Congress the power to establish the terms of copyright. As copyright is defined and enforced on a national basis, the next section looks at copyright in the U.S. A later section will examine international agreements. The U.S. Copyright Office maintains a useful document that covers the basics of copyright protection at http://www.copyright.gov/circs/circ1.html#wci. There are also any number of excellent books and articles that provide detailed analyses of this topic. Finally, there is a huge volume of information about it on the Internet.

A copyright grants the exclusive right to copy a work of expressed authorship, with certain limitations and exceptions. It covers any form of IP, including literary and dramatic works, artistic and musical works, audio and video recordings, films, broadcast and cable-transmitted material, and computer software. In short, it applies to any creation that has been fixed in a tangible medium. As Barlow noted, copyright protects the bottle that contains the IP, but it does not cover the wine. So copyright does not protect ideas, processes, systems, methods, concepts, or principles no matter the bottle that it happens to come in.

---

5. D Mendis. *The Historical Development of Exceptions to Copyright and Its Application to Copyright Law in the Twenty-first Century*, vol 7.5 Electronic Journal of Comparative Law. December 2003, http://www.ejcl.org/ejcl/75/art75-8.html

Copyright becomes effective upon creation of the work, the moment the IP is expressed; no registration, notice, or publication is required. Before 1978, publication was the key to obtaining copyright, but the Copyright Act of 1976 changed that requirement. In addition, in 1989, the U.S. conformed its laws to the international Berne Convention and dropped the requirement for copyright notice, the '©' mark found in many instances of published material. Prior to 1989, copyright notice was required, however, and it still applies to older works.

The period of copyright protection has been frequently extended since the adoption of the Constitution, which protected copyright for 14 years. Today, copyright protection for material created after January 1, 1978, lasts for the author's lifetime, plus 70 years after the death of the author. IP created on a 'work for hire' basis is protected for an even longer period – 120 years from the time of creation or 95 years from its first publication, whichever is shorter.

In order to qualify for copyright, the IP must be original. This means that it must originate from the author and not simply be copied from other works. The amount of creativity in the material must be more than trivial.

The legislation that establishes the basic legal framework for the protection of IP and copyrights is the Copyright Act of 1976 is Title 17 of the U.S. Code. Congress has amended the statute 50 times since then, mostly adding types of IP such as architecture and semiconductors, responding to new technologies and networks, extending the period of copyright, and clarifying specific points of the legislation.

The DCMA

The biggest change to copyright law since 1976 came in 1998 with the Digital Millennium Copyright Act of 1998, called DMCA. It implemented the treaties signed by the U.S. in 1996 at the World Intellectual Property Organization (WIPO) conference in Geneva and also addressed additional concerns. The DMCA was generally supported by the entertainment and software industries and opposed by scientists, academics, librarians, and consumer and civil rights groups.

The Major Provisions of the DMCA

- Make it a crime to circumvent anti-piracy measures incorporated into commercial software

CONTINUED ▶

CONTINUED ►

- Outlaw the manufacture, sale, or distribution of code-cracking devices used to illegally copy software

- Permit cracking copyright protection devices to conduct encryption research, and test product interoperability and computer security systems

- Exempt nonprofit libraries, archives, and educational institutions from anti-circumvention provisions for under certain circumstances

- Shield Internet service providers from copyright infringement liability for transmitting information over the Internet; however, they must remove material from users' web sites that appear to infringe copyright.

- Require webcasters to pay licensing fees to record companies

The most controversial part of the DMCA was the anti-circumvention provisions. In the years following the DMCA's adoption, situations developed that revealed shortcomings in the law. In 2003, the Copyright Office announced exemptions from the prohibition against circumvention of technological measures that control access to copyrighted works:

(1) Compilations consisting of lists of Internet locations blocked by commercially marketed filtering software applications that are intended to prevent access to domains, websites or portions of websites;

(2) Computer programs protected by dongles that prevent access due to malfunction or damage and which are obsolete.

(3) Computer programs and video games distributed in formats that have become obsolete and which require the original media or hardware as a condition of access. A format shall be considered obsolete if the machine or system necessary to render perceptible a work stored in that format is no longer manufactured or is no longer reasonably available in the commercial marketplace.

(4) Literary works distributed in ebook format when all existing ebook editions of the work (including digital text editions made available by authorized entities) contain access controls that prevent the enabling of the ebook's read-aloud function and that prevent the enabling of screen readers to render the text into a specialized format.

Since the passage of the DMCA, there have been five additional important enactments that amend U.S. copyright law, summarized in Table 2.2.

ENACTED LEGISLATION	MAJOR PROVISIONS
Family Entertainment and Copyright Act (P.L. 109-9) signed April 27, 2005	Made it a crime with a 3-year prison sentence for "camming" – to bring an AV device into a theater to copy a film from the screen.
Intellectual Property Protection and Courts Amendments Act of 2004 (P.L. 108-482) signed Dec. 23, 2004	Increases penalties for using counterfeit labels on copyrighted materials that appear to be genuine but are not.
Satellite Home Viewer Extension and Reauthorization Act of 2004, signed Dec. 7, 2004	Permits satellite companies to provide local broadcast signals to subscribers in the local TV station's market, "local-into-local" service, and distant stations to eligible subscribers.
Individuals with Disabilities Education Improvement Act of 2004 (P.L. 108-446) signed Dec. 3, 2004	Amends section 121 of the copyright law to allow publishers to provide copyrighted materials in "specialized formats," such as Braille, so they are accessible to people with disabilities.
Copyright Royalty and Distribution Reform Act of 2004 (P.L. 108-419) signed Nov. 30, 2004	Reformed the operation of the Licensing Division in the Copyright Office, which collects and distributes the royalty fees collected from cable and satellite operators and streaming websites who must pay for compulsory and statutory licenses to retransmit copyrighted programming from radio and TV stations and networks.

TABLE 2.2 *Additional Enactments to U.S. Copyright Law Since 1998*

Exceptions to Exclusive Copyright

As mentioned in the beginning of this chapter, the framers of the U.S. Constitution established copyright with a purpose in mind: "...to promote the Progress and Science and useful Arts..."   This purpose was also met by permitting some exceptions to copyright. Over the years, there have been revisions to the law, but as of 2005, the exceptions, are:

- Fair use

- Reproduction by libraries and archives

- Effect of transfer of particular copy or phonorecord

- Limitations on exclusive rights: Exemption of certain performances and displays

- Secondary transmissions and ephemeral recordings

Fair Use

The Copyright Act, section 107, provides for the "fair use" exception. Fair use can be invoked as an exception to exclusive copyright when the original material is used for purposes of criticism, comment, news reporting, teaching or education, and scholarship or research. Fair use, called "fair dealing" in Canada and the U.K., is the most important, and oft-cited exception to author's or rights holder's exclusive copyright. The criteria used to determine whether a given use is fair are:

- The purpose and character of the use

- The nature of the work

- The extent of the work copied – whether the use is "transformative" or merely duplication

- The impact of copying on the work's commercial value

Courts may also look at how available the original work is, practices within the industry from which the work springs, and whether the copy was undertaken in the good faith belief that the use was fair or was a deliberate infringement of the copyright.

The Audio Home Recording Act, 1992

The AHRA, an amendment to the federal copyright law, gave specific meaning to "fair use" in the digital world. It affirmed consumer's right to reasonable use of media they had purchased – or licensed, as the case may be. Consumers could copy media an infinite number of times – but they cannot copy copies. This restriction is accomplished by a form of protection called the Serial Copy Management System (SCMS), which allows digital recorders to make first-generation copies of a digitally recorded work, but does not allow a second-generation copy to be made from that first copy. All digital recording devices recognize SCMS.

The legislation allows up to $8 per new digital recording device and 3 percent of the price of all digital audio tapes or discs, as a royalty tax. (Computers are not considered digital audio recording machines.) The tax is paid by the manufacturers of the products to the U.S. Copyright Office and distributed to CONTINUED ▶

CONTINUED ▶   copyright owners. In return, copyright owners and holders agree to waive forever the right to claim copyright infringement against consumers using audio recording devices in their homes for noncommercial purposes. The justification for consumers being able to do this recording is based on the fair use exception to copyright law.

Reproduction by Libraries and Archives

The Copyright Act (17 U.S.C.), section 108 lays out detailed provisions for the library and archive exception to copyright. The major points are that it is not an infringement of copyright for a library or archives, or any of its employees acting within the scope of their employment, to reproduce no more than one copy or phonorecord of a work, except for security; distribution to another archive; or replacement of damaged, lost or stolen copies and the material is not reasonably available — in which cases, the library or archive may make three copies.

The rights of a library or archive to distribute the copy or phonorecord of copyrighted material holds only under the conditions that the there is no commercial advantage; the library or archive is open to the public and any person doing research in a specialized field; there is notice of copyright; the material is not distributed to the public in a digital format outside the premises of the library or archives; there is notice of where orders for the work are accepted and an order form. The library or archive cannot have any substantial reason to believe that the material could be used in ways that would infringe on the exclusive copyright held by the content owner.

The exception for libraries and archives do not apply to musical, pictorial, graphic, or sculptural works, or to motion pictures and other audiovisual work, other than those dealing with news. However, copies may be made of pictorial or graphic works published as illustrations, diagrams or similar adjuncts to works that are covered under section 108.

Effect of Transfer of Particular Copy or Phonorecord

The Copyright Act (17 U.S.C.), section 109 embodies the "doctrine of first sale." It allows people who have acquired copyrighted works to sell them or dispose of them without permission. However, they may not rent, lease, or lend them for direct or indirect commercial advantage. This stricture does not apply to nonprofit libraries and educational institutions.

Limitations on Exclusive Rights: Exemption of Certain Performances and Displays

The Copyright Act (17 U.S.C.), section 110 is sometimes called the "educational exception."

It allows for the use of copyrighted material in the course of face-to-face teaching activities of a nonprofit educational institution, in a classroom or similar place devoted to instruction, as long as it is a lawfully made copy. It must be directly related to the course and its use must take place in a classroom or place normally devoted to instruction.

Additional criteria include brevity, meaning that only the minimum amount of material that is needed may be use; spontaneity, which requires that the inspiration and decision to use the work and the actual moment of its use are so close together as to preclude seeking and obtaining permission to use the material; and the cumulative effect the use has on the value of the copyright.[6]

This provision also allows the use of copyrighted works at places of worship and other religious assembly, as long as there is no direct or indirect commercial advantage or admission charge, unless the proceeds, after deducting reasonable costs of producing the performance, are used exclusively for charitable purposes. There are also some rather complex allowances for the use of copyrighted materials in commercial establishments.

In 2002, Congressed passed the Teach Act, creating Section 110 (2), which expanded the rights of educators to use copyrighted material in distance education. However, the right to use the copyrighted material is more restricted than it is in a face-to-face setting, especially for audiovisual and musical works. Only "reasonable and limited portions" of the material may be used, says the legislation. The use has to be under the direction or supervision of the instricture as a regular part of mediated instructional activities by a government body or an accredited nonprofit educational institution. It must be directly related to the course and it is limited to officially enrolled students. The institution must have policies regarding copyright and provide notice that the material is copyrighted.

Secondary Transmissions and Ephemeral Recordings

The Copyright Act (17 U.S.C.), section 111 and section 112 deal with the technical requirements for distribution of copyrighted signals. For example, when a cable system delivers its signals to a hotel, the establishment re-transmits them to

6. W Garrity. Classroom Copying Guidelines, posted at http://www.dartmouth.edu/copyright/.

individual rooms; this activity is called 'secondary transmission' and it is allowed under this section. Like the other exceptions to copyright, there are many conditions that accompany the exemption.

Section 112 is the "broadcast exception," which permits a transmitting organization that holds a license to display the work, to make an ephemeral copy of it for the purposes of that transmission. Like the other exceptions, it is surrounded by a veritable thicket of requirements, including destruction of the copy within six months.

Finally, Sections 111, 114, 115, 116, 118 and 119 of the Copyright Law limit copyright by establishing compulsory licensing in specified situations, such as cable and satellite retransmissions of broadcasts for private home use.

FCC Broadcast Flag Mandate

Broadcast flag is a content protection system for television signals that was developed as part of the industry's transition to a digital television system, including transmission and reception. The agency responsible for overseeing this transition is an agency of the U.S. government, the Federal Communications Commission (FCC). The U.S. government has an interest in the transition of television to digital because it will release valuable bandwidth now used for the transmission of analog TV signals.

The FCC recognized early that the ability to receive compelling content would be the incentive for consumers to move to digital receivers. But content owners didn't want their most compelling (and valuable) content to be transmitted over the air in the clear, so that it could be copied in high definition digital formats. Anyone with a digital personal video recorder (PVR) and a computer would be able to compress the material and put it on a hard drive, accessible to peer-to-peer subscribers. As bandwidth to the home increases, content owners could see the same problem with casual copying undermining the value of their libraries, much as had happened to the music industry.

To solve this conundrum, the FCC queried vendors, content owners, and TV industry companies to provide information about potential systems for content protection. As the FCC order put it: "Content owners assert that content protection mechanisms are needed to assure the availability of high value digital content to consumers in a secure, protected format. Others express concerns that the use of technical measures to protect content will inhibit consumers' ability to enjoy programming when and where they choose. In order to advance the DTV transition, a delicate balance must be struck between these sometimes competing interests."[7]

---

7. FCC Notice and Order

The answer that drew the approval of the FCC was called a "redistribution control protection system," which would allow consumers to copy broadcast material to tape, digital recorders, discs, and hard drives – but would not allow them to retransmit the material. This idea is similar to the Serial Copy Management System, authorized under the Audio Home Recording Act of 1992.

The FCC "broadcast flag mandate" as the order became was called, required that all products that could receive a television signal – demodulate it – would be required to comply with the requirements of the broadcast flag. The flag itself is simply bits of data that appear in the digital TV signal, itself a string of digital data. The Demodulator Compliance Requirements required that all HDTV demodulators 'listen' for the flag (or assume it to be present in all signals). Content with a flag could only be output to "protected outputs," or would only be output in a degraded form. Degraded was defined to mean a picture with a visual resolution of 720 pixels by 420 lines or less – less than one-quarter of HDTV's highest resolution.

On November 4, 2003, the FCC issued its Report and Order that mandated broadcast flag for all demodulator products, that is, HDTV receiving devices. As its authority for this action, the FCC cited it's broad mandate to facilitate the transition to a digital television system: "Pursuant to the doctrine of ancillary jurisdiction, we adopt use of the ATSC flag as currently defined for redistribution control purposes and establish compliance and robustness rules for devices with demodulators to ensure that they respond and give effect to the ATSC flag," said the report and order.[8]

There was an immediate firestorm from two sources, consumers and consumer groups and consumer electronics manufacturers. Consumers and their representatives said that the mandate would forever tie HDTV to devices approved by Hollywood, stifling experimentation and technological innovation, and making HDTV signals off-limits to hobbyists.

The Electronic Frontier Foundation, a consumer watchdog group that monitors the digital environment objected to the way the broadcast flag had been developed and adopted. The main body of the proposal was drafted in a private (closed and secret) negotiation between seven Hollywood movie studios, five electronics companies, and one computer trade association. (Other entities did have input, but were not a part of the core negotiations.) This proposal was discussed by various organizations and received partial support from a few dozen other companies. It's worth noting that all consumer advocates and several large electronics manufacturers broadly dissented

---

8. Ibid.

from the proposal. In addition, watermark vendors who participated in the discussion continued to insist that the broadcast flag mechanism was technically ineffective.[9]

Critics from the consumer electronics and information technology industries also made procedural objections. They argued that the FCC lacked jurisdiction to order manufacturers to put ATSC broadcast flag recognition capabilities into their products. They noted that the Communications Act granted the FCC jurisdiction over transmission equipment, not reception equipment.

The American Library Association filed suit against the FCC, citing these and other arguments, including the points that the rule overstepped the bounds of copyright law and that the FCC adopted the broadcast flag rule without any evidence that there was a problem in redistribution of digital content.[10] On May 6, 2005, The U.S. Court of Appeals for the District of Columbia decided that the FCC had "exceeded the scope of its delegated authority" with the broadcast flag mandate. "We can find nothing in the statute, its legislative history, the applicable case law, or agency practice indicating that Congress meant to provide the sweeping authority the FCC now claims over receiver apparatus," the three-judge appeals court panel said in its opinion.

Broadcast flag might just be another footnote in some musty archive except that the entertainment and media companies are now lobbying Congress to amend the Communications Act, granting the FCC jurisdictional authority over reception devices for content protection purposes. If they are successful, all the arguments save the procedural ones will reappear, and it is possible that broadcast flag could again become mandated.

Key Court Cases

The wave of technology that has revolutionized the media and entertainment industries owes much to a 1984 Supreme Court decision in *Sony Corp. v. Universal City Studios*, often called the "Betamax case."[11] The movie company, Universal

---

9. Post on the Broadcast Protection Discussion Group of the Electronic Frontier Foundation, July 4, 2002: http://bpdg.blogs.eff.org/archives/000148.html

10. United States Court of Appeals, for the District of Columbia Circuit, No. 04-1037, *American Library Association et al. v. Federal Communications Commission and the United States of America*. Online at: http://pacer.cadc.uscourts.gov/docs/common/opinions/200505/04-1037b.pdf

11. U.S. Supreme Court, *Sony Corp. v. Universal City Studios*, 464 U.S. 417, 1984. Online at: http://caselaw.lp.findlaw.com/scripts/getcase.pl?court=us&vol=464&invol=417

City Studios, sued Sony Corporation of America, arguing that Sony's videocassette recorders, VCRs, enabled copyright infringement and, beyond that, the company's marketing campaign encouraged and promoted infringement.

The case went to the Supreme Court, which decided that a company could not be held liable for marketing a technology that some customers may use to infringe copyright. There was one other requirement – the technology must be capable of substantial non-infringing uses. The decision paved the way for such successive technologies as photocopiers, personal computers, routers, CD burners, personal video recorders (PVRs), iPods, and minidisc recorders to come onto the market without the threat of lawsuits from copyright owners.

The Audio Home Recording Act reaffirms that decision as well as the rights inherent in fair use. It recognized that consumers could exercise personal use of the media they paid for. As noted earlier, they have the right to time shift and to make personal copies for their own use, as long as that use is noncommercial.

The Betamax decision has been recently revisited in *MGM v. Grokster*. Grokster and co-defendant StreamCast Networks are peer-to-peer services that do not have a central directory or server. (Napster, a predecessor P2P service, inserted a server between peers and operated a central directory of the music files that members stored on their hard drives.) Grokster and StreamCast were entirely distributed, so that peers communicate directly with peers across the open Internet.

MGM sued the two companies, arguing that the services exist almost entirely for uses that infringe copyright. In short, they said non-infringing uses were *not* substantial. Further, MGM said the defendants knew that copyright infringement was the main reason users downloaded and used the companies' software, allowing them to operate and maintain a commercially viable, profitable network.

The Supreme Court decision is expected to hand down a decision in June, 2005. The defendants said there is substantial non-infringing uses of P2P networks, providing evidence that the Internet Archive relies on P2P networks to distribute more than 17,000 concert recordings from more than 700 bands, all authorized for P2P sharing among fans. The U.S. Court of Appeals of the Ninth Circuit found that P2P file-sharing software is capable of, and is in fact being used for, non-infringing uses. However, citing the Betamax case as precedent, the court ruled that the distributors of Grokster and Morpheus software cannot be held liable for users' copyright violations.

A&M v. Napster

Few people are offering even guesses as to how the Supreme Court will rule in the case. However, an earlier case that was heard in the Ninth Circuit of the U.S. Court of Appeals went against the P2P software company, Napster. In the 2001 case of *A&M v. Napster* the plaintiffs made many of the same arguments they have made in the Grokster case: That the company knowingly encouraged, facilitated, and profited from copyright infringement; that there were no substantial non-infringing uses; and that the P2P service had damaged the value to their copyrighted works, causing them economic harm.[12]

The Ninth Circuit Court found Napster, Inc. guilty on both contributing to copyright infringement by aiding and abetting the activity, and by causing vicarious copyright infringement that resulted in economic harm. They cited the use of a central directory, and the interpolation of a Napster download between peers that managed the download. The court declined to grant Napster a compulsory license, instead holding the company liable for the violations and the economic harm.

Napster shut down, and an attempt at relaunch failed. Its assets were purchased by another company. However, Napster has since re-relaunched as a paid P2P company.

The DeCSS Cases

Two cases make up what are collectively called the DeCSS cases, *University City Studios, Inc. v. Reimerdes* and *DVD Copy Control Assoc. v. McLaughlin, et al.* They are of special interest because they test the anticircumvention provisions of the Digital Millenium Copyright Act (DMCA) of 1998. The Content Scrambling System (CSS) is a copy protection for DVDs. DeCSS is software that will "crack" the copy protection and allow unfettered access to the DVD contents.

In *University City Studios, Inc. v. Reimerdes*, an Internet web site published a link to a software program DeCSS, which could be used to "hack" the Macrovision protection on film industry-marketed DVDs. The plaintiffs, University City Studios, argued that by posting and linking to DeCSS, the magazine provided a technology to circumvent the access and copy controls on copyrighted works. The defendants said that the software enabled fair use of DVD media and allowed movies to be played on operating systems that did not support Macrovision and, hence, would not play. They also said that the DeCSS code is free speech that warrants protection under the First Amendment.

---

12. A&M Records, Inc. v. Napster, Inc., 239 F.3d 1004 (9th Cir.). 2001. Decision online at: http://www.law.cornell.edu/copyright/cases/239_F3d_1004.htm.

The plaintiffs won their case. In 2001, the Second Circuit Court of Appeals ruled that Congress had the legitimate authority to regulate the uses of of DeCSS code.[13] The appeals court further upheld the permanent injunction granted by the district court. 2600 Magazine was barred from posting or linking to DeCSS code.

But the issues involved in anti-circumvention aren't really resolved. In the *DVD Copy Control Assoc. v. McLaughlin et al.* case, the association (DVDCCA) filed suit in a California court against a Texas resident for posting the code on the Internet, demanding he come to California. The suit claimed that the DeCSS code that was distributed on the Internet violated the proprietary trade secrets of the DVDCCA, which had adopted CSS as its method of copy protection for DVDs. The DVDCCA was granted a preliminary injunction against the posting of DeCSS. However, in 2004, the California state appeals court lifted that injunction, ruling that DeCSS code is free speech and cannot be subjected to prior restraint under trade secret laws.

When the case went to the California Supreme Court, that court held that the DVDCCA could not demand a nonresident with no connections to California to appear in a California case. So the circumvention issues were never decided in this case. The U.S. Supreme Court allowed the state decision to stay.

As a footnote, the individual who reverse-engineered CSS to produce DeCSS software was a 16-year old resident of Norway, Jon Lech Johansen. He was prosecuted in Norway for violation of the Criminal Code sect. 145(2), an anti-hacker provision that makes it illegal to break the security of a computer or a database in order to access data. The court found Norwegian court acquitted Johansen.

MGM Studios, Inc., et al. v. 321 Studios

There were three cases filed against 321 Studios, all by movie studios. At issue was software created by 321 Studios, DVDX Copy that "ripped" DVDs and allowed consumers to make first-generation copies of DVDs. The company defended itself by saying that it was allowing consumers to back up their own copies, therefore not aiding copyright infringement. Further, they argued that their software had the implicit consent of copyright owners, since consumers are allowed to "decrypt" their own DVDs, else every DVD viewing would be illegal.

---

13. Universal City Studios, Inc. et al. v. Eric Corley and 2600 Enterprises, Inc., Docket No. 00-9185. Decision online at: http://cyber.law.harvard.edu/openlaw/DVD/NY/appeals/opinion.html. The original case was: Universal City Studios, Inc. v. Reimerdes, 111 F. Supp. 2d 346 (S.D.N.Y. 2000).

Not so, ruled courts in both California and New York. In February of 2004, the California stated: "This Court finds that 321's software is in violation of both § 1201 (a)(2) and § 1201 (b)(1) [of the Copyright Act], because it is both primarily designed and produced to circumvent CSS, and marketed to the public for use in circumventing CSS."[14] The violation of Section 1201 stemmed from circumventing the CSS copy protection, not decrypting the contents of the DVD, as argued by 321 Studios. As a result of the court decision, the company pulled its software from the Internet, ran out of money, went bankrupt and went out of business.

Eldred, et al. v. Ashcroft

In 1999, Eric Eldred, owner of Eldritch Press, which offers free online access to public domain works, joined with other plaintiffs to file lawsuit which challenged the Copyright Term Extension Act (CTEA) of 1998. Sometimes referred to as the "Sonny Bono law," the bill significantly extended the duration of copyright. For works created after 1978 or created but not published before 1978, it extended the duration of copyright from "the author's life plus 50 years" to "the author's life plus 70 years." For copyrighted works created and published before 1978 and still within their original or renewed copyright period, the law extended the term to 95 years.

The suit argued that the CTEA was unconstitutional because it exceeded Congress's power under the Copyright Clause of the U.S. Constitution and because it violates the First Amendment by limiting speech without providing any supporting any important government interest. The plaintiffs lost their case in every court, the district court, the D. C. Circuit Court of Appeals, and in the Supreme Court.

External Influences on Copyright

In her informative paper on exceptions to copyright,[15] Irene Segal Ayers points out that there are also forces external to copyright law that exert an influence. She cites freedom of speech, freedom of the press, and antitrust laws as examples of such forces, noting that the use of copyrighted material in the exercise of free speech is

---

14. U.S. District Court, District of Northern California, 321 Studios v. MGM Studios, Inc., et al. No. C 02-1955 SI. Feb. 19, 2004. Decision online at:
http://news.findlaw.com/hdocs/docs/mgm/321mgm22004ord.pdf

15. I S Ayers. *The Future of Global Copyright Protection: Has Copyright Law Gone Too Far?* Online at: http: //lawreview.law.pitt.edu/volumes/vol62i1/Ayers-new.pdf.

usually justified as a "fair use," while news organizations typically cite both fair use and the dichotomy between ideas and expression.

The impact of antitrust laws is more indirect. In *United States v.Microsoft Corp.*, the U.S. District Court for the District of Columbia held that the Microsoft's copyright in its software was not a justification for anticompetitive practices. In this case, Microsoft forbid PC manufacturers from modifying its product without permission. If the manufacturer did so, Microsoft refused to license its software to that company. The U.S. government argued that this practice constituted an anticompetitive practice with respect to companies that published other Internet browsers, such as Netscape. The court ruled that the company could not use its copyright to deny PC makers the right to make other software available to its customers.

International IP and Copyright Treaties

All types of IP are protected on a national basis. Thus, the scope of protection and the requirements for obtaining protection will vary from country to country. There are, however, similarities between national legal arrangements. Moreover, the current worldwide trend is toward harmonizing the national laws.

In the late 19th century, there was a movement to recognize ownership of intellectual property to establish an international system for copyright. The Paris Convention for the Protection of Industrial Property (1884) and Berne Convention for the Protection of Literary and Artistic Works (1886) established offices to administer copyright agreements. In 1893, the two organizations joined their efforts to form the United International Bureaux for the Protection of Intellectual Property, which became known by its French acronym BIRPI.[16] Only a small number of nations participated in these agreements until 1970 when WIPO became a specialized agency of the United Nations.

Table 2.3 summarizes the important points in the key international treaties and agreements that have an impact on IP and copyright protection.

Trade Related Aspects of Intellectual Property Rights (TRIPS)

The first step towards creating a widely-recognized international framework for protecting IP and copyright came in 1994, when the General Agreement on Tariffs

---

16. World Intellectual Property Organization: http://www.wipo.int/about-wipo/en/gib.htm#P29_4637

TREATY OR AGREEMENT	MAIN PROVISIONS
Berne Convention for the Protection of Literary and Artistic Works (1886) *Note: Now administered by WIPO.	Signatories must grant the same protection to works originating in any contracting state as it does to works originating with its own nationals. Protection must not be conditional upon compliance with any formality (such as registration). The duration of protection is the end of the 50th year after the author's death. Protection extends to all works in the literary, scientific, and artistic domains. The duration of rights is 50 years. Rights include exclusive rights of authorization to: translate; to make adaptations and arrangements; to perform in public; to recite; to communicate to the public the performance of such works; to broadcast; to make reproduction in any manner or form; to use the work as a basis for an audiovisual work; and to reproduce, distribute, perform in public, or communicate to the public that audiovisual work.
Rome Convention for the Protection of Performers, Producers of Phonograms, and Broadcasting Organizations (1961) *Note: Administered jointly by WIPO, the International Labour Organization (ILO), and the United Nations Educational, Scientific, and Cultural Organization (UNESCO)	Protects performances, phonograms (recordings), and broadcasts. Performers such as actors, singers, musicians, dancers and others who perform) must consent to the broadcasting and communication of their live performance, including fixation in recordings, and reproduction of that fixation. Producers hold the right to authorize or prohibit the direct or indirect reproduction of their phonograms. Broadcasting organizations have the right to authorize or prohibit rebroadcasting, fixation, and reproduction of fixations of their broadcasts.

TABLE 2.3 *Key International Treaties and Agreements*

TREATY OR AGREEMENT	MAIN PROVISIONS
Geneva Convention for the Protection of Producers of Phonograms Against Unauthorized Duplication of Their Phonograms (1971) *Note: Administered by WIPO in cooperation with the ILO and UNESCO.	Reciprocal protection by contracting states against the importation and distribution of unauthorized copies of phonograms.
	The duration of protection is at least 20 years from the first fixation or the first publication of the phonogram.
Brussels Convention Relating to the Distribution of Programme-Carrying Signals Transmitted by Satellite (1974)	Contracting states must prevent the unauthorized distribution of program-carrying signals transmitted by satellite.
	Distribution is unauthorized if it has not been expressly authorized by the originating organization.
	This convention does not apply to the distribution of signals from a direct broadcast satellite (DBS).
WIPO Copyright Treaty (1996)	Signatories are bound to provisions of Berne Convention and 1971 Paris Act of the Berne Convention.
	The treaty covers computer programs and compilations of data, such as databases.
	Authors have the exclusive rights of distribution, rental, and communication to the public, subject to limitations and exceptions.
	There must be legal remedies for circumvention of technical copy protection and management measures.
	Each signatory must adopt measures that ensure the application of the treaty, effective enforcement procedures, deterrents, and adequate remedies for infringement

TABLE 2.3 *(Continued)*

and Trade Uruguay Round created the World Trade Organization (WTO) and established the Agreement on Trade-Related Aspects of Intellectual Property Rights (TRIPS). Agreements between WIPO and the WTO meant that WTO members could use that organization's dispute apparatus to enforce the IP and copyright rules within WIPO treaties and conventions. In 1996, WIPO member nations agreed the WIPO Copyright Treaty, which provided protection to copyrighted works, and to

TREATY OR AGREEMENT	MAIN PROVISIONS
WIPO Performances and Phonograms Treaty (1996)	Protects the IP rights of performers and producers of phonograms.
	Protections must be reciprocal among signatories.
	Remuneration to both performers and producers may be single payments.
	In recorded performances, performers are granted the exclusive rights of: reproduction, distribution, rental, and availability, subject to limitations and exceptions.
	For performances that are not recorded, performers have the rights of: broadcasting, communication to the public, and fixation (recording).
	Performers have the right to be identified and to object to any distortion, mutilation or modification that would be detrimental to their reputation.
	Producers of phonograms have the rights of reproduction, distribution, rental, and availability, subject to limitations and exceptions.

TABLE 2.3 *(Continued)*

the WIPO Performances and Phonograms Treaty, which dealt with the digital transmission of copyrighted works.

TRIPS covers copyrights, patents, trademarks, industrial designs, trade secrets, semiconductors, and geographical indications. TRIPS signatories must comply with the agreements in the Berne Convention, except with respect to the requirements on moral rights. It also:

- Defines computer programs as literary works and databases as compilations and places them under copyright.

- Requires signatories to give owners of computer programs and sound recordings the right to authorize or prohibit the rental of their copyrighted material.

- Sets a protection of sound recordings at 50 years and requires signatories protect existing sound recordings.

- Sets a minimum 50-year term for protection of motion pictures and other company-authored works.

Enforcement Requirements

In the Uruguay Round agreement, the World Trade Organization (WTO) replaced the General Agreement on Tariffs and Trade (GATT). Under the WTO, all the dispute resolution mechanisms that had been in effect under individual agreements (goods, services, TRIPS), were pulled together under the WTO umbrella. If a dispute settlement panel finds inadequate IP or copyright protection or enforcement in a member country, the signatory bringing the complaint has the right to retaliate against the violator in other trade sectors.

However, members must provide expeditious, fair, and equitable remedies to deter further infringements. Injunctive relief and other effective provisional measures should be available through the member states' judicial system and adequate compensation for damages to the rights holder should be available. Such damages might include attorney's fees, recovery of profits, recovery of statutory damages. Members must provide border measures that include attorney's fees, recovery of profits, recovery of statutory damages. Members must provide border measures that include release of goods by customs authorities, indemnification by the importer and owner of the goods, and the right to inspection. Finally, criminal procedures and penalties must be in effect for cases of willful commercial copyright infringement.

3 The Content Revolution

A decade ago, in 1996, there was no iPod. Napster was still three years in the future. Interactive cable still two years away. People who had high-speed access to the Internet were almost all using systems in the workplace; few people had broadband at home. There was no Wi-Fi. In 1994, only 15 million people had cell phones; by 1999, 104 million people in the U.S. had them. There were no color screens, personalized downloadable ringtones and image backgrounds, photo sharing, or SMS services.

Hotels didn't have pay-per-view. Hotel rooms didn't offer Internet access at any speed. Guests had to configure their modems to account for the need to dial "9" before calling the number of a local dialup service.

Only two years before, in 1994, the first consumer-level digital camera came on the market, the Apple QuickTake 100 camera. It could be connected to a home computer with a serial cable. Then in 1995, Hitachi's MP-EG1, the first camera to output moving pictures (in MPEG format) came to market and Panasonic and Sony introduced the first digital video cameras to the consumer market.

In 1996, the cost of a Quantum 3.2GB hard drive was $469.00, or 17.3 cents per megabyte, so editing on the PC was not an easy task. There was no TiVo, no personal video recorders at all. No widescreen TV or high definition TV, no home theater, or SurroundSound. Unbelievably, there were no commercially available DVD players or DVDs for another year!

Moreover, there was no content, except for a few companies in Seattle and Silicon Valley. Sure, there were movies, TV programs and shows, books, vinyl records, CDs, a few console games, and software programs. But these products were not called content. Only in the computer industry were media and entertainment products lumped with productivity software and given that term, and the people who create material are called "content providers," words still considered hideously derisive, desiccated, and soulless by many artists and creative professionals.

Nevertheless, today everyone in each of the media and entertainment industries is now aware of their output as content. And the transition from outlet-specific descriptors and formats to content is not merely semantic. People who create material for one media and entertainment channel and media platform recognize that their work will be formatted for cross-platform delivery, and multiple formats within each channel. For example, a successful motion picture or television property is likely to be compressed into MPEG2 for DVD, with simultaneous release of widescreen (16:9) and standard screen (4:3) versions. It may be repackaged for airlines use, ad-supported television, VCD (video CD), and console and online games, undergoing the appropriate surgical procedures for each platform incarnation.

Beyond mere formatting, the very nature of a product may change. For example, music companies have exploited a whole new category of product and revenue stream from "ringtones," small excerpts from existing popular songs that play when a purchase-to-download buyer's cellphone rings. The ringtone market is estimated to be between $1 and $3 billion, and it doesn't cannibalize any of the revenue from hit tunes. Nicolas Nardone, general manager of the French music label Small, was quoted as saying that in Great Britain, the music ringtones market is as important as the CD singles market.[1] Although the estimated market size and for ringtones may be somewhat overblown, this development underlines the unmistakable changes that have come and continue to impact the content marketplace, namely that "slice-and-dice" is the future, with prices geared to usage.

At the same time, the amount of content is exploding, much of it under the rubric of "personal publishing." While some people can make all the elements of their productions on their own, others purchase pre-produced building blocks. Tools like Sony's Acid software program, which allows people to piece together small musical phrases called "loops" into sophisticated compositions, allow

---

1. E Shibuya. Music business revenues via the ringtones market. Jan 25, 2004. Available at:http://www.smartmobs.com/archive/2004/01/25/music_business_.html.

anyone to create their own, royalty-free background music. Or, for the less adventurous, about $50 will buy a CD of background music for a home video from www.royaltyfreemusic.com. Similarly, professional photographs and illustrations are available for purchase-to-download for $1 each on www.istockphoto.com.

The same proliferation of content is occurring with video material. A 2003 study by the Yankee Group reported that businesses are incorporating rich-media communications into core business operations. Interviews with executives indicated that they saw significant increases in key performance metrics of customer support departments by using live chat and Internet-based video communications.[2]

The growth of rich media usage and its proven effectiveness as a means of communication points to a future where both businesses and individuals will want to purchase clips of movies and TV programs. The Hollywood community is not ready for such a shift, whether one considers business processes or managerial attitude. Permission to use every clip requires an individual contract that takes weeks, even months to execute, and are usually available only at a substantial cost. But ultimately attitudes will change. Just as music labels do not stand in the way of consumers using ringtones, movie executives will come to appreciate the potential for new revenue streams that will not detract from the value of their principal products.

The adoption of digital technologies to acquire and to deliver content in multiple formats and for multiple platforms is progressing rapidly throughout most parts of the industry, bringing in its wake new products and new revenue streams. The digitization of the motion picture industry started at the beginning of the production process (acquisition) and the end (distribution). Now it is making inroads in the middle of the process: editing, mixing, and processing.

Content Creation: Then and Now

Many content-producing sectors are all-digital. However, there are other sectors where acquisition and other parts of the production process are analog. For examples, some musicians play on acoustic instruments. And motion pictures, high-end television programs, and large-format photographs are still acquired using analog technology, such as film. A great deal of still photography, video games, and local broadcast production of TV and radio programs now originate digitally.

2.Yankee Group, Rich Media Applications Become Mainstream Among Enterprises. August, 2003. http://www.marketresearch.com/product/display.asp?xs=r&SID=35401418-324254555-290428305&ppg=4&kw=support&productid=942904&view=sta#

Despite the technological changes, the stages of content creation that were formalized in the motion picture industry nearly a century ago still prevail. The stages of the process provide a useful rubric for understanding the content creation process, whether it is analog or digital. The stages are:

- Development

- Pre-production

- Production

- Post-production

- Pre-distribution

The term "content lifecycle" has been coined to describe these stages of content creation. The lifecycle differs from one type of content to another. For example, the above lifecycle applies to motion pictures and television programs; video games and other interactive have a somewhat different lifecycle, as we shall see later in this chapter.

The activities that typically take place in these stages of motion picture and television creation have not changed very much, although they have been refined as the industry has matured. For example, the development stage has become a more prolonged, complex, and deliberate process as product development and marketing research came to the forefront after World War II, and affected virtually every industry.

Technology also drives changes in work processes. For example, over several decades the technology and processes for analog production in 35mm and 16mm formats were well-understood and highly integrated. Video production was standardized by 1953 and it too was integrated. But as digital technologies have penetrated production, the creation of content has become fragmented across a disparate production infrastructure, particularly in the motion picture sector.

Each of the stages of content creation takes place in a "silo" of activity, which means that each part is isolated from the other parts of the overall process. Hardware and software appropriate to each stage were developed at different times and with different needs. The machines and programs used in one part of the process can ingest and process material created, gathered, or acquired in another stage or location, but they often cannot process information about the material.

Tracking material requires information about it, so that loss of the data that describes the content makes it difficult to track it, to automate controlled access to it, or to audit who had access to it after its use. All these functions make it possible to provide higher level of protection and security for content while it is being prepared for distribution.

The next sections will consider the stages of production for motion pictures and other entertainment and media products, and how content is protected, or not, in each stage. Popular filmed entertainment products, such as movies and TV programs, often initiate a cascade of new products and revenue streams, so securing this material before it gets to market is also protecting downstream revenue.

Ideas and Concepts

The concept or idea stage is the origin of a content product. On the whole, there is little incentive to steal an idea in a community where there are far more ideas than productions. Some writers can come up with several ideas a day, a treatment a month, so there is really no shortage ideas. Moreover, some of the most prolific and creative people in the industry prefer to produce their own ideas; they are not dependent on others for them. Nevertheless, as we shall see in the next section, there are some instances of the theft of ideas once a creator's idea is expressed and circulated to studios and production companies for consideration.

There are only a few means of protection for creators. They can provide copies and pay a fee to the Writers Guild to register" their work. It is placed in a sealed enveloped, and the Guild provides numbered receipt for the property. Another method also involves the creator placing the work in a sealed enveloped; but in this instance, the author simply addresses the envelope to himself or herself. Once the envelope arrives, it is left unopened, and the Post Office date stamp serves as a record of when the work was expressed. Since the assertion of copyright is no longer necessary, a dated computer file will probably will do as well.

Well-known writers with a track record can pitch their ideas to the development executives in studios and production companies. The leave-behind document for a pitch is usually only a few pages that provide a working title and sketch the central idea, potential audience, the characters, the story arc, and the main plot points. New writers usually have to write a completed script.

Development

The development stage is where creative and business people shape and agree upon an idea for an entertainment or media project. The idea can come into being directly from the mind of the creative person, who "makes a pitch" to a studio, network, or production company. Or it may come from the business side of the house, when executives identify a potential market for a particular type of product.

At some point, the decision-makers will sift through the ideas that have been submitted to them and evaluate the potential attractiveness, value, and feasibility of the projected final product. They will ask the creators of their selected ideas for more detailed work, such as a "treatment." The treatment is a document prepared by the writer before the actual script is written. It is a detailed presentation of the story idea, including its elements of attraction to a specified audience, and its themes, characters, plot points, and story arc. Many changes are made to the treatment before executives commission a script.

At the same time, one or more artists may prepare "storyboards" based on the treatment. Storyboards are artistic renderings and drawings that depict major scenes in the projected script, conveying the look and feel the film will have when it is finished.

In the digital environment, the activities are almost the same as they were forty or fifty years ago, except that the work is done on computers and much of the communication is conducted over networks. Storyboards are now created on "previsualization" software that presents much more detailed, realistic storyboards than were possible in the past.

People may use either PCs or Apple computers, although in the corporate world, PCs predominate. Scriptwriters use relatively inexpensive specialized software on either type of computer. By contrast, previsualization requires much more expensive software and the storyboards are likely to be produced on Mac computers.

Protection and Development

Protecting content in development means preventing someone from stealing a commercially viable idea and selling that idea to a production company, studio, network, gaming company, music label, or other entity that has the means to actually produce and distribute it. One incentive to the theft of ideas at this stage is a procedure called "turnaround."

When a studio or production agrees to develop an idea, they give the creators an option on the property. As meetings take place to discuss the script, the casting, and the hundreds of activities that must take place to mount a production, one or more executives spend time on the project. They must account for that time, and the accounting department aggregates those hours. If the option runs out CONTINUED ▶

CONTINUED ▶   and another entity wants to option the property, that new buyer must pay "turnaround costs," the amount that the previous studio or production lodged as expenses against the project. Stealing circumvents those payments.

Stories about the theft of story ideas are rampant in Hollywood, and it is sometimes difficult to ascertain the truth. The most famous incident is the Art Buchwald case. He is an American humorist, nationally known for a long-running syndicated column that featured commentary and political satire. In 1982, he won a Pulitzer Prize for his work.

Buchwald wrote a screenplay titled *King for a Day*, and teamed up with Alain Bernheim to pitch the idea to Hollywood studios. In 1988, Buchwald and Bernheim sued Paramount pictures for credits and profits from *Coming to America*, a popular motion picture starring Eddie Murphy, claiming that Paramount had stolen the idea. Buchwald and Bernheim won the case and Paramount settled.

Similarly, longtime documentary producer Ben Moses came up with an idea for a film based on a radio DJ, Adrian Cronauer, whom Moses had known in Vietnam where he served in the military as a public information officer. He thought about the idea for many years and in the late 1970s, developed a treatment for a script, *Good Morning Vietnam*. The Walt Disney Company optioned the property and produced the film, starring Robin Williams. The studio refused to give Moses any story credit for his idea, although he was hired as a producer.

Moses protested this denial of credit to the Writers Guild of America (WGA), which arbitrates writers' claims. The hearing was about to start, and Disney stood firm in its decision. At the last minute, Moses' attorney found a lawsuit where someone had sued the studio, alleging that Disney had stolen the idea from him, and Disney had cited Moses as the creator of the idea in defense against this action! The WGA awarded a story credit to Moses.

Although a thorough discussion of digital rights management technologies appears in a later chapter, it is important to note here that some kinds of DRM would benefit creators. For example, a story idea or treatment could be password-protected, and it could be linked to an executable program that would send an email to the creator every time the file was opened. If every person who was sent the file was given a unique password, the DRM system would provide an audit trail of when the property was opened, who opened it, how long it was opened, how long that individual spent on each page.

Pre-production

In pre-production all the elements needed to actually produce content are strategically pre-positioned for production. The work includes:

- Finalizing the script

- "Breaking down" the script into actors' and performers' parts; necessary talent, creative partners, and crew; locations; lighting needs; wardrobe, hair and makeup; sets and backgrounds; props

- Locating, negotiating, and arranging for all the required elements, as identified in script breakdown

- Negotiating and executing contracts for required performers, talent, and crew

- Set production schedule

- Identifying and negotiating for downstream licensing partners and deals

Today, almost all of this work is summarized on computers and stored digitally, even if it results from face-to-face, telephone, or email communication. Digitization has introduced a number of important efficiencies into the pre-production phase. A few years ago, when artists wanted to be hired on a project, they submitted their work in bulky portfolios that were messengered to producers' offices. The work sat in a conference room over a period of weeks while executives considered who they would hire. Most artists lived in Hollywood or New York and could drop in for a subsequent interview.

Now this entire process occurs online. Artists submit their work from their homes and studios anywhere in the world by emailing files or a link to a website. The portfolios reside on a web site or the files go to an assistant who makes them available online to executives. Similarly, preliminary location scouting may occur online, with scouts looking at photos for leads to locations before physically inspecting them.

Even many of the casting calls for actors —"cattle calls" — have gone online. Casting agents look at actors' photographs online, making preliminary selections before calling them in for an interview.

Similarly, business processes are computerized. Some companies simply store contracts and other business documents. However, there are sophisticated entertainment and media contracts management systems that automate contracts and agreements that deal with rights creation, segregation and application as part of an industrial contract workflow process. In the entertainment and media industry, contracts and rights include such issues as licensing, clearance, audit, geographical and temporal exclusivity, finance, and royalties.

This capability offers intrinsic value in business-to-business rights management scenarios, in which exclusivity, non-exclusivity and co-exclusivity restrictions to intellectual asset use are subject to change with each new acquisition, sale or proprietary grant, says Jaguar Consulting. The company's System 7 software is built upon a contract database that standardizes the administration of rights management administration across all types of contracts, properties and business models for businesses that must manage intellectual property. Table 3.1 lists some of the rights associated with creating and distributing contract by companies in the entertainment and media industry.

DISTRIBUTION RIGHTS	COPYRIGHT
Rights licensing	Copyright year
Production company	Copyright channel
Theatrical	Expiration date
Home video	Copyright assignment
PPV	
• Pay TV	
• Cable	**RESTRICTIONS**
• Network	Cut and edit
• Syndication	Merchandising
Term	Dubbing language
Territory	Dubbing music
Foreign language	Underlying agreements
Holdbacks	Promotion and advertising
Sub-distribution	Sub-titles
Music	Film clips

TABLE 3.1 *Table 3.1 Typical Rights, Copyright, and Restrictions Covered in Entertainment and Media Contracts*

According to Jaguar, attempts to produce software for contracts management have foundered due to the inability to address the multiple business and licensing models needed for IP management. System 7 defines "licensed Assets, Territories, Rights, Restrictions, Distribution Channels, Contractual Parties, Languages, and Deal Types

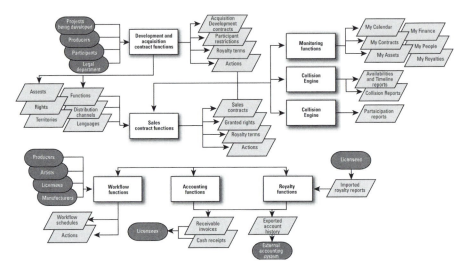

FIGURE 3.1 *Jaguar Consulting's System 7 software functions (Permission from Jaguar Consulting)*

in an unlimited number of levels and interrelationships."[3] Moreover, before DRM systems can operate efficiently, there must exist a definition of the parameters of usage and payments, which occur at the contractual stage. Figure 3.1 offers an overview of the processes that contracts management software must address.

For the most part, the pre-production stage does not require digital rights management technologies to protect copyrighted material. However, companies creating content are vulnerable to negative effects if competitors, outsiders, and employees learn the details of their business plans and arrangements. For this reason, some form of content management and security of the business documents that underlie content creation may be desirable. DRM systems could do the job, but so can some content and document management systems that incorporate a security element and audit capability.

Production

The production phase of content creation is where the various elements that will one day become a product actually come into being. In addition to recording on audiotape and videotape, or exposing and developing 35mm film, production also includes the creation of illustrations, drawings, animation cells, and special effects.

3. *Jaguar Consulting, Rights Management on Every Desktop*, at: http://www.jaguartc.com/news/jn05112004.asp#item1

For the most part, studio-backed motion pictures and scripted television programs are shot on 35mm film, then digitized and stored on high-capacity drives to be edited on digital editing systems. Many independent films are shot on videotape, either high-definition or 24p standard definition cameras. The film development lab or video post house that is storing the film or video makes a relatively inexpensive film print or a video version for viewing the day of or the day after the shoot, appropriately called "dailies."

Dailies are vulnerable to unauthorized distribution. In July of 2005, the U.S. Copyright Office proposed regulations for "pre-registration" of unpublished works like movies and music albums, which have had a history of pre-release infringement. In many cases, the material ends up on a P2P file-sharing network. The regulations would provide for pre-registration of a copyright while the work is being prepared for the marketplace.

Other elements of creative works may also be leaked. On average, 40% of studio films are composed of digitally-created special effects. Studios and production outsource specialized work to skilled artisans working in boutique digital facilities. The assignments and deliveries may take place anywhere in the world by a globally dispersed workforce. The computer workstations and software needed to do high-quality work is very expensive, creating material in 2k x 2k or 4k x 4k format. (2k x 2k means 2,000 vertical lines of resolution by 2,000 horizontal lines of resolution; similarly, 4k means 4,000 vertical and 4,000 horizontal lines of resolution.)

The machines used to do this work often require proprietary software with output to standard formats or even film. The implication of using these proprietary systems is that until there is a final product, it may be difficult to view it or process it on any other kind of system. So although most the work of the development and pre-production stages occurs on desktop Windows PCs and Macs, the lack of integration with business and development processes means that material may remain isolated in the production silo.

For independent films, workers are likely to create the drawings, illustrations, animations, and special effects for independent films on fast desktop computers (usually Macs, but increasingly with Windows PCs), running relatively inexpensive software. The output resolution is far lower than studio films, either at high definition TV (720p or 1080 x 1,920) or standard definition DV (720 x 486) quality.

In the production stage, there is a potential for theft, disappearance, alteration, or unauthorized distribution of copyrighted material, right out of the gate, so to speak. Particularly with widely awaited motion pictures like a *Star Wars*, even the early graphics, special effects, and compositions have great value to eager fans.

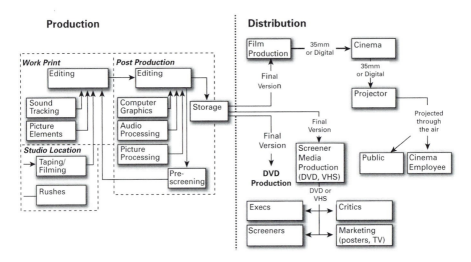

FIGURE 3.2 *Post-production and Distribution Flow (Permission from Lorrie Cranor)*[4]

The distribution of creative work across multiple facilities and companies (and hard drives) is another factor in the theft or loss of copyrighted material. Computer networks and high speed connectivity allow studios and production companies to hire people working almost anyplace in the world. The work that they undertake on their local machines may continue to reside on their hard drives, or in nearline or offline storage, long after the work is completed, with or without the permission of the company that commissioned it. The computer, workstation, and storage may not have the level of security that a studio or production company would impose on equipment under their own control.

Post-production

In this stage of production, editors make a final product out of the pieces of the produced material, the editing process. It is in this stage, as the project nears completion, that the threat of theft is the greatest. And since post-production is a lengthy, complex process, many opportunities exist for the determined thief to steal all or part of a valuable motion picture, as shown in Figure 3.2.

The first version of the product is called the rough cut. The rough cut may have blanks where elements are missing, or early versions of material that will later be

4. S Byers, L Cranor, et al. *Analysis of Security Vulnerabilities in the Movie Production, and Distribution Process.* Telecommunications Policy. Volume 28, Issues 7-8, August-September 2004, Pages 619-644. Available at: http://lorrie.cranor.org/pubs/drm03-tr.pdf.

improved may be used in place of the yet-to-be-delivered final version. The elements have not been color corrected so that they match, a process known as "color grading." Even so, there may be a big market for early versions of highly-anticipated films, even though they are not yet finished.

The post-production process is both creative and technical, involving both picture and sound. The film that has been shot is developed, resulting in an original camera negative. Usually only the good takes are printed, so the frame numbers are not entirely sequential. A film work print can be struck with frame numbers matching those of the negative, but today many productions use a telecine from the original negative camera roles to make video work prints.

The editor cuts together a rough cut, including a rough audio track mix, which goes to the director, producers, and other executives. It is at this point that a motion picture becomes vulnerable to theft because the rough cut is often similar enough to the final version to satisfy the business model of professional pirates or the curiosity of fans.

When all the players reach creative agreement on a final version, the editor generates an Edit Decision List (EDL) with key code numbers. A negative cutter conforms the camera original negative to the EDL, inserting the material from all special effects and optical effects. The conformed negative is used to strike an answer print, which is screened by the director and a professional colorist. They make notes on the fly about how to best make match the colors in the various scenes. Since the images have likely originated from many sources, there are often many adjustments.

The colorist makes the changes and re-films the conformed negative, striking a new answer print. If it is approved, a final color-timed interpositive is struck that serves as a protection master and as a film element for the final telecine transfer for video versions for distribution to other outlets. The interpositive is also used to make an internegative, the dupe neg, or multiple dupe negatives, to make as many prints as are needed for theatrical release. A contact printer is used to make the prints.

Digital Intermediates

In recent years, filmmakers have begun to replace this complex process with what is termed, "digital intermediate," or DI. The DI process is:

- Shoot and develop film

- Scan negative scanned via telecine and digitize to data

- Store data   CONTINUED ▶

CONTINUED ▶

- Edit on video and electronically insert effects and digital opticals

- Color correct (or grade) images

- Assemble final edited version electronically, using Edit Decision List

- Record finished version back to film

- Process and print film

Distribution follows post-production, and is not part of the creation process at all. Between post-production and distribution stands a link that is a kind of pre-distribution, pre-release phase, during which multiple prints of the final version are made for theatrical release or video release in a variety of venues, such as cable TV, satellite TV, airlines, and so forth. In addition, studios and distributors feed the promotion, publicity, and marketing machine to build excitement for the coming theatrical release. Video copies go to critics, entertainment-oriented television and radio programs, marketing partners, the advertising and public relations agencies, and judges for important film awards.

Insider Piracy

In the last decade, studios and post-production companies have recognized the potential for piracy from their facilities and adopted measures to improve the security of their processes and facilities, including the machines within them. Today, the potential damage to a picture's profitability through leakage is extraordinarily high. Just a decade ago, when a copy of a motion picture was stolen, it could be used to counterfeit VHS tapes that deprived a studio of some rental revenue. These counterfeiters faced many of the same costs as legitimate distributors. Now the Internet distributes a film to millions of potential consumers who would otherwise pay for a ticket or a rental, undermining the every potential revenue stream of the entire life cycle of the film.

A study by AT&T Research reviewed pirated 285 popular motion pictures that were released in 2002 and 2003 and were found posted on the Internet. Examining the condition of the copies and text and watermarks on the images, the researchers were able to determine the origin of the films, the source from which   CONTINUED ▶

CONTINUED ▶   the online movie files had been taken.[5] The analysis showed that 77% of pirated copies originated from insider sources, including pre-release versions and screener copies for critics, publicity, and advertising.

Of the total, only 5 were in a pre-release condition, indicating they leaked out from somewhere in the post-production work flow. On average, the movies had been posted on the Internet 100 days after their theatrical release and 83 days before DVD release. Seven of the motion pictures were posted prior to their theater release date. The study notes that:

> Particularly during production, many current security problems can be traced to the chaotic workflow. Policy must be developed that clearly delineates the process by which content is obtained or accessed, who is authorized to view or access it, and how failures in the process are reported. This policy, among other things, would codify the chain of custody... [6]

The study points to physical security measures that studios and production (and post-production) facilities could take to prevent leaks of motion pictures:

- Making an employee responsible for accompanying copies when they are taken off-site

- Define the requirements for off-site environments where copies may be taken

The study also provides a list of electronic security measures that could be employed in online environments:

- Adequate network security, with evidence of completeness

- Security measures on individual computers, such as physical separation from the Internet

- Frequent routine security audits of networks

- Removable storage devices that must be returned at the end of the work day

- On-site security personnel

The study also suggests that digital rights management may prove a useful means of controlling unauthorized distribution of motion pictures by insiders during the creation process. The researchers provide guidelines for the design of a DRM system that would meet the needs of studios, production companies, and post-production facilities. The security requirements for such a DRM system will be covered in Chapter 5.

---

5. Ibid., p. 6

6. Ibid., p. 13

Distribution and Consumption

Nowhere are the effects of digitization in the media and entertainment industry greater than in distribution and consumption. The astounding savings and dazzling speed of electronic transport are enough to make entertainment executives weep with joy, that is, when they are not quaking in fear. Because the digital distribution environment offers the same fabulous advantages to content pirates and infringers that it does to legal owners and distributors of content. Entertainment and media companies are still very uncertain how they can take advantage of the opportunity without having their business models eviscerated by the opportunities the same technologies offer to everyone else.

For music labels, online piracy threatens the profitability of albums. Previously labels could average out production costs by bundling together more expensive singles with cheaper album tracks. This allowed for a higher total album sale price. With the rise of online access, consumers can now "cherry pick" the best songs for free. Competing with free means charging a very low unit price for online singles, which undermines the profitability of the industry unless it can vastly increase legitimate sales of tracks, reduce production costs, or create an entirely new value proposition to cover its costs in the same way albums did. The labels fear that low-priced online sales will undercut profits to a greater extent than even savings on production and distribution costs and sharing in ancillary revenue streams can make up for, especially considering the loss of album sales.

> "There's concern because the legs for a film develop in the first three to four weeks. That's when you figure out what downstream windows will look like. You don't want to preview a film to the closest one million potential fans – there's an element of keeping it under wraps for marketing. These products are not made to be viewed on a small screen with small speakers; they are developed for impact in a theater. The buzz is associated with entire presentation and you can de-buzz a film quickly with release on a PC or even a TV." — Brian Seth Hurst, Opportunity Management

The effects of piracy and casual downloading on filmed entertainment content have been far less severe than they have been for the music industry. The files are so much larger that downloading is time-consuming and memory-intensive. In addition, the Hollywood film industry is less dependent on a bundling strategy. The television industry has created viable broadcast and network business models that reward consumption. And TV content creators are now profiting from DVD packages that bundle an entire season of shows – a daunting download at almost any speed. This new source of revenue points to a new way of thinking about content – that it has multiple lives.

The Content Lifecycle

As mentioned earlier, the content lifecycle differs by content type. Interactive content, which has a more intricate relationship between content programming and delivery platform, provides a good example of how the lifecycle may vary. In 2003, the revenue brought in by video games exceeded that of the theatrical box office revenue from motion pictures. Video games incorporate moving images, presented in an interactive format.

There are many similarities between creating motion pictures and video games: creating story lines, writing dialogue, casting, designing visuals and directing the cinematic portions of the game. The methods for creating video games are still evolving. As a result, the following version of the lifecycle of video games is subject to change:

- Concept/idea

- Development: Establish functional requirements for interface, game engine, and technology, write story and script, technical documentation, and licensing of game engine and technology

- Programming: Write code for game play, interaction, etc.

- Production

- Asset integration: Similar to post-production

- Testing and Quality assurance

Like the movie industry, video game makers use big names and spend big money to produce blockbuster hits. Spin-offs of successful motion pictures and comic books are common, as are prequels, sequels, and clones. Getting a video game to market nearly doubled between 2000 and 2004, when it cost $10 million or more: $5 million to $8 million to produce, another $5 million or for marketing and promotion, and $1 million or more for licensing fees if the game is based on a motion picture property. Of the more than 600 games released in 200, only eight to 15 of them sold 1 million or more copies. However, since games sell for $40 each (as compared to a first-run theater ticket at $10), a hit will bring in $40 million or more. Revenues from a mega-hit game that sells more than 10 million copies will bring in revenues that rival a blockbuster movie.

The Many Lives of Content

There is an iterative aspect to the content lifecycle that is not captured by simply detailing the various steps of content creation, as presented by many content management vendors. Decades ago, a studio created a movie. Perhaps there was a sequel, or a follow-on movie, like the numerous Andy Hardy movies that starred Mickey Rooney and Judy Garland. Perhaps the movie came from a book. Perhaps songs from the movie became popular, or a popular song was incorporated in the motion picture. For the most part, these efforts were not coordinated; they were simply situational opportunities that executives could exploit and then move on to the next project.

The view of content as having multiple life cycles emerged after Ted Turner's purchase of part of the MGM library. He was mocked for paying $1 billion for what was considered a defunct library. Turner laughed all the way to the bank as he used that library to launch the TNT and TBS networks.

Now it is well-understood that content has many lives: first as an initial product, then as an asset that can be reincarnated – repackaged, re-expressed, and repurposed, then distributed, consumed, and experienced in multiple, co-existing forms in many venues and on a virtually unlimited number of displays and devices. The implications of a content life cycle are enormous. A hit isn't just a single product; it is a franchise that may spawn many more profitable offerings.

Today, studios and production companies examine every idea in terms of its extensibility to other media, platforms, and products. Ideally, on its initial release, a hit movie would lend itself to downstream sources of revenue: sequels, prequels, DVD sales and rental, music CD, TV shows, video game, board game, comic book, and musical stage play. The music can be sliced into polyphonic ring tones and sold for $2.50 per user. Images can be licensed as screen savers for computers, PDAs, and cell phones. It's even better if the popularity of the movie will support licensing for key rings, sheets, pot holders, suitcases, dolls, and an unimaginable host of other items. And this is just the first release. Later, the motion picture and all of its elements could be re-used, re-purposed, and re-created to initiate an entirely new lifecycle.

The traditional creation phases of content are development, production and post-production, distribution, and consumption. Now content owners must add reincarnation (repackaging, re-expressing, and re-purposing) new lives when the resulting product is recreated, re-distributed and experienced by a new audience or within a new context.

Repackaging means taking the content and changing its meaning to the consumer by bundling it with other material, updating its appeal to contemporary society, or improving it through processes not available at the time of production. Colorizing, film restoration, and digital renovation, and theming are all ways to repackage content. However, there may be few changes made to the content in terms of its overall flow or number and type of images and sounds.

> "We've found that DVD's extend the life of content. We can market our library by putting together films and programs in themed packages that give us new marketing opportunities with clear business models." — Mary Lou Bono, VP, Marketing, Home Video at Rhino Entertainment/Warner Strategic Marketing.

Re-purposing content means using content to meet some new objective that is different from its original one. Examples include such activities as licensing a Beatles song as a background for a TV commercial; playing a popular love song at a wedding, placing one or two stanzas of a poem at the beginning of a book chapter. Typically repurposing means some editing of the content to fit the time or space requirements its new creative role, but the content is recognizable as a form of the original.

Re-expressing content means reworking it for a different media platform or device. It is likely to entail a complete overhaul of the content so that storytelling method, user involvement, and functionalities are perfectly situated in the new environment. The game, *Enter the Matrix*, is a re-expression of the movie, *Matrix Reloaded*. It is an individual work, quite different from its parent although related to it.

Media Asset Management, Digital Asset Management and Content Management

There is nothing set in cement about the terms media asset management (MAM), digital asset management (DAM), and content management (CM). They are often used interchangeably, although MAM is more often used in the context of traditional media such as movies, broadcast, and music, and DAM is the more common term for Internet applications, such as web site development and management. MAM and DAM usually refer to systems for managing the elements that are used to create a completed content product. For example, the shots, animation cells, special effects, music, and sound effects that go into a motion picture are all assets. The final film is content. MAM and DAM systems

Content management (CM) is an integrated business and technology strategy to create, manage and distribute content. Thus, a content management system (CMS) describes a specific hardware and software infrastructure that goes beyond MAM and DAM and carries the completed content products into delivery and distribution outside the creation organizations. Theoretically, an enterprise-wide system could integrate records management, document management, contracts management, financial and business systems, enterprise resource planning (ERP) media asset management, search engines, and content output formatting.

However, such integration does not yet exist. Entertainment and media companies still have silos of computerization for ERP and financial systems. A few have media asset management for particular departments such as marketing and promotion or for a specific show, such as *Entertainment Tonight*, a production of Paramount Television, which does not have integrated content management for the overall company.

The functions of a CMS that is independent of many of the other business process systems are to organize content, organize information about the content, automate content-centric workflows, and provide some level of security and audit trail of the use of content within the organization or organizations that are engaged in creating or distributing content. Note that CM organizes two classes of "objects" the content and information about the content. The content itself may be called "essence," as opposed to metadata, nomenclature adopted as part of the standard promulgated by the Society of Motion Picture and Broadcast Engineers (SMPTE).

Metadata is the key to organizing content, as shown in Figure 3.3. Metadata means "data about data." In other words, in a digital environment, the content (or essence) is itself data. Metadata is data that describes the content. Metadata enable search engines. Metadata vary with respect to their quality, quantity, granularity, descriptiveness, searchability, and availability. Indeed, the value of the overall CMS is dependent on the quality of the metadata it uses.

FIGURE 3.3 *Life is Easier with Metadata*

Consider the search function on a personal computer. The user calls up "Search" and can fill in blanks about the file – its name, file extension, and the date it was created or modified. All this information is metadata. When users do not know any of this metadata, they must search the essence, the entire contents of the file, a much more time-consuming and processor intensive task.

When a member of a work team must locate a particular piece of content within the digital bowels of an organization, the task would be daunting, perhaps even impossible, without metadata. Indeed, information work without some kind of structured guide to the data in storage is difficult to imagine. Perhaps that is why that when Viacom surveyed departments and sub-departments on its Paramount Studios lot, the company found that employees had created more than 30 database projects on their own, just to track and retrieve information for the work they were tasked to carry out.

As noted earlier, no entertainment and media company has a unified content creation, distribution, and financial digital infrastructure. However, some web companies and some departments within content-producing and distributing organizations do have end-to-end integrated platforms. It is likely that companies in this industry are likely to move towards enterprise-wide infrastructure integration as system design becomes more sophisticated and hardware and software standards evolve, as shown in Table 3.2.

INTEGRATED CONTENT CREATION AND DISTRIBUTION		
MEDIA ASSET MANAGEMENT OR DIGITAL ASSET MANAGEMENT	**CONTENT MANAGEMENT AND DIGITAL RIGHTS MANAGEMENT**	**CONTRACTS MANAGEMENT AND RELATIONSHIP MANAGEMENT**
Create Content	**Distribute Content**	**Monetize Content**
Original and Repurposed Material	*Wholesale* *Retail* *(B2B)* *(B2C)*	*Business Processes*
Step 1: Acquisition	Step 1: Encode	Step 1: Process Revenue
• Capture, create or acquire assets	• Apply appropriate markup language: HTML, SGML, XML	• Process payments from consumers
• Generate acquisition metadata: date/time, etc.	• Embed languages	
	• Code user player types, bit rates, end-user devices	

TABLE 3.2 *Integration of Media Asset Management and Digital Asset Management, Content Management, Digital Rights Management, and Financial Accounting*

INTEGRATED CONTENT CREATION AND DISTRIBUTION		
MEDIA ASSET MANAGE-MENT OR DIGITAL ASSET MANAGEMENT	**CONTENT MANAGEMENT ANDDIGITAL RIGHTS MANAGEMENT**	**CONTRACTS MANAGEMENT AND RELATIONSHIP MANAGEMENT**
Create Content	**Distribute Content**	**Monetize Content**
Original and Repurposed Material	*Wholesale* *Retail* *(B2B)* *(B2C)*	*Business Processes*
Step 2 Ingest 1. Digitize asset, if analog 2. Parse (by text keyword, scene change, lighting change, lyrics, key change, etc.) 3. Capture existing metadata	Step 2: Transcode Format for consumption • Enable content customization • Link to metadata database • Embed callouts for targeted ads	Step 2: Track and Audit • Track content and con-sumer usage • Collate and report session data per partnership agree-ments
4. Generate metadata that describe Asset • Filename, name, number, informal handle • Brief description in natural language • File format detail • Creation software detail • Attach descriptive meta-tags 5. Generate low resolution proxies for search, browse, and retrieval 6. (If ingested material is a finished program, encode for distribution.)	Step 3: DRM • Intellectual property pro-tection (IP) - Digital watermark - Encryption • Digital Rights Management (DRM) - Specify business rules that apply to use of con-tent (Subscription, pay-per, ad-supported, etc.)	Step 3: Pay Referral Partners • Calculate referral payments to affiliates and other sources

TABLE 3.2 *(Continued)*

INTEGRATED CONTENT CREATION AND DISTRIBUTION			
MEDIA ASSET MANAGE-MENT OR DIGITAL ASSET MANAGEMENT	**CONTENT MANAGEMENT ANDDIGITAL RIGHTS MANAGEMENT**		**CONTRACTS MANAGEMENT AND RELATIONSHIP MANAGEMENT**
Create Content	**Distribute Content**		**Monetize Content**
Original and Repurposed Material	*Wholesale (B2B)*	*Retail (B2C)*	*Business Processes*
Step 3: Edit 1. Check out asset from storage • Collect user information • Content request information • Authenticate user ID/account status authorized users to retrieve assets via meta-tags 2. Assemble rough cut 3. Edit and assemble program (Includes repurposing and re-expressing of existing assets and programming 4. Check-in asset into storage • Invoke version control 5. Collect user session data	Step 4: Package for Delivery • Modulate and encode, as needed for channel • Apply distribution wrapper or format - SOAP - ICE		Step 4: Pay Fulfillment Partners • Refer merchandise orders to fulfillment partner(s) and allocate payments

TABLE 3.2 *(Continued)*

INTEGRATED CONTENT CREATION AND DISTRIBUTION		
MEDIA ASSET MANAGE-MENT OR DIGITAL ASSET MANAGEMENT	**CONTENT MANAGEMENT ANDDIGITAL RIGHTS MANAGEMENT**	**CONTRACTS MANAGEMENT AND RELATIONSHIP MANAGEMENT**
Create Content	**Distribute Content**	**Monetize Content**
Original and Repurposed Material	*Wholesale* *Retail* *(B2B)* *(B2C)*	*Business Processes*
Step 4: Secure Approval • Circulate edited version and secure necessary approvals.	Step 5: Deliver to Distribution Point • Insert ads • Transport to playout server or publish to edge servers • Automated intake by receiving sites	Step 5: Pay Royalties • Calculate royalties • Pay appropriate royalties to content creators, owners, and license holders

Step 5: Storage
• Store new asset or program, as well as previous version(s).
  - Tiered storage: Online, nearline,
    offline		

	Step 6: Distribute
	• Distribute to end-users/consumers
	  - Broadcast
	  - Opt-in push
	  - On demand
	• Monitor transmission
	  - Quality of service data
		Step 6: Mine data
		• Mine data about user and usage to promote additional content
		• Share data with Customer Relationship Management (CRM) partner.

TABLE 3.2 *(Continued)*

Just as the means of managing content are changing, the work process and lives of the workers who create content are changing as well. They no longer have to live in a few centers of media production, such as Hollywood, New York, Miami, London, Paris, Berlin, Rome, Mexico City, Bombay, Shanghai, or Hong Kong. They are likely to work anywhere in the world, never meeting the other people who work on the project.

The Work of Creating Content

From its earliest beginnings, the work on motion pictures was often done by ad hoc groups, one-time teams that form and re-form from project to project. During certain time periods, such as the late 1940s and 1950s, studios hired permanent employees and created pictures almost entirely on the lot, but work groups assembled for the length of time needed has been the more common working arrangement. Even so, most of the workers lived near a center of production and secured work through local face-to-face networking.

Today, the same ad-hoc team formation takes place, but the workers may never come together at all, except in the live action production phase. Geographically distributed work groups that form a collaborative team is a working style that increasingly permeates the entertainment industry. In pre-production, work groups are distributed around the world. Music and graphics files zip across the network between collaborators as people separated by thousands of miles work together.

Real-time two-way online collaboration compensates for distance. London has become an enormous post-production center for both Europe and the U.S. Two-way high speed networks link London post-production facilities through services such as Sohonet, which offers secure Ethernet IP connectivity services at 10 Mb, 100 Mb, and 1 Gb fiber, with cost competitive connections to Los Angeles, Australia, New Zealand, and Amsterdam. Working with partners, Sohonet connects to all major U.S. and European cities as well, with sufficient bandwidth to allow simultaneous collaborative work and approval functions.

One of the first instances of online collaboration occurred in the final editing of Jurassic Park. Director Steven Spielberg was shooting *Schindler's List* in Poland when his approval was needed on some edited sequences of *Jurassic Park*. Spielberg and the Los Angeles-based editing facility were linked via the Sprint 'Drums' network, an ISDN line that carried the material at 128 megabits per seconds. It was primitive by today's standards, but sufficient for the work on *Jurassic Park* to go forward.

Concept	Single individual
Development	Individual or team
Preproduction	Small work group (3-50)
Production	Medium-sized work group (2-500)
Post Production	Medium-sized work group (1-500)
Marketing	Small work group (1-50)
Sales	Small work group (1-50)
Distribution	Small work group (1-50), plus thousands of exhibitors and hundreds of thousands of retailers
Consumption	Consumers – lots of them! Music industry: Gold album=500,000 • Platinum album=1,000,000 • Diamond album=10,000,000 TV industry: 2004 - 1 share point = 1% = 1,096,000 households tuned to a specific program Motion picture industry: Box office. For an example of box office revenue on a release weekend, see Table 3-3. Video games: Hit=1,000,000 Megahit=10,000,000

TABLE 3.3 *Creating and Consuming Content*

"Follow the Sun" Production and Post-production

In computer software development, a "follow the sun" creation strategy means that distributed groups work around the clock in different locations around the world. A team starts at 9:00 in the morning, say in California. Eight hours later, a Chinese group picks up where they left off. Nine hours after that, a group in London gets to work, and at the end of their day, they send the work back to California. Every worker puts in an eight or nine hour day; there is no overtime, yet work continues on a 24-hour basis.

In the entertainment industry, animation projects lend themselves to this kind of production. It already occurs between workers in California and Japan, seven hours apart. Many post-production processes are also suitable for distributed work

#1 FOR WEEK OF 6/12/05: MR. AND MRS. SMITH, IN 3,424 U.S. THEATERS			
	DATE FRIDAY 6/10	DATE SATURDAY 6/11	DATE SUNDAY 6/12
Day #	1	2	3
Box office (daily gross)	$17,474,908	$18,895,207	$13,972,763
% Change	NA	8.1%	-26.1%
Avg per theater	$5,104	$5,518	$4,081
Total gross	$17,474,908	$36,370,115	$50,342,878

TABLE 3.4 *Box Office Revenue for One Film over a Summer Weekend in 2005*

and around-the-clock activity. As bandwidth increases and the cost of transport goes down, there is likely to be more such arrangements.

One reason filmed entertainment can be so profitable is that the number of people it takes to produce a motion picture or program is very small in comparison to the potential number of consumers of the final product. Table 3.3 summarizes the number of people involved in the various stages of the initial release lifecycle of motion pictures, including its consumers. Table 3.4 details the box office revenue of a typical film in the spring of 2005, demonstrating the revenue-based power of the mass consumer market.

The Content Economy

The digital, networked marketplace has changed some of the basic building blocks of the economic foundation upon which the content marketplace was built over the previous hundred hears. These fundamentals include such aspects of the market as supply, demand, value and pricing, fungibility (the extent to which consumers can substitute one product for another), and competition.

One way to consider all these issues together is to examine the risks of creating and distributing content. The motion picture business has always been a high-wire enterprise with both the risk of a flop and the chance of a soaring upside. In the 1960s, 1970s, and even the 1980s, the levels of risk decreased somewhat because multiple downstream distribution windows allowed almost every motion picture to recoup the cost of its production.

More recently, risks have not only increased, they're changing. With the advent of digital technologies, creative individuals and independents are starting to develop and distribute their own filmed entertainment on their own. To start, the supply of sophisticated, high-quality content may increase dramatically in the next few years.

Prosumer high definition production equipment means that with a dream, perseverance, a circle of friends, and an investment of less than $30,000, anyone can make a movie. And when garage producers can distribute their own trailers across the Internet for pennies and send DVDs to consumers for less than $4.00. How long can it be before one of them in Dallas, Des Moines, or San Diego creates and distributes a feature that makes millions? Three years? Five years? Ten years?

To see how the distribution of risk is changing, consider the risks of developing and creating a project in the film industry between 1950 and 2000. Creative people were the ones who took a chance on finding a buyer in a very limited market for their ideas, often toiling without compensation in the early stages of bringing forth their wares. Production risks were offset by insurance and completion bonds. And, in any case, before the advent of communication networks and high-quality, low-cost digital equipment, studios were able to entirely monopolize the means of production and reproduction.

Now the distribution of risks in the entertainment industry is changing in subtle ways that demand careful attention. Nowhere is this trend more evident than in the areas of project acquisition. The headlines tell the story.

- Mel Gibson acts on his own to produce a blockbuster…without any studio backing

- *Blair Witch Project* and *My Big Fat Greek Wedding* become huge indie hits

- Bollywood and Beijing churn out regional features with stunning regularity, establishing robust (and profitable) local production facilities, striking an independent path from the US entertainment industry

In the old days, the biggest risk was to buy a property that didn't become a hit. But, with the downside cushioned by multiple downstream distribution windows, the more serious risk is failing to buy a project that becomes a hit. Moreover, in the new environment, creative people can bypass studios altogether, raising the possibility that they could suffer the loss of the very engines of popular culture: vibrant, passionate ideas that underlie hit movies and programs. Studios don't create ideas, people do. Studios and major production companies may not even get a chance to bid on exciting properties as even insiders opt out of what they see as a repressive creative regime.

For example, recently a successful comedy screenwriter with four hits to his list of impressive credits produced a hilarious send-up of popular religions with his own money. Shooting on HDTV and editing on his own computer, he made the film he always wanted to make for only $120,000. He's showing the trailer to reps and distributors now. Check out the upcoming Discovery Channel show, *Final Cut*, which will give independent productions submitted by viewers an initial distribution forum. And how long will it take for podcasting to become a source for visual content?

It is just the beginning of the flowering of independent production of visual media. The 2005 National Association of Broadcasters convention saw sub-$5000 high definition television cameras on the exhibit floor. Apple's new G5, loaded with Final Cuts Pro 4, edits the resulting footage in native HDTV in real time. Specifications are in the final stages of approval for new single-sided DVDs that will hold an entire HDTV-quality feature movie.

While studios will continue to produce high-cost, high-value content, alternative producers will take advantage of the lower cost of production, permitting them to create material at a much-decreased risk. In this environment, studios can expect many more content-producing entities to enter the market. Some of them, especially those that have backing, funding, and participation from Hollywood veterans, will be able to compete with studios.

These events listed above are the harbingers of a tectonic shift in the rich media sectors of the entertainment industry. Hollywood may still avoid the flaccid response that Detroit made to lower cost competition in the 1960s: 'Consumers like the big, flashy models,' said U.S. automakers. 'They'll never switch to these teensy tin vehicles from Japan.' Instead, the rise of lower cost indie hits could motivate Tinsel Town studios to do what they do best: Make dreams come true. Established studios and production companies can support, encourage, finance, and assist the coming legion of entertainment producers, lending the best of them their powerful marketing engines and distribution muscle.

Huge advantages can accrue to existing entertainment and media companies if they shed the risks of development and production to independents working in new and niche markets that are too small for studios to enter. At the same time, studios can reduce independents' risks in the areas of marketing and distribution. For this strategy to pay off, Hollywood will need to be open to a greater range of producers and projects than it has ever been before, a kind of share-the-risk, share-the-spoils philosophy with an expanded circle of producers who create material for different audiences at different price points.

The Integrated Content Creation and Distribution Platform

So far, this chapter has considered three infrastructure components that would make up an integrated content creation and distribution platform: Asset and Content Management + Digital Rights Management + Contracts Management and Accounting Systems, as shown below in Figure 3.4. But there are two additional elements to consider: devices and networks. Devices and networks change the creation, delivery, and consumption of content, mediating between content creators, owners, and distributors and consumers of the entertainment and media products.

Just as content producers and distributors worry about profiting from content, network providers worry about making money from the transport of content. Traditional telephone companies bring in enormous revenues from their sophisticated billing systems that let them bill customers for each call. Such billing is only possible because of the underlying ability to capture information about every telephone call, resulting in a document called the Call Detail Record, or CDR.

When a person initiates a call, telephone company software collects data about the location of each party, the time of day, the length of the call, and the type of call. Once a month, the company aggregates all the CDRs and sends the customer a bill.

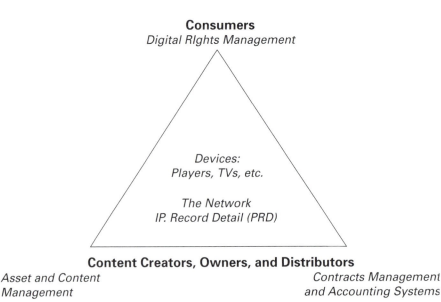

FIGURE 3.4 *An Integrated Infrastructure for Online Content Distribution*

Even though IP networks ride on the telephony infrastructure, network providers do not collect this kind of information. The telephone company generates a CDR only for the call to the ISP (for dialup customers) or charges a flat fee for broadband access, which does not require any CDR at all. But the telephone (or cable) company is not able to get more money from the customer who works online all day and downloads all night than from the customer who sends email to their grandchildren once a week.

It is certainly possible for telephone and cable companies to monitor their customers' activities to generate an IP Detail Record (IPDR), and as broadband becomes ubiquitous, there may be some profit pressure on network providers to do so. Certainly they will be looking to find ways to insinuate themselves between content and consumers as a way of increasing revenues.

The next chapter looks at the high stakes and the multiple stakeholders involved in the content industries and the technologies that depend on them. Participants in the commercial content industries, communications giants, consumers, and society as a whole

4 Content Protection and Digital Rights Management Technologies

Content owners can protect the material they own with a single technology, but they often combine multiple schemes. In addition, as noted early, protecting content (and copyright) differs from managing copyright. Some of the technologies explored in this chapter protect content. Some manage rights and may even incorporate the terms of contracts with links back to systems that handle the distribution of royalties to the parties who are entitled to receive them. And even though the two tasks are not the same, there are some schemes that do both.

Although this chapter covers the various content protection and digital rights management techniques and technologies, entire books and manuals can and have been written about each of them. So it is impossible to discuss any one of them in detail. Research on the Internet will turn up relevant white papers and standardization documents, allowing those who are interested to get the further information they seek. The chapter ends with a consideration of how, in a general way, these techniques and technologies can be combined into systems of protection and management. The next chapter will look at actual implementations of protection, rights management, and monetization systems.

There are many different approaches to securing content against unauthorized use, but it is possible to group them into four general categories:

- Protecting the content itself
- Protecting access to the content

- Limiting or blocking the copying of the content

- Protecting against transporting the content from one device or drive to another

Technologies that Protect the Content Itself

Most of these techniques involve some modification of the content in order to make it secure from unauthorized use. Depending on the method, there may be such additions may include tags, headers and other strings of digital data, and invisible graphical or data elements. Or it can involve transformation of the content by encrypting or encoding it in some way. An exception to this general rule is 'digital fingerprint' schemes, which do not modify the content. Rather, they measure the content and create a record of its unique parameters (such as waveforms) and looks for that fingerprint in the stream of content that flows across a given point in a network or device.

SECURITY TECHNOLOGIES	DESCRIPTION
Direct Protection of the Content Content Identification and Unique IdentifierSystems	Utilizes techniques that protect the content directly. They do not prevent access to the content, nor do they manage rights to the content, although they are usually used in combination with technologies to accomplish such ends. An essential process for protecting content is identifying it. So this section begins with systems that provide unique identifiers for individual works and, in some instances, for the constituent parts of an individual work.
Digital Watermark	Embedding information in content that allows the material to be identified. Usually the watermark and the information are hidden
Digital Fingerprint	Using the characteristics of a particular piece of content to create a unique signature of that content. A filter examines a data stream, seeking a match to that unique signature, it's "fingerprint."

TABLE 4.1 *Techniques to Protect Content*

SECURITY TECHNOLOGIES	DESCRIPTION
Encryption	Digital content is data. Data can be altered in a methodical way so that it cannot be consumed. Before the data is changed, it is called "plain text." After it has been encoded, it is called "cipher text." In order to experienced encrypted content, the user must decrypt it by means of a "key" or password.
	The two types of encryption. Symmetric encryption techniques use the same key to encrypt and decrypt; asymmetric encryption techniques, sometimes called public-key encryption, use different keys for encryption and decryption.
Symmetric Encryption Algorithms Algorithms	An algorithm is a set of instructions that, when applied to a string of data, transform that data into a different string. Some well-known algorithms for symmetric encryption are Advanced Encryption Standard (AES), Data Encryption Standard (DES), triple DES, and Skipjack. RSA is an example of an asymmetric encryption algorithm
CSS	
AACS	
Asymmetric Encryption Algorithms	
Keys: Public keys and Private keys	Keys unlock encryption. In the digital world, they are composed of a series of characters, alphabetic, numeric, or symbolic. A public key can be known and accessed; a private key is a secret. Public and private keys are different but related. One of the keys is used to encrypt plain text into cipher text; the other key is used to decrypt the cipher text into plain text.

TABLE 4.1 *(Continued)*

Identification

Without identification of intellectual property, there can be no protection of it. And the ability to protect content can be enhanced greatly when identification is extended to each copy of the content, not just the original. The International Standards Organization working group to develop standards for metadata says that the Digital Item (an identified digital object) is "the fundamental unit of distribution and transaction."[1]

A package of digital content includes metadata and essence. Essence is the actual content. Metadata means "data about data"; in other words, it is information about the content. Identifiers are metadata.

For many reasons, the shorter an identifier is, the better. A short identifier is easier to attach, embed, and transport. Yet it must convey enough information to provide unique identification of a given piece of content; that is, it must distinguish effectively between one digital object and another. One way of limiting the amount of information that must be carried by the content itself is to list the identifier in a database that holds more information about the content, its attributes, and its provenance. Added to the identifier is a pointer to the database where information about the content is stored.

In the digital world, there is a great deal of ambiguity about the boundaries of an item. One reason is that there can be so many items within items. For instance, take a music CD. The CD is an item. Each individual track could be an item. The lyrics to each song could be an item. And, in the age of sampling, each musical phrase or each note could be an item. The question of how finely to identify the elements of a digital item is referred to as the granularity of an identifier.

Most content owners would like identifiers to persist over time. This means finding a way to permanently attach them to the content or to embed them within it. When the content is highly granular, such as audio, it may prove impossible to identify every possible element within the content. Even if it were possible to identify it, it might not be practical to attach or embed the identifier in every element.

Identifiers tend to be domain-specific. For more than three decades, most industries, industry segments, networks, and media channels developed and used its own system of identifiers, as shown in Table 4.2.

Unique Material Identifier (UMID)

The Society of Motion Picture and Television Engineers (SMPTE) adopted the UMID as its standard (SMPTE 330M) for identifying audio-visual material. The

---

1. Borman, J., Hill, K. (ed). *MPEG-21 Overview v.5*. Published by the Requirements Group, International Standards Organization, WG-11, October 2002. Available at: http://www.chiariglione.org/mpeg/standards/mpeg-21/mpeg-21.htm#_Toc23297968.

DOMAIN	IDENTIFIER SYSTEMS AND LANGUAGES
Metadata	MPEG 21, MPEG 7, Dublin Core, MARC, <indecs>, P/META (EBU), TV-Anytime
AudioVisual	UMID and Extended UMID, MPEG-7, ISAN and V-ISAN, DMCS, P/META
Music and Audio	GRid, MPid, MWLI, ISMN, ISRC, ISWC, CAE/IPI
Multimedia	UMID, MPEG-21, DOI, <indecs>
eBook	OEBF, DAISY
Print Media (Books, periodicals, journals, magazines, newspapers)	Onix, NewsML, PRISM, ISSN, ISBN, PII, SICI, EPICS, CrossRef, ISTC,
Libraries, Archives, Museums, and Education	METS, MARC , MODS, FRBR, CIDOC, Dublin Core, IMS, SCORM, IIM, NITF

TABLE 4.2 *Identifiers and Their Domains*

UMID offers considerable granularity for audio-visual material. It applies to components as small as a single frame of film or video.

The Basic UMID contains 32 bytes of identification information. The first 12 bytes are a label that signals the presence of a UMID identifier and content. The next 3 bytes define the length of the material, and the final 16 bytes specify the unique numerical identifier of the content. The Extended UMID adds an additional 32 bytes of information, that include the time, date, and place of creation, and codes to identify the country and organization or origin, and user, as shown in Figure 4.1.

SMPTE has also standardized a metadata dictionary (MDD) that describes the all the data elements within the industry. The organization also created a registry for defining sets of data and metadata for storage and exchange. Figure 4.2 shows how UMID identifiers fit into the overall structure of the MDD.

The SMPTE metadata methodology calls for KLV (key, length, value) encoding for the data elements and sets, which allows for searching of these variables without searching the entire content package.

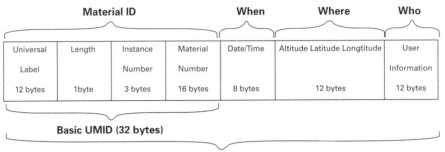

FIGURE 4.1 *UMID Header*

International Standard Recording Code (ISRC)

The ISRC is approved by the International Standards Organization (ISO) as an international identification system for sound recordings and music video recordings. Each identifier is unique and is permanently recorded into the product. The embedded information includes the country of registration, the registrant's code, the last two digits of the year in which the material was registered, and a five-digit unique number, called its Designation Code. The ISRC is used also used as part of a digital watermarking copying protection method.

Digital Watermarking

Watermarks have been used by centuries by papermakers to identify their products. They created the watermark by making an impression on the paper that could be seen when it was held under or in front of a light. A series of engineering groups

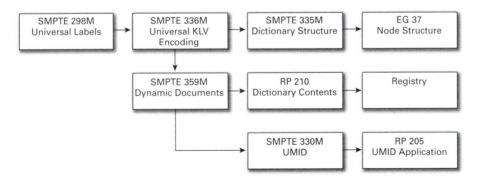

FIGURE 4.2 *SMPTE Use of UMID*

has worked to create a way to create a digital watermark to identify digital content and to embed information that would allow the control of copying as well.

Watermarking is Not Encryption

Watermarking is not encryption; unless encrypted in a separate process, the content is in the clear. Digital watermarks are composed of scattered bits of "noise" that are permanently embedded in each audio or video frame. The scattering prevents anyone from finding and changing these bits. Sometimes digital watermarking is called 'data embedding,' 'data hiding,' or 'steganography.' In order to be functional in the real world of media and entertainment, the watermark must be robust enough to withstand considerable processing after they have been inserted , such as compression, digital to analog conversion, signals modulation for terrestrial broadcast and satellite and cable distribution.

Watermarks are invisible to the eye and inaudible to the ear, but devices with watermark detection technology can recognize them. Beyond identification, they can also convey information. For example, forensic watermarks can be used to identify content that was distributed to a specific venue or exhibition and a tampered device.

In addition, Copy Control Information (CCI) can be built into the watermark to signal to a playback device a set of instructions about the copying allowed by the content owner. Using watermarks to control copying will be discussed further in a later section of this chapter that covers copy protection technologies.

The leader in watermark technology is Digimarc, who has made license deals with Activated Content, AudioAudit (recently acquired by Nielsen Media Research), MediaGrid, Royal Philips Electronics, Signum, Teletrax (under sublicense from Philips), Technicolor (under sublicense from Philips), Verance and Verimatrix. The Verance watermark is incorporated into DVD-Audio protection, Sonic Solutions software for DVD production, and is used by Universal Pictures, Sony Pictures, and Microsoft

Digital Fingerprinting

Digital fingerprinting takes a different approach to identifying content. Rather than attaching or embedding metadata to content, this technology takes a unique "fingerprint" of each bit of content. It is based on the assumption that every piece of content is, in itself, unique. By extracting information about the material – its length, or the type, size, strength, and frequency of its waveforms, its lines, colors, or other characteristics can be used to create the fingerprint.

There is some confusion about the difference between digital watermarking and fingerprinting. Table 4.3 details the differences.[2]

DIGITAL WATERMARKS	DIGITAL FINGERPRINTS
Embeds information into the content.	Does not embed information into the content.
Does not extract information from content.	Extracts information from the content.
Must be embedded prior to distribution.	Does not require embedding; hence, it can be applied to existing legacy content.
Can identify each copy of content.	Cannot differentiate between exact copies.
Cannot be updated if the watermark is successfully hacked.	Updating is not necessary.
Watermark can be extended to new content.	New fingerprint must be extracted from new content

TABLE 4.3 *Differences Between Watermarks and Fingerprints*

Several companies offer products that use digital fingerprint technology to identify audio tracks, including Audible Magic, Gracenote, and Snocap. Snocap has signed deals with Sony BMG, Universal and EMI. Snocap is not a seller of music. It will operate and maintain an automated central clearinghouse for companies that are selling music online. A copyright owner registers its tracks with Snocap. The company extracts an acoustic fingerprint from the track and places metadata about it in a database. The music service checks the Snocap database for authorization to sell the track and the terms and conditions that apply to the sale.[3]

So far, there are no commercially available content-based fingerprinting technologies for video material. However, Seiko has applied for a patent to extend fingerprinting to video. According to the patent application:

---

2. Ku, W., Chi, C. *Survey on the Technological Aspects of Digital Rights Management.* Available at: http://www.comp.nus.edu.sg/~kucheech/files/isc04.pdf.

3. Green, H. *Shawn Fanning's New Tune: Snocap.* Business Week Online, December 3, 2004. Available at:http://www.businessweek.com/technology/content/dec2004/tc2004123_8817_tc119.htm

A method for detecting a copy of a digital image initiates with dividing a suspected copy of a digital image into sub-images. Then, the average intensities associated with each of the sub-images is determined. Next, the average intensities are transformed into a series of coefficients. Then, a rank matrix from the series of coefficients is defined. Next, the rank matrix from the series of coefficients is compared to a rank matrix of a query image to determine if the suspected copy is an actual copy of the digital image. A computer readable media, a computer system and computer code configured to be executed on a computer system are also provided. [4]

The Seiko-Epson patent application indicates that digital fingerprinting of audio-visual material may occur in the near future. The company has applied for a similar patent in the U.S. The application notes that not only will this method identify content, it will also identify copies made from an original because of small differences that occur in the process of making the copy.

Encryption

The basic idea behind encryption is that data is modified systematically so that it can be restored to its original state if the systematic source of the modification is known. For example, suppose the plaintext word 'encryption' is modified by advancing each letter one place in the alphabet, resulting in the cipher text string 'fodszqujpo.' A decrypter who knows the formula will simply apply it to restore the cipher text string to its original plaintext. This single-digit key is absurdly simple, considering the complexity of actual encryption algorithms.

Symmetric Encryption Algorithms

The simple example above shows how a symmetric encryption technique works. The same 'key' or decryption code is used both to encrypt plaintext into cipher text and to decrypt cipher text into plaintext. Real-life symmetric encryption schemes are usually referred to as 'block ciphers' because they don't just use strings of data as cipher keys; they put the data into multiple cells, or blocks. Symmetric standards include the Digital Encryption Standard (DES), the Advanced Encryption Standard (AES), Skipjack (superseded by AES), and RC5.

---

4. Seiko Epson Corporation (Japan). *PatentView/EP1345160. Software Patent: Method and apparatus for content-based image copy detection.* March 13, 2003. Available at: http://gauss.ffii.org/PatentView/EP1345160

DES was developed in response to a request for a cryptographic algorithm from NIST (then the National Bureau of Standards) in the early 1970s. The agency had three main requirements for the algorithm: cheap, available, and secure. The NBS accepted a submission from IBM, the Lucifer algorithm, which had a 128-bit cipher key, but cut the length of the cipher key in half to 56-bits. Since the algorithm would be used to protect sensitive government information, export versions of the algorithm were limited to a cipher key length of 40 bits.[5] Tropical Software describes how DES encryption works:

DES encrypts and decrypts data in 64-bit blocks, using a 64-bit key (although the effective key strength is only 56 bits). It takes a 64-bit block of plaintext as input and outputs a 64-bit block of cipher text. Since it always operates on blocks of equal size and it uses both permutations and substitutions in the algorithm, DES is both a block cipher and a product cipher.

DES has 16 rounds, meaning the main algorithm is repeated 16 times to produce the cipher text. It has been found that the number of rounds is exponentially proportional to the amount of time required to find a key using a brute-force attack. So as the number of rounds increases, the security of the algorithm increases exponentially.[6]

As the processing power of computers has exploded on millions of desktop computers, DES became vulnerable to iterative, exhaustive key searches by persistent and clever hackers. Triple DES was an attempt to prolong the usefulness of the algorithm, which used three 64-bit cipher keys. However, Triple DES decryption proved to be very slow and vulnerable to attack.

As a result, NIST embarked on a search for a new encryption algorithm that would be called the Advanced Encryption Standard (AES). In 2000, NIST received 15 submissions and approved one of them, the Rijndael Algorithm. The standard is promulgated by the National Institute of Standards and Technology (NIST), a federal agency that works with industry to develop and apply technology, measurements, and standards.[7] The new requirements for an advanced encryption algorithm were that it support 128, 192, and 256-bit cipher keys, that it offer fast decryption, even with limited computer resources.

---

5. *Tropical Software, DES Encryption – Overview.* Available at: http://www.tropsoft.com/strongenc/des.htm

6. Ibid.

7. See the NIST website at: http://www.nist.gov

The U.S. government considers AES sufficiently secure for secret information, which can be encrypted with a 128-bit cipher key. Top Secret material requires the use of 192-bit or 256-bit keys.[8] In AES, plaintext is broken into sequences of 128-bit blocks. The bits are converted to bytes, composed of 8 bits – 1 parity bit, and 7 payload bits. The size of the encryption key, or cipher key, is a sequence of 128, 192, or 256 bits. Depending on the size of the cipher key used, the encryption technique is called AES-128, AES-192, or AES-256. Figure 4-1 is a simplified illustration of the first stage the four-stage AES encryption. The original cipher key is expanded into a series of sub-keys that iteratively re-encode the output of the previous encoding, a process of multiple rounds of encryption.

The number of rounds, or encryption iterations, varies for each of the AES-128, -192, and -256 techniques. Each round of encryption (except for the first round, which skips the first stage) involves four stages. To begin, in the SubBytes stage, each byte is replaced with another byte that is formulated through the "S-box," a matrix of values calculated from a lookup table and then mathematically manipulated, as shown in Figure 4.3. Then in the ShiftRows stage, all the rows except the first row are shifted by some set amount. In the third MixColumns stage, the numbers in each column are manipulated to spread the values across each cell in the column. Finally, a Subkey is generated from the cipher key for each round of the encryption process, and it is applied in the last AddRoundKey stage.[9]

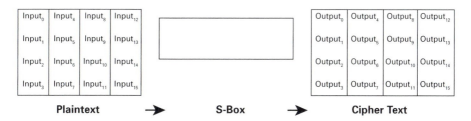

FIGURE 4.3 *The First Stage of AES Encryption, the SubBytes Stage*

RC5 is a symmetrical algorithm created by Ronald L. Rivast, perhaps the most well-known cryptographer in the world. He taught cryptography at the Massachusetts

8. National Security Agency (CNSS), CNSS Policy Number 15, Fact Sheet 1. Available at: www.cnss.gov/assets/pdf/cnssp 15 fs.pdf

9 Wikipedia, Advanced Encryption Standard. Available at: http://en.wikipedia.org/wiki/AES#The_SubBytes_step

Institute of Technology and created the RC5 cipher in the early 1990s. RC5 is a fast, simple encryption technique that allows adjustable block sizes, key length and the number of rounds to fulfill alternative security goals set by users.[10]

Content Scrambling System (CSS)

The discredited CSS is a proprietary algorithm for DVDs that uses weak 40-bit encryption to protect the discs. DVD players and drives contain a decryption module, and the system uses several keys, including an authentication key, a player key, title key, disc key set, and a decryption key.

CSS employs a cascade of encryption algorithms. The purpose of authentication is to make sure that the player or drive has not been tampered with before decrypting the content. The title key is the decryption key for the content, the disc key decrypts the title key, and the player key, one of 400 keys allocated to each DVD player maker, decrypts the disc key.

CSS-enabled DVD players and drives and CSS-protected discs appeared in 1996. About three years later, Jon Johansen cracked the CSS algorithm and released the DVD ripper program, DeCSS, allowing people to access decrypted DVD content and to copy it.

Advanced Access Content System (AACS)

AACS provides a good example of how complex encryption schemes have become. It is an industry effort designed to protect next generation DVDs. IBM, Intel, Matsushita, Microsoft Corporation, Sony, Toshiba, The Walt Disney Company and Warner Bros. released the first preliminary draft of the specifications for AACS in April, 2005. AACS incorporates stronger encryption than CSS (128-bit encryption, compared to 40-bit encryption) and it also includes key revocation and renewability features.

Encryption and decryption of the content is accomplished using the symmetric Advanced Encryption Standard (AES) chaining block cipher (CBC) mode of operation. Data blocks are 128 bits and keys lengths are 128 bits.[11] AACS calls for an

---

10. Network Sorcery website. Document available at:
http://www.networksorcery.com/enp/data/rc5.htm#Description

11. Intel, et al. *Advanced Access Content System (AACS) Introduction and Common Cryptographic Elements, Revision 0.90.* April 14, 2005. Available at:
http://www.aacsla.com/specifications/specifications.htm.

AES-based one-way cryptographic function as well as a hashing function to condense representation. Content owners are responsible for encryption, using a secret, random title key for each piece of content. A secret, randomly-generated volume identifier on each piece of pre-recorded media prevents bit-by-bit copying. Finally, the usage rules that the content owner wishes to apply to the title are also stored on the medium.

Key management is handled by AES with the electronic code book (ECB) mode of operation. The system includes a cryptographic message authentication code (AACS-MAC) and a pseudo-random number generator. Digital signatures utilize the RSASSA-PSS scheme, but AACS devices are not required to generate such signatures.

AACS offers the features of key revocation and renewability. The key management system has three components:

- Secret device keys – 128 bits each

- Media Key Block – variable size, but always multiple of 4 bytes

- Media Key – 128 bits

AACS issues a set of secret device keys to every AACS device. The keys may or may not be unique to the device. The AACS licensing authority also issues a Media Key Block (MKB) that resides in the device. A device key, working together with the MKB, generates the media key needed to unlock the content. If content owners or distributors believe that the device keys have been compromised (or tampered with), the AACS scheme allows updating of the MKB, so that the device keys and the MKB will no longer produce the appropriate media key – effectively revoking the device keys.

An AACS licensed replicator calculates the title key via a cryptographic hash of the media key, the volume identifier, and the usage rules, and uses the result to encrypt the title's title key. Decryption proceeds in reverse: The product reads the stored MKB and, together with its device keys, calculates the media key. The calculated cryptographic then uses the media key, the volume identifier, and the usage rules to calculate the title key, which decrypts the content.

Recordable media have an additional MKB, called the extended MKB. Its purpose is to provide more up-to-date revocation information for a particular media type or application. The device writes the extended MKB on the medium itself as a read/write file for each application, so there may be multiple extended MKB files on a single piece of media.

The AACS system is far stronger than CSS. But it may not work as well as its proponents would like. On April 16, 2005, Edward W. Felton, a professor of computer science and public policy at Princeton University, posted a comment on his weblog, Freedom to Tinker (www.freedom-to-tinker.com):

> *I can reverse-engineer a few players to get their DeviceIDs and keys, and then build those into my product. The licensing authority will respond by figuring out which DeviceIDs I'm using, and revoking them. Then the players I have sold won't be able to play new discs anymore, and customers will shun me.*
>
> *This plan won't stop filesharing, though. If somebody, somewhere makes his own player using a reverse-engineered DeviceID, and doesn't release that player to the public, then he will be able to use it with impunity to play or rip discs. His DeviceID can only be blacklisted if the licensing authority learns what it is, and the authority can't do that without getting a copy of the player. Even if a player is released to the public, it will still make all existing discs rippable. New discs may not be rippable, at least for a while, but we can expect new reverse-engineered DeviceIDs to pop up from time to time, with each one making all existing discs rippable. And, of course, none of this stops other means of ripping or capturing content, such as capturing the output of a player or infiltrating the production process.*
>
> *Once again, DRM will limit competition without reducing infringement. Companies are welcome to try tactics like these. But why should our public policy support them?*

Asymmetric encryption

As we have seen, there are difficulties with symmetric systems, despite the best efforts of experts to develop such schemes as AACS. The keys must be transmitted with a great deal of security, and if one party is careless, it doesn't matter how careful the other party was. Or, if the keys become known, it may not be possible to trace the source of the violation, whether the leak came from some doing the encryption or the decryption.

Asymmetric encryption schemes avoid these and other problems by using two keys, one to encrypt the plaintext and another to decrypt the cipher text back to plaintext. One example of asymmetric systems is that of a night deposit service of a bank. The customer has a key for the deposit door, uses it, and puts in cash, checks, credit card slips, receipts, and sensitive business information. The next morning, a bank employee uses another key for another door to take out the material. The customer trusts that the bank exercises care and supervision of the key and any employee is responsible for emptying the night deposit box.[12]

Asymmetric encryption may use a public key to encrypt content and a different public key to decrypt it. This technique can work when both keys are generated on-the-fly, so both the encryption and decryption processes are unique to that particular transaction. However, this requires the maintenance of an enormous database of keys. More frequent is for companies to encrypt the message with a private key, then to distribute a public key to the consumer.

	PUBLIC KEY ENCRYPT	PRIVATE KEY ENCRYPT
PUBLIC KEY DECRYPT	One time pad: Since each key can be known, the encrypt/ decrypt scheme must be unique for each transaction, with both keys generated on-the-fly.	Authentication: Requires digital signature, certificate, or other means of identification for decrypter to prove identity. Some studios and labels encrypt their content in this manner.
PRIVATE KEY DECRYPT	Confidentiality: Anyone can encrypt, only private key holder can decrypt.	Paradoxical Security: Seemingly secure, but if algorithm is hacked, the key holders will never know since there is no public testing of it.

TABLE 4.4 *Relationships of Public and Private Keys*

Encryption as part of a DRM system

Encryption requires supporting infrastructure. At minimum, a symmetric encryption scheme involves encrypting the content before distribution. The playback/display device must be able to recognize the encryption, store the decryption key, and decode and display the content. In this most simple case, that part of

---

12. Solomon, E. and The Open Group Security Forum. *Working with PKI and Related Technologies.* 2001.

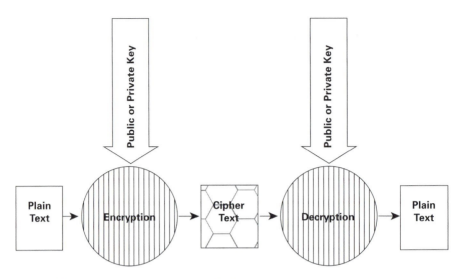

FIGURE 4.4 *Typical Entertainment Industry Encryption Scheme: Public/Private Key Encryption and Decryption*

the device where the key is stored must be tamper-resistant so that the key cannot be discovered and moved to another device.

More complex protection systems require more extensive infrastructure. The supply side may not require anything more than encryption technology. But the playback/display device must have a unique identification that can be remotely accessed. It may also need some way to receive a decryption key and authorization messages. It must be capable of acting on those messages and of actually decrypting the content.. If the device receives the key for each purchase or even each instance of viewing of the same purchased content, there must be some kind of communications infrastructure. The device might be called upon to count the number of uses. These types of more complex protection systems involve protecting access to the content as well as the content itself, covered in the next section.

Access Protection Technologies

These DRM technologies block access to content unless the user is authorized to consume it or the machine is authorized to play or display it. They may be used in tandem with technologies that protect the content itself and other schemes, or they may be used alone. Most often, blocking access is just one of several layers of protection. Authentication and authorization are the prelude to access. Table 4.5 shows access protection technologies.

SECURITY TECHNOLOGIES	DESCRIPTION
Access Protection **Authentication and authorization**	Protecting access to content requires some mechanism for allowing or blocking access. Authentication is the process by which it is determined if a person or device should receive authorization to play or display the content. Authentication does not provide access in and of itself; it usually precedes the granting of authorization, which is the actual provision of access to content.
Access and security languages and architectures	Access and security languages are written as part of the content metadata. They trigger compliant systems to authenticate users and systems and to authorize access to content, based on rights, permissions, and conditions. The rights information may also be part of a rights expression language (REL) or it may reside as part of a database. Languages: Keynote, Binder, SAML, XACML, PERMIS Architecture: Shibboleth
Conditional access	A system used by cable and satellite services to provide access to content under the condition that the person has either paid for it in advance or agrees to pay for it when the he or she receives a bill.
Regional coding	Almost all DVD players check for regional coding, which is contained in a permanently encoded single byte of information on the disc. Only a disc coded for a given region in the world will play on a player sold in that region.
Physical Protection	EZ-D, DVD-D
Product activation	A technique used by computer software companies to insure that the software is installed on only the number of machines that are authorized for use

TABLE 4.5 *Access Protection Technologies.*

Authentication

Authentication answers the question: "Are you who you say you are?" But "you" might mean a person, a device, another computer, or a network. Providing a PIN number for a bank card is one form of authentication that is familiar to most people.

Computer users who go online are accustomed to a variety of authentication procedures that they probably do not even think about. For example, when users sign onto an account, they are usually asked for a username or email address and a password. Knowledge of these two strings of data authenticates that the individual signing on is the person who has the right to access the account. If the user decides to change the password, he or she might have to answer a further question like "What is your mother's maiden name?" or "What are the last four digits of your social security number?" or some other question that (presumably) only the person who opened the account can answer. A further authentication procedure might be to send the new password to the email account the user has provided.

The task of identifying individuals is frequently required of authentication systems, particular when e-commerce, financial or legal transactions, or other situations where personal identity is essential. But that is not always the case. Many entertainment content protection systems authenticate the device rather than the person. Authenticating the device offers advantages to purveyors of entertainment. The process can be entirely automated, so the consumer doesn't have to do anything like enter in a PIN number or answer questions – both of which would require a keyboard or other input device. Moreover, device authentication has the added virtues of being somewhat less expensive and requiring a smaller database than the infrastructure needed to authenticate personal identity.

Authorization

Authorization answers the question: "What is this consumer allowed to do?" The answers might range from: Copy freely, copy once, copy X number of times, copy never, copy part, copy original but cannot make copies of that copy, and so forth.

The consumer may be unaware of the authorization process, as it is typically automated within the playback/display device, or with exchanges between the head end and the set top box. In cable and satellite systems authorization is automated and, once the purchase transaction is completed, the content simply starts playing either on-demand or at its scheduled starting time. In computer applications, users may be notified of authorization. For example, when they download content, they may receive messages like: "click on this link to download the movie (or TV, game or software)," indicating that authorization has been given.

Security Languages: KeyNote, Binder, and Security Assertion Markup Language (SAML)

The use of security languages descend from the computer environment, underlying the establishment of a trust management system. These systems offer mechanisms to specify security policies and credentials. Credentials put forth a particular delegation of trust and eliminate the need for public key certificates; unlike traditional certificates, which bind keys to names, credentials may be role-based, binding keys directly to the authorization to perform specific tasks.

Trust management unifies security policy, credentials, access control, and authorization. Access that relies on a trust management system simply notifies a compliance checker to allow a given action. Policies and credentials are written in standard languages that are shared by all trust-managed applications; the security configuration mechanism for one piece of content all have the same semantic and syntactic structure. Trust management policies are easy to distribute across networks, eliminating some of the architectural components required by other approaches, such as access control lists, certificate parsers, and interpreters.

KeyNote and Binder are security languages that allow people within a network called "principals" to grant and restrict access to content to other individuals, and to restrict access to content. In other words, they tie persons to privileges. both logical languages. Binder is less nature than KeyNote, but it is more capable of expressing complex, concise rights, permissions, and conditions. They may provide the language for certificates, which reside on a digital device, and reference the rights that users have to access and consume content. Other standards for certificate statements include X.509, SDSI/SPKI, and PGP.

In contrast with KeyNote and Binder, the SAML is not so much a security language as it is a format for writing certificates and transporting certificates. It has a very limited vocabulary – Permit, Deny, Indeterminate – and a limited set of conditions. Both KeyNote and Binder allow many more assertions.

Access Languages

Developed by the Organization for the Advancement of Structured Information Standards (OASIS), the eXtensible Access Control Markup Language (XACML). It expresses authorization policies in the XML format. XACML is a general purpose language that issues permit/deny decisions to requests for access within a digital domain. It automates authentication and authorization when both sides of the exchange have established a trusted relationship.

More than 600 companies participated in OASIS, which developed common tools to make explicit a wide range of access policies through an extensible, evolutionary, and expressive language. Like SAML, XACML is XML-based and there are efforts underway to put the two languages together to create a single language that would express both security and access policies.

PrivilEge and Role Management InfraStructure (PERMIS)

PERMIS is an initiative of the European European Community that would simplify Web usage by allowing a single "sign-on" across the Internet. Users could have only one Internet ID and password. The system identifies and authenticates individuals, and maintains a record of what they are authorized to do or access. PERMIS may base that authorization on an individual's attributes, a role, or a group membership. There is some movement to conform PERMIS to XACML, eliminating the proprietary vocabulary elements of PERMIS with XACML's XML-compliant terms.

Security Architecture

A digital infrastructure for entertainment requires extensive communication between content creators, distributors, and aggregators. Shibboleth is an architecture whose purpose is to provide the structure for such inter-organizational exchanges. One feature is that it automates authentication and authorization between trusted groups – and their computing environments. Shibboleth maintains a record of an individual's privileges to access content and shares them across organizational servers. The system eliminates the need for multiple passwords and sign-ons across entity boundaries.

Shibboleth is widely used in research and academic environments, including the National Science Digital Library and Penn State. As with other access implementations, there is a move to combine Shibboleth with XACML because the markup language allows for complexity, specificity, and flexibility.

Public Key Infrastructures (PKI)

Authentication and authorization are both invoked in PKIs. The previous section mentioned that complex encryption schemes require infrastructure. If the key unlocks the door to digital content, where can the content owner or distributor hide that key so that only the person who paid for the content can get it and unlock the material? Public key infrastructure provides the networked answer to that question.

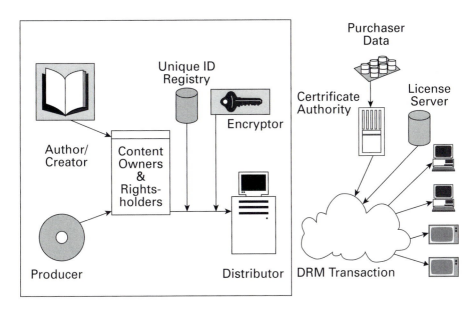

FIGURE 4.5 *Generic Public Key Infrastructure*

PKIs require end-user devices that are connected to a network. They link to a payment database to reference the terms of purchase, an identity database to authenticate the device or user, a certificate server which provides the matching public decryption key, a licensing server that delivers the key to the consumer, the content server that serves up the material, and the end-user device. Figure 4.5 illustrates a generic diagram of how a PKI functions following the purchase of digital content. We will consider specific implementations of PKIs in the next chapter.

The process shown in Figure 4-5 can be described as follows: The certification authority (CA) is one of the components of a PKI. It accesses a database to authenticate the purchase, the device, and the integrity of the user's key. Usually this service is performed by a "trusted third party," or TTP, a company that provides and manages the PKI. When the device accesses the PKI, the certification authority checks the database. If the purchase is recorded and the device is deemed appropriate for the content, then the CA issues a certificate to another database, the licensing server. The certificate will contain additional information, including data about the subscriber, the certificate authority's digital signature, and its public key.

The certificate is stored on the licensing server, which downloads the decryption key to the content purchaser's device. The license is proof of authentication and authorizes the device to decrypt and display the content.

If all of this infrastructure seems complex, be assured that it is. Indeed, cumbersome seems an apt description and service is often slow or even interrupted altogether. There are some estimates that the use of asymmetrical encryption over a PKI may be as much as 100 times slower than symmetrical encryption schemes that do not require infrastructure. However, keep in mind that speed is measured in nanoseconds in the network world, and the Internet is providing a useful testbed for troubleshooting PKIs, where they operate with ever-greater speed and efficiency.

PKIs offer advantages or no one would invest in them. First, they provide a transaction audit trail that can underpin later legal claims if consumers violate the terms of the license they have purchased. Sometimes this function is called "non-repudiation," meaning that consumers cannot argue that they did not receive notification of the terms and conditions to which they have agreed. Also, content owners don't have to rely on consumers to keep their decryption keys secret because the consumer keys are public. It is enough that content providers keep their encryption keys secure.

Conditional Access (CA)

Many consumers are familiar with access protection provided by CA systems because they are customers of the cable or satellite TV services that use them. Both types of subscription services deliver all the channels they offer to the customer premises; CA ensures that they see only the ones they have paid for. CA systems authenticate the set-top box and authorize payment based on the database within the subscriber management system (SMS).

An important aspect of the information that has been compiled in the database is that it comes from face-to-face interactions with the consumer. It is validated by credit checks and the installation of equipment at the subscriber's home premises, during which the installer obtains an actual signature from the customer. In short, authentication of the device rests on a background check that is as thorough as exists for most financial transactions at the consumer level.

The components of a CA system include the SMS, encrypted signals, a provider-specific set-top box (STB), and a security module within the STB. The satellite or cable operator has a contract with a CA vendor who provides the necessary hardware and software for CA. That equipment must be integrated into the operator's delivery system.

The Process of Conditional Access

- Subscriber requests a TV channel or program

- Subscriber Management System (SMS), which contains account information, looks up the customer's account and sends two types of messages for encryption into the entire program stream

    - Entitlement control messages (ECMs) – Information about what the customer wants to see;

    - Entitlement management messages (EMMs) – Information about the subscriber's account – the status of the account, what they have paid for and so forth.

- Scrambled (encrypted) TV program signals and authorization data is transmitted from headend or satellite.

- STB filters signals and divides them between program streams and authorization messages.

- Scrambled authorization signals go security module within STB

- Security module decrypts authorization data and authorizes decryption of signals

- STB decrypts program stream and sends them to play/display device.[13]

For many years, consumers were able to bypass CA systems by buying black market "descramblers," that would decrypt all the program streams. Cable operators categorized the people who received programs illegally, a practice called theft of signal, as:

- passive (hooking up an existing live cable TV connection and failing to notify the cable operator)

- active (buying and hooking up a descrambler) and

- partial-piracy (paying for basic service, then receiving program signals through active or passive means).

To deter signal theft, the cable industry instituted routine audits of households for illegal hookups, reducing the rate of theft from about 10% to about 4.7% in 2004.[14] The growth of digital cable service has also slowed such theft because digital signals are more difficult to steal. One reason is that the STBs used for digital service

---

13. See definition of "Conditional Access" at:
http://searchsecurity.techtarget.com/sDefinition/0,,sid14_gci331380,00.html.

14. Davis, J. *EchoStar deals smarter cards*. Rocky Mountain News, August 29, 2005.

maintain constant communication between the headend and the STB and operators can monitor the identity of the decoder that the consumer is using.

Regional Protection Control (RPC)

The marketing of motion pictures is based on the concept of release windows. Studios release pictures in stages, based on revenue per viewer. For example, the first release window in domestic theaters brings in $7.50 to $10.00 per ticket, depending on the venue. Airlines and hotels get movies in about three to six months and they are also likely to be purchased on a per viewer basis, so the fees might average $4.00 per person. The pay-per-view and video-on-demand windows come next, within six and nine months, also with prices at about $4.00. The pay television window comes three months later, followed by release to basic cable or broadcast TV in a year or two. Internationally, studios release movies in windows appropriate to each country, beginning shortly after the release in the U.S.

In recent years, there has been some movement towards day-and-date release, or releasing films on the same day (or date, depending on time differences) in all territories of the world. (Ironically, this strategy is a response to counterfeit DVDs and peer-to-peer file-sharing over the Internet.) However, day-and-date release is still the exception. *The Matrix I* was the first such release in November, 2004.

So for the most part, there are still some differences in release dates in different countries, and studios want to control the downstream windows for home video sales and rental in different countries. Moreover, there are variations in the contracts with foreign distributors, and in some instances they want to be able to negotiate exclusive markets.

RCP is a way to insure these traditional business models. The agreement over DVD standards between consumer electronics manufacturers and the studios included codes that would allow DVDs to be played only in certain regions. Each player has a code that identifies the region in which it was sold. Only discs that have a matching code for that region will play in it; discs that do not have that code will not play. As a result, some discs will only play in players sold in the matching region. However, discs that do not have any regional coding will play on any player everywhere.

There are eight codes, defining seven regions. Most studio film will play only in one region:

- U.S. and U.S. Territories, Canada

- Japan, Europe, South Africa, and Middle East

- Southeast Asia and East Asia

- Australia, New Zealand, Pacific Islands, Central America, Mexico, South America, and the Caribbean

- Eastern Europe, Indian subcontinent, Africa, North Korea, and Mongolia

- China

- Reserved

Special international venues (airplanes, cruise ships, etc.)

Some consumers react very negatively to regional coding, especially people who travel to different regions and want to play their DVDs wherever they happen to be. For example, people who live in the U.S. but travel frequently to Europe might buy a DVD there and want to be able to play it when they return home. Consumer demand for region-free DVD players proved sufficient for there to be at least seven such players brought to market by 2003, usually at a higher price point than a region-enabled player.

Studios noted the appearance of these products and responded with Regional Code Enhancement, which places a region code on the program disc ("smart discs") and checks that the player has a matching setting. If the player does not have the same code, the disc will not play, and the player displays an error message. Some of the studios that have released discs with RCE coding including Fox, Buena Vista, Touchstone, Miramax, MGM/Universal, Columbia TriStar and Warner Bros.

One problem with RCE is that some players do not respond properly to the disc's query, and discs that should play do not. Nor has RCE stopped people from circumventing regional restrictions. Some players can be "hacked." And the Internet is rife with advertisements that claim that code-free players are now capable of disabling RCE.

Physical Protection

There have been two attempts to limit access to DVDs by making them inoperable after some period of time. The first product was called Divx, a contraction of the company that brought it to market, Digital Video Express. The Divx disc required a Divx-enabled DVD player that was also connected to a telephone line. The player called a central database to report usage. Once the consumer played the disc the number of times he or she had paid for, the central database would send a message to prevent the disc from playing again, and it would stop working. Consumers didn't have to return the disc; they just threw them away.

The latest incarnation of the disposable, self-destructing DVD was called EZ-D. The company that made it, Flexplay, partnered with Buena Vista Home Entertainment, a Disney company, for a trial. The EZ-D system did not require a telephone connection, nor was it disabled by messages. Rather, when consumers opened the disc's shrink-wrap packaging, exposure to the air would cause a gradual chemical reaction that would make the disc unreadable over a 48 hour period. The disc would for 48 hours, then the user would discard it.

Environmentalists were outraged, and consumers were unimpressed. Disney discontinued the trial in January 2004. The product never came to market.[15]

Product Activation

This technique is used by computer software and video game companies to product their programs and applications. Users install the software, then register it online. In the registration process, they provide the product key that came with the product and then receive an activation code, either immediately or via email. Many software applications allow two installations, one for the desktop and the second one for a portable computer.

Typically, the software provider takes a "snapshot" of the computer from which that and all subsequent registrations are made. Essentially, this is an authentication process. If the number of installations exceeds the number allowed by the license, the activation code is withheld. Sending the activation code is an authorization process.

Product activation works well for computer software applications and game programs because users are accustomed to input devices. Entertainment viewers may not have convenient means of inputting information, nor are they used to such procedures. As a result, entertainment marketers have been reluctant to put demanding activation procedures between entertainment content and its consumers.

Copy Protection

In a world of peer-to-peer services over broadband networks, it may not be enough to simply protect the content, even if it is combined with some kind of access protection. Someone could buy a movie that is already digitized, use a legitimately obtained key to unlock it, gain authorization to play the material – and then copy it to a DVR or DVD recorder and put it on a hard drive so that millions could download the film over the Internet.

---

15. Dean, K. *Disposable DVDs Go to the Dumps*, Wired News. May 21, 2003. Available at: http://www.wired.com/news/digiwood/0,1412,58906,00.html.

Even when a digitized movie is encrypted, it has to be decrypted and converted to analog for play and display. The reason is that people's perceptive system – their eyes and ears – are analog. So material must always be in an analog form so that it can be consumed. With today's computers, it is easy to convert an analog stream into a digital file. People merely plug a cable into the analog outputs of their TV, DVD, or VCR and connect them to the analog inputs of their computer's video card. The card digitizes the analog picture into a file of digital pixels, in real time, a file that now has no encryption or access control on it so that it can be copied freely and uploaded to the Internet.

Content owners refer to this potential for circumventing content security schemes the "analog hole."

So whether the movie is distributed in an analog or a digital format and even if it is encrypted, content owners believe that some kind of copy protection must be added to the mix of protection technologies. At the same time, federal legislation requires that people be able to make backup copies and copies for their other home devices. Moreover, sometimes it is in the interest of content owners to allow consumers to make copies under certain conditions, such as passing along a portion of content to friends.

Thus, although it is simple enough to prevent all copying, the goal has been to find a way to limit copying while allowing some flexibility for both content owners and consumers. The next section covers established copy protection schemes such as Macrovision, new flexible techniques like the content generation management system (CGMS), and a variety of device or medium-specific methods. Finally, it will look at the Optikey system that uses physical means and filtering to prevent copying. These techniques are summarized in Table 4.6.

SECURITY TECHNOLOGIES	DESCRIPTION
Copy Protection	Blocks copying of content. Many of these techniques call for a combination of identification of content or devices (or both), encryption, and authentication to prevent copying.
Macrovision	Also called Analog Protection System (APS) or Copyguard. It provides analog copy protection for tapes and DVD discs. When users try to copy the material with a VHS recorder, the picture is distorted and afflicted with light and dark sequences.

TABLE 4.6 *Copy Protection Technologies*

SECURITY TECHNOLOGIES	DESCRIPTION
Copy Generation Management System (CGMS)	CGMS information embeds copy control information (CCI) in the output video signal. Such instructions may prohibit any copying ("copy never"), allow users to make one copy but not subsequent copies ("no more copy"), make unlimited copies from the original ("copy once"), or make any number of copies ("copy freely"). The equipment making the copy must recognize and respect the CGMS information.
Broadcast Flag	A proposal to add flexible copy protection to over-the-air broadcast content.
SCMS	Copy protection for MiniDiscs and video content that can prevent both initial copies or second generation copies (copies of copies). Each disc carries information that specifies if the content can be copied.
CPPM (Content Protection for Prerecorded Media)	CPPM protects DVD-Audio.
CPRM (Content Protection for Recordable Media)	A technology to protect the content on DVDs, CPRM uses the unique identifiers on blank DVD discs to prevent copying from the original disc.
Physical Protection	These methods use some kind of physical means to prevent copying. The digital watermark has grown into something more than simply identification, and the Optikey system takes an entirely different approach.
Digital Watermark Copy Control Information	The Digital Watermark Copy Control Information embeds copy control information (similar to that specified in CGSM) in a digital watermark.
Optikey Analog Authorization System	The Optikey Analog Authorization System uses physical means, combined with filtering, to prevent copying.

TABLE 4.6 *(Continued)*

Analog Copy Protection (Macrovision)

When consumer electronics manufacturers wanted to market DVD players, content owners were worried that consumers would be able to make copies of the high quality video that DVDs carry. Macrovision's ACP was developed to satisfy these concerns. As part of the agreement with owners, manufacturers of DVD players and computer video cards incorporate a circuit that recognizes ACP "trigger bits" in the MPEG-2 program stream on a DVD disc. This information signals the presence of Macrovision, activating the ACP system that turns off the unit's composit outputs, thereby preventing copying the DVD video to VCRs, DVD recorders and personal video recorders.

The trigger bits to activate ACP are inserted when the DVD is authored. The content owner must pay Macrovision a few cents per each ACP-protected disc. The exact amount the owner pays per disc depends on the level of copy protection used by the owner. The greater the protection, the higher the cost.

Macrovision inserts artifacts that either prevent copying altogether or result in a copy that is nearly impossible to watch. Such artifacts can include stripes of color (called 2-line or 4-line Colorstripe, depending on the size of the stripe), distortion, rolling, and alternating bands of light and dark (AGC modification).

Users determined to defeat copy protection may be able to succeed against ACP. Players can be modified to ignore it. Or ACP may not be effective with some graphics cards.

Copy Generation Management System (CGMS)

CGMS extends alternative levels of permission to copy content. It can allow them to make backup copies, as required in federal legislation. The CGMS system requires the entity that prepares the material for distribution to insert two bits of data into the content stream. The data, termed Copy Control Information (CCI), defines the extent of copying permitted, as shown in Table 4.7. CGMS-compliant play/display devices must be able to recognize and act on the CCI.

COPY CONTROL INFORMATION (CCI)	BIT 0	BIT 1	COPYING ACTIVITIES PERMITTED
No Control	0	0	Unlimited copying

TABLE 4.7 *Copy Control Information in CGMS Two-Bit Payload*

COPY CONTROL INFORMATION (CCI)	BIT 0	BIT 1	COPYING ACTIVITIES PERMITTED
One Generation	1	0	Unlimited number of copies from the original but cannot make copies of copies.
No More Copying	0	1	Can make one copy from original and only one.
No Copying	1	1	Cannot make any copies

TABLE 4.7 *(Continued)*

There are two types of CGMS: CGMS-A for analog output and CGMS-D for digital output.

Digital recording devices typically detect encryption and deny copying privileges to encrypted content. Material that is not encrypted or watermarked can be recorded freely, although some devices, especially those manufactured before 2003, will not ever record encrypted content onto removable media. However, when CGMS-compliant devices find encrypted content, they read the embedded CGMS CCI before making this decision.

The analog standard, CGMS-A encodes the CCI data on line 21 or line 20 of the video signal, part of the vertical blanking interval (VBI). CGMS-A is recognized by most digital camcorders and by some computer video capture cards. In professional production domains, time-base correctors (TBCs) regenerate lines 20 and 21, stripping the CGMS-A information from the analog signal.

If a recording device, including a video capture card in a PC, does not have the capability to detect the presence of CGMS-A trigger bits, the device will not "know" that CGMS-A information is present. These devices will record and play back content despite the presence of the CGMS-A information. However, they may detect encryption and deny copying privileges on that basis.

The digital standard, CGMS-D, is very important. It is incorporated into the Digital Transmission Copy Protection (DTCP) and the High Definition Multimedia Interface (HDMI) protocols that protect content across digital connections such as IEEE 1394/FireWire.

In June, 2005, HBO began protecting its copyrighted content with CGMS-A. The company's customers can make one copy – digital or analog – of HBO or

DVD Copy Protection Effect

		Impact					
		VHS VCR Recording	DVD Recording	Analog Input to PC DVD Recorder	Digital-to-Digital Copy pn PC	DV Camcorders Analog In	Digital VCR Analog In
T **e** **c** **h** **n** **o** **l** **o** **g** **y**	CSS	N/A	N/A	N/A	100% effective, except for DECSS.	N/A	N/A
	CGMS	None	Nearly 100% effective with 40% of DVD players. About 0% with VHS.	Unknown	Unknown	Nearly 100% effective with 40% of DVD players. About 0% with VHS.	Nearly 100% effective with 40% of DVD players. About 0% with VHS.
	ACP	Very effective: virtually 100% of new VCRs tested since 2000.	100% Effective	Effective in major brands.	Not Effective	Nearly 100% effective with nearly 100% of DVD players.	Nearly 100% effective with nearly 100% of DVD players.

FIGURE 4.6 *Comparison of Protection for Different Entertainment Devices and Formats*

Cinemax linear broadcast content, but they cannot make copies of the copy. Nor can they make any copies of HBO or Cinemax on-demand programs.

Some studios have chosen CGMS as copy protection for DVDs. For example, Warner Bros. did not put Macrovision protection on *The Matrix*, *Harry Potter and the Sorcerer's Stone*, and *The Lord of the Rings: The Two Towers* DVDs. Five of the eight largest studios use Macrovision on all their DVD releases, Warner Bros. and Sony use Macrovision on some titles, and MGM does not use it. When they use CGMS, studios usually combine it with encrypting the content.

Microsoft's Windows XP Media Center Edition (MCE) also uses CGMS-A. Consumers can record, watch, and backup the material that plays on their media center PC, but they cannot distribute it to others or watch it on another device. Since most broadcast content is not CGMS-A protected, it can be copied freely. But when content owners or broadcasters choose to add CGMS-A CCI, they will be able to restrict consumer copying. Figure 4.6 shows some popular consumer device and formats, and the protection techniques that protect them.

Extended Copy Control Instruction Messages (ExCCI)

SMPTE standard 401-M is a standard for an extended copy control instruction set known as ExCCI. It is a more complex formulation of the 4 trigger bits that are part of the CCI in CGMS.

PRIMARY FUNCTIONS SUPPORTED BY EXCCI	
Control of Analog Outputs (Composite & Component)	Enable/Disable
Control of Uncompressed Digital Outputs	Enable/Disable
Control of Compressed Digital Outputs	Enable/Disable
Control of Analog Protection System (APS, e.g., Macrovision)	Provision made for selection of additional systems Control data provided for each system
Control of CGMS-A	No control: copy freely Limit copying of content on analog output: • One generation • No more copying • No copying
Control of CGMS-D	No control: copy freely Limit copying of content on analog output: • One generation • No more copying • No copying
Image Constrain	Limit output image pixel count Constrain HDTV content to EDTV resolution
Redistribution Control	Preclude Internet redistribution
Copy Control Assertion	Asserts control of number of copies Signals use of CGMS-A and/or CGMS-D
Copy Move Count	Number of moves allowed for permitted copies
DVB Usage State Information (USI)	Makes it possible to harmonize or duplicate European (DVB) DRM specifications in the ExCCI
Domain Control	Control of locations in which use is permitted • Transfer of copies • Move of instances • Viewing

TABLE 4.8 *Major Functions Supported by ExCCI*

PRIMARY FUNCTIONS SUPPORTED BY EXCCI	
Control of Digital Protection Systems	Wide range of digital output media considered • Presence indicates acceptability for distribution or use • Opaque data carried for control of each system • Opaque data carried for control of each system • Dynamic Document™ functionality used for extensions • Quick update (3-6 months) • Online mechanism to discover new systems • Supports links to system data and control • Supports unlimited number of systems (variable payload length)

EXTENDED VIEWING FUNCTIONS	
Control use of temporary recordings	Example: PVRs
Playback Count	Number of times playback is allowed
Delayed Start Time	When first viewing is allowed
Longevity Time	Within what time period from delayed start
Pause Time	How long a pause can be
Viewing Window	Time period from first use in which content must be viewed
Instance Play Time	How much content can be viewed before session counts as an instance of play
Copyright Notice Text	Assertion of copyright. Provision for multiple character sets
Reserved Space for Future Extensions	

TABLE 4.8 *(Continued)*

Table 4.8 presents the major functions that are supported by ExCCI, as summarized in a 2005 presentation by S. Merrill Weiss.[16]

Clearly to support all these functionalities, ExCCI requires far more than the 4 bits used in the first formulations of CGMS. The ExCCI packet is composed of quad-digital-word fields or multiples of them. The fields are described in a table.

The CCI is treated as metadata and carried with the content. (In the SMPTE world, content is called "essence.") When the program stream enters a professional production or post-production facility, the metadata are separated from essence. Within SMPTE-compliant facilities, the ExCCI can be handled as metadata, including transport, processing, storage, and encoding and decoding.

Although studios believe that ExCCI will offer them, there are critics of the complex instruction set, including David Broberg.[17] He writes that think that decisions about the usage rules embedded within the ExCCI packet should originate with content distributors rather than content owners. Today's marketplace requires flexibility, and owners are often too far removed from the day-to-day demands of the commercial arena to make optimal choices for the marketing, sale, and use of content products. Moreover, he is similarly concerned about the lack of flexibility and security flaws that result from ExCCI messages carried within the MPEG stream.

Serial Copying Management System (SCMS)

Record companies insisted on the addition of SCMS to some digital devices such as Digital Audio Tape (DAT) machines and the minidisc. The purpose of SCMS is to prevent the creation of perfect digital copies of pre-recorded content. The technique allows an unlimited number of first generation digital copies from the original but inhibits subsequent copying of the copies. It does not prevent analog copying.

SCMS works by a changing a small portion of the data when material is copied. Original prerecorded CDs, digital tapes, and minidisks have a copy bit placed on them, which plays at the frequency of 75 frames per second. The original's copy bits may signal three states:

---

16. Weiss, S. M. *Extended Content Control Information (ExCCI) Packet — The Studio Side of DRM.* (Powerpoint presentation, Jan. 28, 2005). Available at: http://www.hpaonline.com/files/public/ExCCI_Packet_Presentation_HPA_Tech_Retreat'05.ppt

17. Broberg, David. *Extended copy Control Instructions – A Bad Idea.* Available at: http://www.geocities.com/ResearchTriangle/3930/techart.htm

COPYRIGHT STATUS	SIGNAL	STATUS IDENTIFICATION	RESULT
Copy protected	11	Continuously on, or high state	Copy once
Not copy protected	00	Continuous off, or low state	Unlimited copy
A copy of original copy-righted material	10	On-off toggle every 5 frames	Copy never

An SCMS protected device looks for bits written on the subcode data that includes:

- Content type: original or copy

- Audio Source: CD, DAT, MD, analog

- Copyright status

Content Protection for Prerecorded Media (CPPM)

CPPM, a copy protection technology that is used only for pre-recorded DVD-Audio. CPPM and the related copy protection technique CPRM (for recordable media) are intellectual property that is owned by the companies that developed them. These companies formed License Management International, LLC (LMI) to license CPPM and CPRM to device manufacturers and content owners and distributors.[18]

CPPM is similar to CSS, but is a functional improvement over it, originally it was called CSS2. Authentication for both copy protection schemes are the same, so existing players can respond to them singly or combined on the same disc. CSS and CPPM located keys in the lead-in area but in CPPM, there are no keys in the sector headers. In the control area of the DVD-Audio disc, each volume has a 56-bit album identifier, as does a CSS-protected disc.[19]

Both CSS and CPPM discs contain a media key block (MKB) that is stored in an unencrypted file. The rows and columns of the MKB data generate an encryption

---

18. A document that defines the 4C Entity's framework for both CPPM and CPRM, the Content Protection System Architecture (CPSA) is available on the organization's web site at: http://www.4centity.com/tech/. The site also has additional, more specific information about the design of these two copy protection techniques.

19. See three excellent articles by Don Labriola about DRM schemes that provide details about CSS, CPPM, CPRM and other techniques on www.extremetech.com.

key from the device keys during the authentication process. The MKB is renewable so that compromised device keys can be revoked, disabling can be updated to revoke the use of compromised player keys. If the device key is revoked, the media key block processing step will result in an invalid key value.

Decryption of a CPPM-protected disc begins with authentication that ensures that there has been no tampering with the device. An enormously complex operation between the device ID, title key, album identifier, and Media Key Block generates an intermediate media key and, finally, the content key, which unlocks the encrypted content. In addition to CCI in the header, CCI is also stored on each sector of the disc, so the encryption key (and therefore decryption key value) may differ for each sector.

Despite its elaborate formulation, in July 2005, there were reports that CPPM had been circumvented.[20] Defeating CPPM did not involve tampering with any of the complex encryption and key management processes called for by the scheme. Rather, the workaround exploited the "analog hole." After the device went goes through its authentication, key retrieval and generation, and decryption procedures, the hackers simply diverted the decrypted audio stream from the PC's speakers to a hard drive.

The circumvention of CPPM requires an array of software tools, including InterVideo's WinDVD 5, 6, or 7, plus *DVD-A ripper*, *PPCM ripper*, and *DVD-A Explorer*, all available on the Internet. The writer noted that the keys used in the WinDVD program were likely to be revoked when content owners realize that its keys were compromised, requiring users of the Intervideo software to update their software in order to play DVD-Audio discs that are protected by CPPM.

Content Protection for Recordable Media (CPRM)

CPRM was designed and promulgated by the 4C Entity, the industry consortium composed of IBM, Intel, Matsushita, and Toshiba, to control copying to such recordable devices as DVD recorders, hard drives, and secure digital (SD) memory cards. It is similar to CPPM – it requires secret device keys to be installed in licensed playback devices. There is also an MKB, but in CPRM, it is located in the lead-in area of the blank disc. The mathematical processing to decrypt copied content is very like the decryption of CPPM.

Each blank piece of media has a unique 64-bit ID, located in the BCA of the disc. The main idea behind CPRM is that it binds a recording to the specific piece

---

20. Byrne, S. *DVD-Audio CPM can be got around with a WinDVD patch.* July 6, 2005. Available at: http://www.cdfreaks.com/news/12061.

of media on which it is recorded. Although most DVD recorders support CPRM, the technique is not recognized by some DVD players.

Blank recordable DVDs have a 64-bit media identifier etched in the burst-cutting area (BCA) or the narrow burst-cutting area (NBCA) of the disc, depending on the recordable format. When the user records protected content onto the blank disc, CPRM encrypts that content with a 56-bit C2 (Cryptomeria) cipher that was generated in from the media ID. The media will play from that disc. But if the content is re-copied to another blank disc, the media ID in the BCA will not match the media ID used to encrypt the copied content, so the content cannot be decrypted.

Physical Means to Prevent Copying

One advantage to using physical means to prevent copying is that they span both digital and analog domains. They require some kind of information to be embedded into the content and a filtering mechanism in the device to recognize that information. One method builds on the digital watermark identifier and embeds copying instructions within it. The second method, the Optikey system, takes an entirely different approach.

Digital Watermark Copy Control Information

DVD-Audio players prevent copying via analog outputs by recognizing watermarks. Using that circuitry, content owners and distributors can go beyond mere identification to specify how consumers can copy material. The Video Watermarking Group (VWM) of the DVD-CCA (DVD Copy Control Association) is responsible for evaluating digital watermarking systems for copy control of the material on DVDs.[21] The group is composed of Digimarc, Hitachi, Macrovision, NEC, Philips, Pioneer, and Sony.

As developed by Verance and the 4C Entity, controlling copying with a digital watermark is achieved by embedding CCI in the watermark, which is itself encoded into the waveform of the audio. The copying instructions are similar to those defined in CGMS: Freely copy, copy once, and no copy. There is also room in the digital watermark CCI for content owners and distributors to create their own copying instructions.

Even when DVD-Audio permits copying, it limits the quality of that copy to 16-bit, 44.1 KHz stereo (Red Book CD-audio quality), not at the original DVD-Audio

---

21. Digimarc, *Protecting Video in the Digital Age*, available at: www.digimarc.com/docs/analogHole/ Protecting%20Video%20Brief%20FINAL.pdf

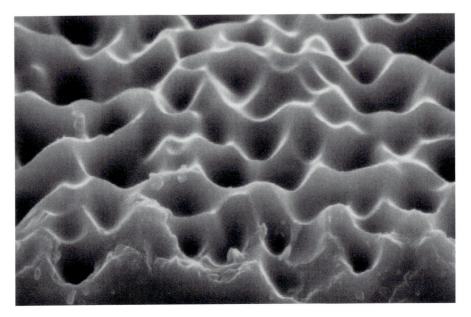

FIGURE 4.7 *Optikey Phase Mask Sub-Micron Optical Fingerprint (Permission from Optikey)*

quality. Recording devices recognize the International Standard Recording Code (ISRC) identifier and store it. When a consumer tries to copy material, the device checks the ISRCs that have been previously saved. If it has already recorded the title once, it will not copy it a second time, even at the lower CD quality.

Optikey

The Optikey Analog Authorization System was developed under a contract with the U.S. National Institute of Standards and Technology, Advanced Technology Program (NIST-ATP) to prevent the copying of ID cards and other important documents. It can be used alone or in conjunction with other content protection technologies.

The system uses a blue laser to generate a speckle pattern on glass, a process the company calls "sub-micron sand-blasting" of an "optical fingerprint," as shown in Figure 4.7.[22] The mark is always different because of slight differences in the oscillation in the laser. Because the surface features of the pattern are sub-micron and extremely complex, they cannot be reproduced. Even a direct copy will fail to reproduce all the features of the original.

---

22. Optikey presentation to Copy Protection Technologies Working Group. Available at: www.cptwg.org/Assets/Presentations%202005/Optikey%20Presentation%20090805.ppt

Measurements of the original, including curve structures, areas under the curve, and other signature elements are stored in the player device. Those measurements are used to create a filter that is stored in the player. A laser diode in the player reads the speckle pattern on the content and measures it against the filter. The laser diode already exists in players to read the content, so only software must be added. As a result, Optikey says adding their ID system is relatively inexpensive.

Removing the optical mark or tampering with it will disable all playback. Content owners and distributors can store 30-50 kB of additional data in the optical signature, such as CCI or other data that would enable rights management. The filter is a data block, based on the original optical mark, so it is renewable and updatable.

SECURITY TECHNOLOGIES	DESCRIPTION
Transport Protection)	Technologies that protect content as it moves between network nodes and devices
DCPS (Digital Copy Protection System)	In order to provide digital connections between consumer electronics devices, while preventing the copying of perfect digital copies, five digital copy protection systems were proposed to the CEA under the umbrella of a Digital Copy Protection System.
DTCP (Digital Transmission Content Protection)	DTCP was developed by the 5C (five companies, Intel, Sony, Hitachi, Matsushita, and Toshiba) for IEEE 1394/FireWire. It was the 5C response to the CEA's request for proposals for DCPS, and it quickly became the leading contender.
HDCP (High-bandwidth Digital Content Protection)	Similar to DTCP, The standard to move digital visual content between devices is called the digital visual interface (DVI). It has no built-in security, so HDCP adds authentication, encryption, and revocation services to the DVI.
HDMI (High Definition Multi-media Interface)	The combination of HDCP and DVI. When an HDMI output senses that the connected monitor does not support HDCP, it lowers the image quality of protected content.
XCA (Extended Conditional Access)	Developed by Zenith and Thomson, XCA is similar to DTCP. However, it works with both one-way and two-way digital interfaces, such as the European EIA-762 RF remodulator standard, and uses smart cards to renew security.

Digital Copy Protection System (DCPS)

In the mid 1990s, the Consumer Electronics Association (CEA) issues a request for proposals for techniques to prevent copying when digital content is moved from one device to another. For example, when content leaves the DVD player and moves to the TV via an analog or digital output, it may be intercepted and copied. The CEA received five proposals, each calling for CGMS-style "flags" that would permit states of *copy freely, copy once, don't copy,* or *no more copies.*" Players must be equipped with DCPS technology, but these techniques could not require any changes to discs.

Digital devices that would only play content, not copy it, could receive and display all data. Digital recording devices would receive only content that is marked as copy-able. If the original material were marked as copy once, DCPS devices must be able to change the copying instruction, the "flag," to *don't copy* or *no more copies*. DCPS technologies came on the market in 2003 and are part of today's high definition consumer electronics products, including TVs, receivers, and digital video recorders.

Five digital copy protection systems were proposed to the CEA to answer questions about how to transport content from one device to another. The most widely-used technique is DTCP (digital transmission content protection).

Digital Transmission Content Protection (DTCP)

DTCP was developed to apply to devices connected by IEEE 1394/FireWire but it will work with other mechanisms of transporting digital signals between devices. The draft proposal, called 5C for the five companies that developed it, was presented in 1998 by Intel, Sony, Hitachi, Matsushita, and Toshiba. Sony released a DTCP chip in mid-1999. This method is licensed to consumer electronics manufacturers by the group's licensing authority, the Digital Transmission Licensing Administrator (DTLA).

Under DTCP, devices that are digitally connected, such as a DVD player and a digital TV or a digital VCR, exchange keys and authentication certificates to establish a secure channel. DTCP provides two levels of authentication: full and restricted. All DTCP devices support restricted authentication. However, full authentication can occur only when the devices have sufficient processing power to carry out the full procedure, such as a computer. Full authentication is typically invoked when the content carries copy bits that market it as copy never or when the process is implemented by the copy owner for any particular content.[23]

---

23. Labriola, Don. *Digital Content Protection, Part III.* Extreme Tech, August, 2003. Available at: http://www.findarticles.com/p/articles/mi_zdext/is_200308/ai_ziff55584

DTCP provides for system renewability. This feature means that if the device receives a message indicating that a given key or the key generator (key selection vector, KSV) has been compromised or hacked, the device can be prevented from receiving content. The term for such messages is System Renewability Messages, or SRM. The delivery of SRMs may occur via new discs, broadcasts, downloads, or new devices, bringing key revocation lists and updated keys to a unit.

If the devices authenticate one another and exchange keys successfully, then the source device (like a DVD player) encrypts the audio/video signal sector-by-sector, on-the-fly as it sends it to the receiving device (like a TV display), which must decrypt it. This keeps other connected but unauthenticated devices from stealing the signal. Content that is not copy protected is not encrypted.

Along with the content, the sending machine transmits CCI. The CCI may be embedded in an MPEG-2 stream or as part of the initial packet header information. Packet header carriage of CCI has the advantage of indicating the copy protection status of the material immediately without processing of the content stream.

The receiving unit uses the CCI to honor the copying instructions. Such authentication and encryption/decryption processes prevent other connected but unauthenticated devices from gaining access to the signal and diverting it to a non-DTCP device.

The DTLA provides equipment manufacturers that license DTCP a Device Certificate for each unit. Certificates support full or restricted authentication (or both), and include a number of keys, such as the a public key or key selection mechanism, device identifier, digital signature, and other data that allow for optional extensions.

High-bandwidth Digital Content Protection (HDCP)

In the late 1990s, the lack of sufficient content protection slowed down the introduction of high definition consumer electronics products to the market, because Hollywood content owners were reluctant to make their high-value content available without what they regarded as adequate safeguards. To break the bottleneck, Intel, working with Silicon Image, developed the HDCP specification to protect material carried over the Digital Video Interface (DVI). The main concept of the scheme was that device manufacturers could implement it on top of the existing DVI technology and protect content as it moves across the connection between two devices.

This transport protection technique calls for a licensing authority, the Digital Content Protection, LLC to license HDCP to consumer electronics manufacturers and distribute the keys. The technique includes system renewability messaging, which means that devices can be updated to revoke keys that have been compromised or hacked successfully.

HDCP involves matching two device identifications with one another and three stages of authentication. Similar to DTCP, HDCP has the ability to renew identification and authentication SRMs can update the systems and data elements and prevent compromised devices from decrypting content. The source device stores a list of revoked keys and vectors that it receives via SRMs. It transmits these messages to downstream devices, either as part of the content stream or as individual messages.

Identification occurs by matching a securely-stored secret key selection vector (KSV) with an array of 40 device keys, one matching each bit in the KSV. The first stage of authentication requires an exchange of KSVs and tells the content source if the reception device is a display or a recorder or transmitter.

If the receiver's KSV does not match one of those stored by the source or it does not contain the appropriate number of bits at the proper settings, the session is ended with no further processing. However, if source accepts the receiver as authorized, the the second stage of authentication takes place: The two devices utilize the device keys and the other's KSV to generate a content key. If the keys and KSVs are genuine, then both devices will generate the same content key independently. This means that the device can encrypt and decrypt the content without having to communicate the content key, which might be vulnerable to discovery in transit. The first stage of authentication concludes with the generation of a secret session key and a rapid exchange of confirmation messages.

The second phase of authentication occurs if the downstream device is has the ability to record or pass-through the content, and not simply a standalone display. If the devices authenticate one another, then the source device sends the encrypted content stream. The third phase of authentication occurs every 128 data frames (once every two seconds) in the vertical blanking interval (VBI) throughout the transfer of material, ensuring that the connection is secure and the devices remain the same. If, for any reason, the two devices do not produce identical values, the source device will stop sending the material.

Extended Conditional Access (XCA)

XCA was an alternate proposal for protecting content in transit, submitted by Zenith and Thomson to the CEA. Its purpose was to offer a way of securing high definition content, moving across one-way digital interfaces that would also be renewable. XCA does so with smart cards that carry the information renew and update content protection data stored by consumer devices.

The scheme was abandoned by Zenith and eventually incorporated in a Thomson intiative called SmartRight.

Technologies to Digitally Manage Rights

This chapter tells the story of DRM: It is nine parts security and one part rights management. The means to manage rights are in the early stages of development and there is little agreement about how to do it. At its broadest, DRM technologies must:

- **Access content identity and rights databases:** As covered earlier in this chapter, owners and distributors have to be able to identify the units of content that they wish to protect and monetize. In addition, DRM systems must be able to tie those copyright-protected content items to the rights, permissions, and conditions (RP&Cs) that pertain to them.

- **Respond to rights languages:** Process the expressions of those RP&Cs, as defined in metadata dictionaries and rights expression languages

- **Interface with business systems:** Interface with payment and financial systems that accept revenue and transmit RP&Cs, as appropriate

- **Manage consumer access:** Provide a system for managing access to the content, based on the RP&Cs, as established by content owners and distributors. This task includes interfacing with content protection technologies and systems in order to signal to them the users' rights of access and use

- **Track:** Track and report usage by content consumers

RIGHTS MANAGEMENT TECHNOLOGIES	DESCRIPTION
Contracts Management	Systems that store information about the terms of contracts and interface with financial systems to account for monies that are expended and received pursuant to contracts. Example: Jaguar
Rights Expression Languages (RELs)	Markup languages that express defined rights so that the rights may be implemented by digital systems in an automated manner. Examples of RELs: ODRL, XrML, MPEG-21 and the Rights Data Dictionary, and DPRL
File Exchange Formats	Systems that incorporate digital rights languages and format content so that it can be transmitted with the appropriate protection and rights information. Examples: XML, AAF, MXF

Contracts Management

If content is to be protected and managed by digital systems, then the actions that the digital machines undertake must be expressed in ways that allow them to receive, process, and act on instructions. Rights that apply to content are generally embodied in contracts and agreements that are likely to cover such areas as overall deals; creative, production, and distribution deals; acquisition agreements, and royalty terms. As mentioned earlier in Chapter 3, Jaguar Consulting markets a product called System7, which provides contracts administration for intellectual property companies. Jaguar's definition of contract-driven processing includes the following activities:

- Scheduled revenue recognition

- Participation statements

- Payment authorizations

- Royalty import/validation

- Advance/guarantee invoicing

- Cash receipts projections

- Unapplied cash management

- General ledger interface

Even if a company does not automate its contracts administration, managing its rights in the digital arena will require explicit statements of RT&Cs that can be expressed digitally and communicated to consumers. Essentially, the management of rights is a function of contractual agreements, and whether management is handled with digital computers or a quill pen and ledger book, those rights must be understood and spelled out before they can be negotiated, licensed, sold, enforced, protected, or violated.

Rights Expression Languages (RELs)

Rights are granted or licensed to consumers. These rights may include such potential actions with respect to content as: display and consumption, copying, modifying, distributing, and marketing and selling. The conditions specified in a contract define the eligibility of a given user or class of users to receive a license to be granted rights. The most common condition is a payment: outright purchase, subscription, pay-per (use, bit, time period), or site license. But other conditions might be demographic, such as age, gender, occupation, or professional status, or depend on some kind of group membership. Some P2P networks demand that users have to give to get they must open shared folders in order to download content.

One approach to attaching machine-readable rights to content is an REL. Many RELs are similar to HTML (hypertext markup language), in that they are contained in brackets (<REL vocabulary>). When the REL is part of the content's metadata it becomes a persistent part of that piece of content, traveling with it as it moves across networks to consumer devices.

The importance of making rights management information part of content metadata cannot be overemphasized:

"Rights management metadata is a part of this metadata management process, and without standards for overall metadata management, DRM processes cannot work effectively in a distributed ecosystem. Rights metadata, as defined in a rights expression language is one type of metadata. RELs provide structure for that meta-data and rights dictionaries provide codes for that structure. They must be consistent and work together.[24]

Most RELs include:

- a vocabulary (semantics), organized into a Rights Data Dictionary (RDD) that express the RP&Cs imposed by the rights-holder

- a structure for the vocabulary (grammar or syntax)

RELs must convey information about the copyrights that apply to a given piece of content in a format that computers can receive, read, process, and transmit. Such rights begin with the identification of the rights holders, licensees, creators, and any others who participate in the rights to the material. RELs express the rights, terms and conditions of the rights that are granted. It is helpful if the language can be persistently attached to the content and is amenable to change and transformation. Some RELs merely express rights, while others also support copyright enforcement. Finally, there are RELs that serve in any environment and environment-specific ones.[25]

There are many RELs, including ONIX, Publishing Requirements for Industry Standard Metadata (PRISM), Creative Commons, METSRights, Adobe Content Manager, Electronic Resource Management Initiative (ERMI), and Federated Digital Rights Management (FDRM).

---

24. Coyle, K. *Rights Expression Languages: A Report for the Library of Congress*, February, 2004. Available at: http://www.kcoyle.net/.

25. Ibid.

Three general purpose RELs that support both rights expression and automated enforcement are Open Digital Rights Language (ODRL), MPEG-21, and XrML. ODRL was accepted by the Open Mobile Alliance for its DRM implementation, but in recent years, XrML and MPEG-21, have come to the forefront. XrML is a more complex and structured language than ODRL, and the MPEG-21 REL is based on XrML, with some modification for audio-visual content. To further address AV content, MPEG developed its own Rights Data Dictionary (RDD). All three RELs are written to conform to XML, although XML parsers would not recognize the rights management tags unless it had access to the XrML dictionary.

Most RELs have a vocabulary and a syntax (grammar) to provide information about the content as part of the content's metadata. The information is likely to include some kind of unique identifier, the name of the content, the role played by the content, comments about it, version, date, type, physical location, digital location, external reference, transaction, and service provider (URI). Permissions expressed in the language usually include:[26]

- Usage - Content can be consumed (Display, Print, Play, Execute).
- Reuse -Content (or portions of it) can be re-utilised (Modify, Excerpt, Annotate, Aggregate).
- Transfer – Use of content can be transferred (Sell, Lend, Give, Lease).
- Asset Management – Content can be managed (Move, Duplicate, Delete, Verify, Backup, Restore, Save, Install, Uninstall).

RELs also express constraints on usage, such as:

- User - Limits usage by identified users (Individual, Group).
- Device - Limits usage by physical devices or systems (CPU, Network, Screen, Storage, Memory, Printer, Software, Hardware).
- Bounds - Limits usage to a fixed number or extent/coverage (Count, Range, Spatial).
- Temporal – Sets temporal boundaries (Date Time, Accumulated, Interval).
- Aspect - Limits usage to distinct features or expressions (Quality, Format, Unit, Watermark).
- Target – Limits how the asset is used (Purpose, Industry, ReContext).
- Rights - Indicates presence constraints which only apply to content with Transfer Permissions and enables the specification (and constraints) on downstream permissions (Transfer Permission).

26. Ianella, R. *Open Digital Rights Language (ODRL), Version 1.1*, September, 2002. Available at: http://www.w3.org/TR/2002/NOTE-odrl-20020919/

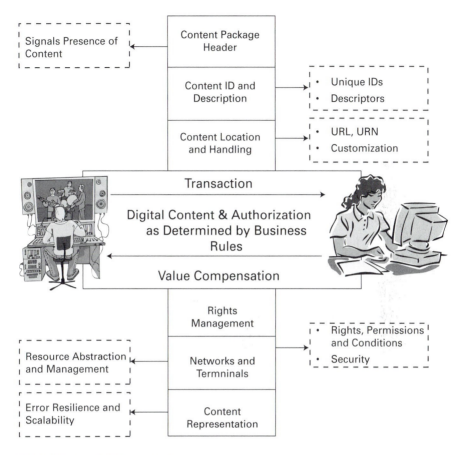

FIGURE 4.8 *MPEG-21 DRM Structure*

One key requirement that DRM systems need to fulfill is not yet incorporated into RELs are the related tasks of tracking and reporting. However, the developers of MPEG-21 intend to make this function part of the standard, and the committee is in the process of creating it (Figure 4.8).

File Exchange Formats

As with all the other aspects of media, there are probably any number of file exchange formats – formats for moving content across networks. This section covers three of the most important used to move rich content: XML, AAF, and GFX.

XML stands for Extensible Markup Language, sometimes written as eXtensible Markup Language. To introduce XML, it is useful to distinguish between and

HTML, the language used to write web pages.[27] HTML displays data and provides techniques to change how it looks; XML describes and carries data. XML is used to describe the structure of information so that machines know how to transmit and store it. The language is extensible, meaning that it can change and grow.

The goal of XML is to solve the problem of incompatible data formats. Whenever data is exchanged between different computing environments, there can be problems of reading and processing that data. Converting the data to the XML format makes the data usable by any system that understands the language. XML is independent of hardware, software and type of application. Any browser can read it. For these reasons, XML is the basis for Wireless Markup Language (WML), which is used to create applications for mobile devices like cell phones and PDAs.

Another format is the Advanced Authoring Format (AAF), developed by Microsoft. It is an exchange format that allows content creators to exchange digital media and metadata across platforms and applications. So it is less a file format for distributing finished work to consumers as it is a tool for creators to share work still under construction. It's ability to cross application boundaries is most useful: An application written in an Adobe program and saved to AAF can be pulled up in a Macromedia application for additional work. Naturally it's success depends on its inclusion within application saving options.

According to Microsoft, AAF offers the following functionalities:

- Allows complex relationships to be described in terms of an object model

- Facilitates the interchange of metadata and/or program content

- Provides a way to track the history of a piece of program content from its source elements through final production

- Makes it possible to render downstream (with appropriate equipment)

- Provides a convenient way to "wrap" all elements of a project together for archiving

The Material Exchange Format (MXF) is a subset of AAF that deals with the exchange of finished content, rather than authoring information associated with content. The Professional-MPEG Forum, with a membership of 130 broadcasters,

---

27. See the excellent tutorials on XML available at: http://www.w3schools.com/.

content creators, equipment manufacturers, and component suppliers, promulgates MXF standards. The Society of Motion Picture and Television Engineers (SMPTE) and the European Broadcast Union (EBU) are both members. The main goal of the forum is to promote interoperability of professional equipment and content.

The standard MXF provides for a standardized way of carrying metadata and both video and audio content (essence). According to the Pro-MPEG Forum, the video formats include uncompressed, compressed (including but not limited to MPEG based coding), standard definition and high definition.[28]

There is a close association between AAF, MXF and MPEG-7. MPEG-7 is an ISO/IEC standard developed by MPEG (Moving Picture Experts Group). Formally called the "Multimedia Content Description Interface," it provides comprehensive audiovisual description tools (metadata elements and their structure and relationships) enable multiple applications to search, filter and browse multimedia content. MPEG-7 has been developed by experts representing broadcasters, electronics manufacturers, content creators and managers, publishers, intellectual property rights managers, telecommunication service providers and academia.[29]

In the next chapter, we will consider how these technologies are combined into systems that carry out most or all of the functions of digital rights management. The chapter will cover approaches to the design and implementation of systems. It will also examine several DRM systems, either in use or in the design stages: Digital Cinema DRM, SMPTE DRM and the Broadcast Flag, DVD content protection and AACS, the DRM system for the next generation of DVD, Windows DRM, and Intertrust.

---

28. More information is available at: http://www.pro-mpeg.org/publicdocs/about.html.

29. More information about MPEG-7 is available at http:www.chiariglione.org/mpeg, http:www.mpegif.com, and http://mpeg7.nist.gov.

5 DRM Systems: Design and Implementation

Creating an end-to-end DRM system requires making choices from the available technologies at every step and then assembling them into an array of security and rights management systems. End-to-end products are simply systems that have been pre-assembled, packaged, and marketed by an organizational entity. In this chapter, we will consider some of these systems and how they have been put together, including the Digital Cinema DRM, SMPTE DRM and broadcast flag, DVD DRM for the current generation of devices and AACS for next-generation devices, Windows DRM, the Intertrust system, the Protected Entertainment Rights Management (PERM), and Creative Commons.

Before covering these systems, the chapter will also look briefly at the standards that necessarily come into play when technologies are concatenated into enormous, multifunctional systems. The array of standards is as bewildering as the technologies they purport to standardize. And content security and DRM truly form an inhospitable maze of international, national, trade, and proprietary standards.

This chapter will look at some issues to take into account when examining DRM for adoption and implementation. It examines where different systems locate the functions needed to handle content security and DRM. And covers the business considerations companies have to look at when selecting vendors and technologies.

For example, the first step will be to decide what works to offer for license. Then license-holders must establish which rights will be licensed. They should understand the threats and risks of making their content available. And they must decide how to address those risks. By a thoughtful structuring of these issues, content owners, aggregators, and distributors will be able to make decisions about the kind of content security and DRM that they need.

Works that Should Be Licensed

Content owners can license any form of intellectual property. However, in the digital world, where consumers can 'slice and dice' content on their computers, a new issue arises: "granularity." For example, take just one painting by Henri Matisse, "La Musique" (1939), viewable at: http://www.ibiblio.org/wm/paint/ auth/matisse/. Using any one of dozens of inexpensive programs, consumers can extract each of the two figures, the guitar that one of them is holding, at least 5 different background elements, samples of and samples of colors. The situation is infinitely more complex with an entire film, which in the course of 90 minutes, presents nearly 130,000 frames to viewers.

The elusive concept of what constitutes a work and who makes that determination is likely to become only more difficult in the future. Faster computer processing power and greater user sophistication presage ever more definitional difficulties. For example, musicians complain that they are hired (and paid) for one session. Then producers take samples from the session and create multiple works. Without signing the contract that gives these rights away, musicians may not be able to get the gig.

An early preview of the decisions facing creators is the sale of ring tones that are lifted from popular songs. Ring tones are the familiar ring of the telephone, signaling an incoming call. According to Ipsos Insight, about 30 million Americans have downloaded ringtones for the mobile phones.[1] So today's music performer contracts include clauses on the royalty split between carriers, labels, performers, song writers, and song publishers.

Rights Granted to License Holders

License-holders can specify the rights that are granted to consumers for each work and any part of the work. Beyond mere consumption, such rights typically include:

- Reproduce or copy
CONTINUED ▶

---

1. Ipsos, *Ringtone Downloading Jumps Fourfold In Past Year*, August 9, 2005. Available at: http://www.ipsos-na.com/news/pressrelease.cfm?id=2750.

CONTINUED ▶

- Publish
- Perform in public
- Communicate in public
- Modify
- Make an adaptation, specifying rights for adaptations
- Loan
- Transfer rights

In addition to granting rights, license-holders establish the conditions for granting the rights. Conditions usually involve monetary compensation, but may also include group membership (Girl Scouts, Lutherans, Masons), role (CEO, stevedore, police officer, age, gender, nationality, and so forth.

Threats to Copyrighted Material

Only after the content owner has decided what material to license, what the license will grant, and what the conditions are for giving the license (essentially established a rudimentary business model) is it possible to assess the potential copyright threats.

A precondition for assessing the business risks of distributing content is a clear and detailed understanding the nature of the threats involved. In the context of content security and DRM, a threat is anything involving a copyright violation that has the potential to damage a license-holder's ability to monetize content. It might be a modification of the work that brings it into disrepute, piracy or theft, an inadvertent release of material, or an unauthorized early release or a release into unapproved markets.

The nature and likelihood of threats to copyrighted products differ from one medium to another, from one company to another. Some typical threats to copyright include all of the situations just described:

- Physical theft

- Professional piracy

- Large-scale casual copying

- Inadvertent early release

- Release into unapproved markets

- Impermissible modification

Although it is common for entertainment executives to characterize threats in terms of an activity such as peer-to-peer networks or professional cammers and counterfeiters, these are not the actual threats. In a business sense, the more serious problems are yet to follow.

The real threats are the negative consequences on content businesses that stem from copyright infringement. The most frequently cited is a drop in the sales of an entertainment product. It might also be a loss of value to the entire cascade of release windows. For instance, if a motion picture is widely counterfeited and distributed prior to its release, not only the immediately theatrical revenues are diminished. It is quite possible that income that would flow from a successful theatrical run would be reduced in all the subsequent downstream windows of home video, pay-per-view, and premium cable licensing.

Executives also need to consider the source of each threat. A professional piracy and counterfeiting operation can be devastating, but it is critical to identify exactly how the good quality material got into the hands of the counterfeiter. A careless employee, an embittered technician, or a bribed theater manager may all provide pathways to the pirate. Each of these possible sources of content leakage requires a different security response.

However, the music industry's struggle with peer-to-peer networking presents an interesting conundrum: The threat comes from their own customers. The jury is still out on whether or not peer-to-peer networking actually causes damage to music sales, or if it does, the extent to which it affects the bottom line. Nevertheless, most music industry executives perceive p2p networks as an enormous threat that has reduced sales volume and industry profits to a significant degree.

Clearly some threats are more serious than others, as measured in the potential for negative impacts on monetizing content, ranging from devastating to irritating. And some threats are more likely than others to occur at all, depending on the work, the audience, the technology, the price, the difficulty of carrying out the threatening activity, and the negative consequences (if any) for doing so.

Assessing Risk

The Australian Department of Communication, Information Technology and the Arts suggests that the likelihood of a given threat actually occurring depends on the level of motivation of the motive of the would-be infringer and the opportunity to do so. Putting these two variables together results in the assessment matrix shown in Table 5.1.

The assessment of risk is based on the likelihood that infringement will take place and the potential impact of the violation, as shown in Table 5.2. The methods

OPPORTUNITY/ LEVEL OF MOTIVATION	VERY HIGH	HIGH	MEDIUM	LOW	VERY LOW
Very high	Certain	Probable	Probable	Possible	Possible
High	Probable	Probable	Possible	Possible	Improbable
Medium	Probable	Possible	Possible	Improbable	Improbable
Low	Possible	Possible	Improbable	Improbable	Negligible
Very low	Possible	Possible	Improbable	Negligible	Negligible

TABLE 5.1 *Likelihood of Threat Occurring*

THREAT	SOURCE	LIKELIHOOD	POSSIBLE REMEDY
Physical theft	Criminal activity	High	Legal, criminal justice system
Professional piracy	Criminal	High	Legal, criminal justice system
Camming	Theaters	High	Watermark, digital fingerprint
Pre-release theft	Employee	Low	Internal security, encryption
	Outside facility	Moderate	Encryption, security agreements with partners
	Reviewers	Moderate	Encryption, dedicated player, watermark, digital fingerprint

TABLE 5.2 *Assessing Risk*

THREAT	SOURCE	LIKELIHOOD	POSSIBLE REMEDY
P2P downloading	Consumer	High	Content security: Encryption or encapsulation, watermark
Casual copying	Consumer	High	Content security: Encryption or encapsulation, watermark
Inadvertent early release	Workforce	Low	Internal security, encryption, watermark
	Reviewer	Moderate	Encryption, dedicated player, watermark, digital fingerprint
Release into unapproved markets by partners/customers	Downstream distributors	Low	Contract enforcement, security, watermark and digital fingerprint, and digital rights management
Impermissible modification	Any	Moderate to high	Digital rights management

TABLE 5.2 *(Continued)*

for addressing those risks open through the analysis of the source of the threat, specifically the level of motivation and the opportunity to carry out the infringement.

No matter what license-holders do or pay, there is no perfect protection against copyright infringement. So the real question becomes: What percentage of loss (risk) are they willing to accept? Executives in the media and entertainment might look at "depletion audits" of alcoholic beverages in the hospitality industry, where about 15% is allowed for breakage, theft and other crime, returned drinks, and

2. Ruggless, R. *Bush twins' woes are backdrop for change in liquor regulations*, Nation's Restaurant News, June 11, 2001. Available at: http://www.findarticles.com/p/articles/mi_m3190/is_24_35/ai_75620218.

promotional giveaways.[2] By comparison, a study of retail operations, conducted by researchers at the University of Florida, found that in 2000 total inventory shrinkage was 1.69 percent of sales.[3]

License-holders need to make careful judgments about just how much copyright protection and rights management their content requires. The closer content providers try to come to 100%, the more it will cost, with each percentage point of closure costing more than the last. Moreover, as DRM becomes more draconian, it imposes greater difficulties for paying customers to consume the content. One of the most effective methods of copy protection is to require the consumer to use a dedicated player to watch the material. Such an action may be possible with the most popular hit movie or song, but for most products, it may be as effective a deterrent to sales as it would be to copyright violation.

Locus of Rights Management

The location of DRM activities is a key consideration when looking at its costs. Any or all of the DRM functions can be out-sourced. The issues are cost, control, and ownership of consumer usage information. The more activity that can be pushed to consumer devices, where either the customer or the manufacturer makes the investment, the less expensive it is for license-holders. The more control and information exclusivity a license-holder wants, the more DRM will cost.

Systems and implementations differ greatly in their approach to locating rights management functions. Often, it is possible to pick one function from column A and another from Column B, so that the resulting distributed system is a hybrid that puts some functions in every possible venue.

Theoretically, all of the DRM activity could take place inside the local machine or the consumer electronics device, and this scenario could take place if these functions were placed on a chip. Some architectures distribute DRM activity, calling for a payment processor, which handles the financial transaction, a license server, which issues permission to the consumer to access the content, and a separate media server, which transmits the content. There are packaged designs that involve third party vendors that handle all the DRM functions, typically using a distributed architecture. Finally, there are registries that take care of some of the first steps required for security and DRM, such as assigning unique identifiers to content products.

---

3. Statistics reported at: http://retailindustry.about.com/
od/statistics_loss_prevention/l/aa001122a.htm.

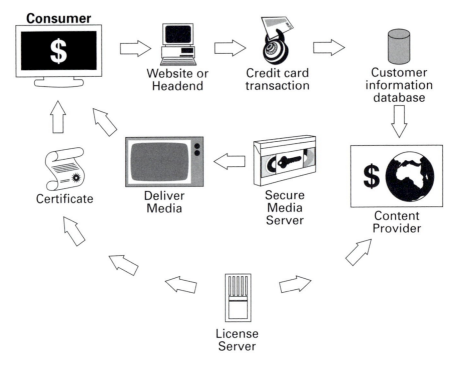

FIGURE 5.1 *License Server Architecture and Process*

Registries

These are systems that register content, assign it an identification number, and stores information about it, including its location. Some registries maintain the content's metadata or store pointers to both metadata and content. Registries are often managed by trade organizations such as SMPTE, government agencies, and other institutions. Conceptually, however, they could be managed by any entity with sufficient professional knowledge, processing capability and storage capacity. A registry may also be maintained by a trusted third party host.

License Server

A license server is a computer where information (payments) from consumers is correlated with the rights (licenses) they have purchased, as shown in Figure 5.1. A content provider chooses a clearinghouse to store the rights and usage rules. The clearinghouse authenticates requests for a license and verifies that the conditions for authorization, access, and consumption have been met. The content itself is usually stored on a separate server that is optimized for serving content.

Some certificates issues by license servers impose the rules license-holders wish to impose, such as restricting the device (or devices) where the user can consume the content. License servers maintain a list of compromised devices and either refuse to deliver the content, or do not issue the necessary permission to decrypt the content on a compromised device. A license server may be part of an overall DRM system operated by any entity such as an organization, company, or trusted third party host.

Trusted Third Party

In any environment, trust is hard to find. When used in a DRM system, the trusted third party acts as a mediator between buyer and seller. It verifies identity and payment, and sends out a certificate to the buyer's device that specifies the terms and conditions of access to the content. Although it entails its own costs, using a trusted third party host is a way for companies that distribute content to avoid the necessity of building an expensive, processing-intensive public key DRM infrastructure.

A trusted third party can also shore up public key technologies by verifying the security of the keys. But more importantly, it can authenticate the identity of the user. This action is necessary because encryption alone cannot guarantee identity, link keys to specific users, or ensure that the key has not been falsified or compromised.

Security models in many industries rest on trusted parties exchanging information, goods, and services because distributing digital content across network platforms means that the license-holder may not know the consumer at all. Even the distributor, whether it's a cable operator, telephone company, or ISP, may not know customers well enough to trust them on behalf of a content provider. In other words, the distributor may not be willing to assume the risks of the license-holder.

Trusted third party technology can protect the anonymity of buyers, shielding access to their financial information from marketers. To do so, the trusted agent strips away any personal or identifying information about the consumer before passing it on. Marketers can aggregate the data but will not know the individual identity of any single buyer.[4]

Trusted third party systems bring their own difficulties. They may be difficult to implement. The anonymity they offer may not be strong enough, or they may renege on their agreement to preserve anonymity and sell or share information.

---

4. Burk D., Cohen, J. *Fair Use Infrastructure for Copyright Management Systems*, 15:1, Fall, 2001. Available at: jolt.law.harvard.edu/articles/pdf/15HarvJLTech041.pdf.

They require substantial communication overhead. And there may be significant delays in the processes of verification, authorization, and certification because they rest on network and server technologies that may not always function optimally.5

Smart Card

A smart card unites DRM activities at a distance and within the local device. Smart cards are very popular in Europe, where they are commonly used for electronic cash transactions and subscription television systems like satellite TV. TV content providers that use smart cards provide consumers with set-top boxes (STBs) that are manufactured with slots for the cards and can read the information on them into the STB's memory. The smart card itself is a plastic card that is the same size as the credit card. Gold contacts on the card carry signals, so communicates with the device in which it is placed.

A small chip inside the card acts as both a microprocessor and memory, allowing it to hold more information than a magnetic strip. And it is far more secure than the strip: Typically, encryption secures the data. The programmable processor can respond with requests for information that are appropriate to the requirements. For example, it can report that there are sufficient funds in an account without providing the total balance in the account.[6]

Smarts cards may have up to 8 kilobytes of RAM, 346 kilobytes of ROM, 256 kilobytes of programmable ROM, and a 16-bit microprocessor. They use a serial interface and get power from external sources, such as the card reader or STB. For cryptography and other applications, the processor uses a limited instruction set.

User Devices

Almost everyone owns a device that has embedded DRM functionality: A cable or satellite STB, an iPod, or a DVD player. The common set-top box manages conditional access, which lets cable operators and satellite companies deliver a bouquet of channels to the STB, but only allowing the subscriber to access the channels for which the household has paid. The STB also stores usage information and sends it to the headend so that pay-per-view (PPV) and video-on-demand (VOD) charges to invoice eventual uses on a pay-per-view and video-on-demand basis.

---

5. Abadi, M. *Trusted Computing, Trusted Third Parties, and Verified Communications*, May, 2004. Available at: www.cse.ucsc.edu/~abadi/Papers/verif.pdf.

6. Information about smart cards is available at: http://www.compinfo.co.uk/ecom/smart-cards.htm

It is worth looking at the security and DRM features that will be built into next-generation STBs, a system called the Secure Video Processor (SVP). It has both hardware and software elements that protect content, as shown in Table 5.3.

INSIDE THE DEVICE	
COMPONENT	**FUNCTION IN CONDITIONAL ACCESS AND DRM BUSINESS MODEL ENFORCEMENT**
HARDWARE	
Chip	Processing for personalization, compliance, and robustness.
	Core Security Functions: Certificates handling, SAC, CryptoTools., time, key management, content license (usage model definition and rules & content keys), export content control, revocation
Secure boot loader	Content processing: Content descrambling and decoding
	Tamper-proof system startup
SOFTWARE	
Chip software driver TRS software	Support microprocessor operation
	Enforcement for domain, proximity, broadcast flag, private extensions)
Memory	Usage model definition, billing information, and conditional access, digital rights management, and distributed system architecture (FTA)

TABLE 5.3 *The Secure Video Processor Open Content Protection System*

The complexity and sophistication of DRM embedded in consumer electronics devices will continue to grow. Consider the television set of 30 years ago. It had a power cord and an antenna connection. That's it. Now look at today's display. It has RCA, S-video, and component video inputs and outputs for hookups to PVRs, DVD players and recorders, game consoles, computers, and even those dinosaurs, VHS videocassette players and recorders. It has a cable-ready hookup. It probably has audio outputs, including mono, stereo, and SurroundSound.

This ever-greater connectivity between consumer devices of all kinds is a source of concern to content license-holders. They demand that consumer electronics manufacturers incorporate DRM into the design of their devices, but they decline to pay anything for it. According to DRM guru Bill Rosenblatt or GiantSteps Media, "Consumer devices and DRM are not going hand in hand. Neither content nor consumer-device manufacturers will pay for implementing DRM in under-$200 consumer devices," he said.[7]

However, some form of security and DRM is incorporated into higher-ticket devices and the software inside them is becoming ever more important. Many devices have an Ethernet connection, which allows the software, including DRM applications, to be updated and renewed.[8] These developments create the possibility of more flexible security and DRM regimes. In addition to altering security settings and renewing device certificates, content distributors can change the pricing, promotion, business and usage rules, and other elements of the security and make changes at any time to the rights protection features they installed at the time the consumer first purchased the content.

Standards

So far, this chapter has looked at decisions that content owners and distributors need to make about DRM systems. But complex technical considerations come into play when technologies are put together into systems. One of the ways that hardware and software from different vendors recognize, communicate, and function together is through standardization. Whether it is something as mundane as plugs and sockets or as abstract as a markup language, standards are technological glue.

There are two broad types of standards: de jure and de facto. De jure standards are reviewed, approved, and promulgated by official standards-setting bodies, like the International Standards Organization, or the U.S. National Institute of Standards and Technology. De facto standards are usually proprietary protocols that have acquired such a commanding market share that they are simply accepted as a standard, even though they were never approved by a standards-setting entity. Microsoft Windows is a good example of a de facto standard.

There are many standards involved in implementing a DRM system, particularly if it is designed to work across the entire content life cycle. Speaking at a conference on DRM, GiantStep's Bill Rosenblatt noted that there is a hierarchy of DRM standards that are not all completed and approved, nor are they necessarily

---

7. Dykstra, G. *The Truth About Digital Rights Management*. Information Today. 19:10, November, 2002. Available at: http://www.infotoday.com/it/nov02/dykstra.htm.

8. Mittag, L. *The future of consumer electronics platforms*. Embedded.com, November 1, 2004. Available at: http://www.embedded.com/shared/printableArticle.jhtml?articleID=51201908.

THE HIERARCHY OF STANDARDS FOR DRM SYSTEMS	
DOMAIN OR APPLICATION	**STANDARD NAME**
Content identification	Digital Object Identifier (DOI)
	International Standard Audiovisual Number (ISAN)
	International Semantic Web Conference (ISWC)
	Unique Material Identifier (UMID)
Content description	Advanced Authoring Format (AAF)
	ONIX for books
	News Markup Language (NewsML)
	Motion Picture Experts Group (MPEG-7)
Expression of rights and contract terms	Extensible Rights Management Language (XrML)
	Motion Picture Experts Group Rights Expression Language (MPEG REL) and Contracts Expression Language (CEL)
	Open Digital Rights Language (ODRL)
	MPEG-21 and Rights Data Dictionary RDD
Copy protection	Analog Protection System (APS-Macrovision)
	Broadcast flag
	Copy Generation Management System (CGMS)
	Serial Copy Management System (SCMS)
	Copy Protection for Pre-recorded Media(CPPM)
	Copy Protection for Recordable Media (CPRM)
Encryption	RSA (based on the names of the inventors, Ron Rivest, Adi Shamir and Len Adleman)
	Blowfish
	Advanced Encryption Standard (AES)
	Digital Encryption Standard (DES)
	Rivest Cipher 5 and 6 (RC5 and RC6).
	International Streaming Media Association (ISMACrypt)

TABLE 5.4 *Hierarchy of Standards Involved in DRM Systems*

THE HIERARCHY OF STANDARDS FOR DRM SYSTEMS	
DOMAIN OR APPLICATION	**STANDARD NAME**
Networks and platforms	Internet standards: HyperText Transport Protocol(HTTP) • HyperText Markup Language (HTML), • Extensible Markup Language (XML), • Java • PRISM: Architecture for distributing, storing, and delivering high quality streaming content over IP networks. Shibboleth: Architecture for inter-organizational sharing Cable and Satellite Industries: • Secure Video Processor (SVP) hardware DRM specifications for set-top boxes
Players and formats	Windows Media DRM Real (HELIX) Motion Picture Experts Group Layer 3 (MP3), Apple's Fairplay: Advanced Audio Coding, (AAC – part of MPEG-4 standard by the Motion Picture Experts Group)
Transaction and e-commerce: **Authentication** **User or device identity**	Microsoft .net Passport Internet Engineering Task Force: Session Initiation Protocol (SIP) Internet – OASIS: Security Assertion Markup Language (SAML) 150 company, nonprofit, and government membership: Liberty Alliance IBM and Microsoft: WS-Federation IBM: Internet Keyed Payment Protocol (IKPP)
Payment mechanisms	Visa and MasterCard: Secure Electronic Transactions (SET) Proposed interoperable electronic transaction standard: • Joint Electronic Payments Initiative (JEPI)

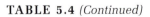

TABLE 5.4 *(Continued)*

THE HIERARCHY OF STANDARDS FOR DRM SYSTEMS	
DOMAIN OR APPLICATION	**STANDARD NAME**
Meta and interoperability standards	Mpeg-21: Framework for standards of networked multimedia that covers all types of content, all formats, all networks.
	Microsoft Windows Media DRM
	Content Reference Forum (CRF)
	Digital Media Project (DMP)
	Marlin Joint Development Association
Home networking	Digital Transmission Content Protection (DTCP)
	High-bandwidth Digital Content Protection (HDCP)
	High Definition Multimedia Interface (HDMI)
	Extended Conditional Access (XCA)
	Consumer electronics manufacturers and CEA - DENi Alliance: • Protected Entertainment Rights Management

TABLE 5.4 *(Continued)*

compatible with standards that govern other functions at other levels. An oft-cited wry comment about the situation is: "The best thing about standards is that there are so many of them to choose from." (See Table 5.4.)

DRM Systems

This chapter now turns to DRM systems that have been issued for entertainment systems. Some of them are up and running, others have merely been published or are in the first stages of implementation so they may be altered by actual experience (Table 5.5). The systems broadly address consumer consumption channels: motion pictures, television, DVD, IP networks, and home networks. Most of the systems came out of trade associations, such as the DRM for Digital Cinema, the SMPTE scheme for television, DVD players, and home networks. One, Intertrust, is a proprietary vendor system, and another is a system by a nonprofit, Creative Commons.

DRM SYSTEM	INDUSTRY/MEDIUM	PARTICIPANTS
Digital Cinema DRM	Motion Picture	
SMPTE DRM and broadcast Flag	Television	
DVD-CCA and AACS	Current DVD and next-generation DVD	DVD-CCA
Windows DRM	Internet/IP Networks	Microsoft
Intertrust	Trusted Third Party Architecture	Coral (NEMO), Marlin
ContentGuard	Standards-based proprietary solution	MPEG REL (XrML)
Permanent Entertainment Rights Management (PERM)	Rights management across home networks	Consumer electronics manufacturers: CEA, Pioneer, Thomson, Sharp, BridgeCo, Onkyo, Kenwood
Copyleft and Creative Commons	Any and all distribution platforms	Copyleft is the opposite of copyright, copyleft specifies that all users have the right to access, use, and modify the content. Creative Commons is a form of copyleft – it is copyright assertion for the rest of us: Small content creators and publishers

TABLE 5.5 *DRM Systems Covered in this Chapter*

Digital Cinema DRM

The Big Seven Hollywood studios: Disney, 20th Century Fox, MGM, Paramount, Sony Pictures Entertainment, Universal, and Warner Bros. established the Digital Cinema Initiative in March 2002. The primary purpose of DCI is to establish voluntary uniform specifications for Digital Cinema, although digital cinema is still in its infancy. In 2004, there were about 36,000 theatrical exhibition screens in the U.S. and only 172 of them were digital. However, as many as 6,000 screens

ACTIVITY	SECURITY/RIGHTS MANAGEMENT
Post-production	Watermarking
	Compression: JPEG 2000
	Encryption: AES-128, capable of using secure cryptographic keys of 128, 192, and 256 bits. Each frame of the picture is encrypted separately
Packaging and Transport	MXF file format (MXF, subtype MXF_J2: Containerization
Delivery to theater	Encryption keys with time/date stamps
	Key management: Key delivery separate from content
Distribution within theater	Link encryption
	Security manager
	Theater Management System (TMS) and Screen Management System (SMS)
	Rights management
Server and Projector	

TABLE 5.6 *DCI Security and Rights Management Specifications*

are expected to go digital in 2006.[9] The growth of the new exhibition format has been inhibited by lack of standards in resolution, color matching (gamut), projectors, file formats, compression algorithms, and security and rights management techniques (Table 5.6). The formation of the DCI reflected the enormous incentive that motion picture studios and distributes have to make the transition from physical distribution of film reels to electronic delivery over networks: Estimates of cost savings to them the cost savings for the industry range from $900 to $2.28 each year.[10]

In July, 2005, the group released the 176-page Digital Cinema System Specification, Version 1.0. It lays out the procedures, policies, requirements, and formats

9. Advanced Media Report, *Digital Cinema Turns Corner.* January 3, 2006. Available at: http://www.weinstockmedia.com/enews/weinstock_media.html#Top_story.

10. White, K. *Security and Digital Cinema: The Last Big Question.* Available at: http://www.webbuyersguide.com/sub/animation/buyingadvice/2674-wbganimation_buyingadvice.html.

for preparing, packaging, transporting, and displaying motion pictures digitally. Although the specification includes all the requirements for delivering movies over networks, current plans call for distributors to ship movies to theaters on a hard drive, with the encryption key delivered separately. The basic elements of the specification are:

- Bandwidth: 307Mbps

- Ingest interface: Gigabit or 1000Base-T Ethernet interface using TCP/IP

- Compression: JPEG 2000

   Security operates at every level of the distribution process.

Packaging the Movie for Transport: Material Exchange Format (MXF)

The DCI specification for protecting the content directly with watermarking and AES encryption are techniques that were covered in Chapter 4. So this section begins with packaging the movie for transport, using the MXF format. The DCI adopted SMPTE MXF standards (377M-393M and EG 41 and EG42).

Essentially, the MXF file format "wraps" or "containerizes" video, audio and other bitstreams (the content or essence). MXF metadata provides instructions for re-assembling the streams into the original whole program. These instructions do not discriminate between essence types and recognize the metadata associated with the essence. (Recall that SMPTE distinguishes between "essence," or program content, and information about the content, metadata.) The MXF metadata define "operational patterns," which includes transport file format and encryption information, similar to MPEG profiles.

Inside the MXF container are the movie "tracks," audio, video, and subtitles. The re-assembly occurs by means of a composition playlist that provides instructions about how the different tracks should be put back together. There are several types of tracks, including timeline tracks, event tracks, and static tracks. All the tracks are synchronized in a container for tracks called a "package."

There are a number of security measures incorporated into the DCI MXF specification. The container must accept encrypted content, although the track file metadata is unencrypted. The metadata includes information that will disclose if the essence or container has been altered since the material was formatted for transport. The spec recommends that distributors divide track files into segments, giving each individual authenticity and error checking codes.

File Header		File Essence	File Footer
Header Metadata	Header Metadata	Essence Container	Footer Partition Pack

FIGURE 5.2 *MXF file format (Recreated with permission from DCI)*

UL Key (16 bytes)	Length (BER)	Value (Variable Length Octets)

FIGURE 5.3 *Example of KLV Coding (Recreated with permission from DCI)*

MXF encrypts every frame of the track, using SMPTE 336M-2001 key-length-value (KLV) encoding. The MXF file format is shown in Figure 5.2.

The KLV packets are encrypted using AES-128, as shown in Figure 5.3. Frame integrity of every frame is verified using the HMAC-SHA1 algorithm. However, frame headers are in plain text – that is, readable by humans.

Distribution of the transport file includes an XML-format packing list that describes everything all material in the package. The entity that creates the packing list provides for authentication and verification via digital signatures.

Security and Rights Management within the Theater

Figure 5.4 shows the flow of content within the theater. The DCI specification says that the high level business requirements for security must:

• Enable the decryption and playback of feature films, based upon business rules agreed upon by exhibitors and Distributors

• Provide persistent security protection against unauthorized access, copying, editing, or playback of feature films

• Provide records of security-related events

Digital cinema theaters are operated with two types of software, the Theater Management System (TMS) and the Screen Management System (SMS). A TMS controls the theater from one central location, enabling management of show programming, troubleshooting, asset management, and showing the status of the digital cinema

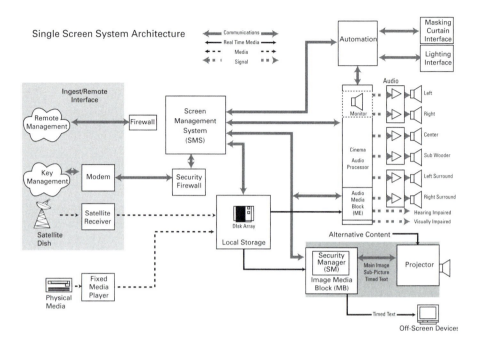

FIGURE 5.4 *Flow of Content within a Single-screen Theater (Recreated with permission from DCI)*

equipment. The SMS allows an operator to load a playlist and to start, stop, and pause the content running in an auditorium. One TMS system may operate a multiplex theater (one with multiple screens), but there must be an SMS for each auditorium.

Theaters must operate an environment that provides persistent security: protection of content, security of data, and support for forensic processes. The specification describes the various employees within theaters and the access they may have to the digital cinema equipment and security apparatus.

Part of the equipment configuration is the "Media Block" (MB). The MB is the device that takes the packaged data from storage, unpacks it, decrypts it, and converts it in real time to data for playback. There are alternate designs for MBs, but if decryption is part of its function, the MB must be physically secure. It also contains the Security Manager and forensic marker decoder.

If the MB is not part of the projection system, the theater must provide physical security for the link between the MB and the projector. In addition, the content must be encrypted as it flows across the link and security must be provided for the decryption and security keys. The specification encourages that standard encryption technologies be used for the link, including TDES [FIPS (46-3) and ANSI standard

X9.32] or AES, with 112 bit keys (for TDES) or 128 bit keys for AES. Every movie showing requires the generation of fresh, time-limited link encryption keys.

As is clear, the primary means of security is encryption and key management, and rights management establish the rules for content usage. Theaters are required to keep a log of every time the content is accessed and to maintain other security event records. At the heart of the security infrastructure is a Security Manager (SM), software that must be present in every auditorium.

The SM is built with open standards and must be interoperable with all the digital cinema management and security infrastructure. Security data enables (or denies) access to the content; this data is entrusted to the SM, which ultimately controls access.

The SM carries out key management as well. When the SM receives a key, that key only works for a specified time period. The SM authenticates the identity and integrity of the security equipment and then enables the keys during the authorized play window. The SMS is not considered secure and does not handle keys.

The importance of the SM is apparent from the breadth of task the specification assigns to the SM:

- Receive, store, decrypt, and validate signatures on Key Delivery Message(s) (KDMs) that are targeted at the SM.

- Enforce the playback time window specified in the KDM by:

    a. Delivering content keys to Media Decryptors along with usage periods fully contained within the KDM time window,

    b. Deleting expired Key Delivery Message(s) (KDMs) and associated keys from (its) storage.

- Reject messages that are not recognized as DCI compliant standardized messages.

- Validate Composition Playlists (CPL), and log results as a prerequisite to preparing the suite for the associated composition playback.

- Process essence (i.e., Track File frame) integrity pack metadata for image and sound during show runtime. Log information necessary to detect deviations from the actual playback sequence from the Track File ID and reel sequence specified in the CPL follows:

- Maintain a list of certificates required to authenticate CPLs and messages.

- Perform remote Secure Processing Block (SPB) and Screen Management

System (SMS) authentication through Transport Layer Security (TLS) session-establishment, and maintain the certificate lists so collected.

    a.   Associate certificate lists with TDLs delivered in KDMs to support the identification of security devices that are trusted/not trusted.

    b.   Maintain encrypted link sessions open for not more than 24 hours between complete restarts

- Support encrypted link sessions within the theater

- Prepare and issue protected content keys to external media decryptor (MD)and forensic marking. Constrain issuance of keys to:

    a.   Suite preparation command received from an SMS that appears on the Trusted Device List (TDL) for the composition being prepared for play-back.

    b.   Usage validity periods of six (6) hours for remote SPBs. Do not allow the six hour period to extend beyond the playback time window

    c.   Authenticated and trusted Secure Processing Blocks (SPBs) per

    d.   Media decryptors (e.g., image, sound, subtitle, link encryption) in SPBs

    e   Specific MDs matching the key type IDs as designated the KDM.

    f.   Receipt by the SM of a valid CPL for the composition being prepared for playback.

- Support Link Encryption (LE) keying (if link encryption is used) by:

    a.   Generating unpredictable keys

    b.   Transferring LE keys only to an authenticated and trusted Link Decryptor Block installed in an authenticated and trusted projector.

    c.   Support link encryption operational processes for combinations of clear and encrypted content.

- Perform suite playback preparations (via SMS) for each showing, within 30 minutes prior to showtime.

- Maintain secure time for a specific auditorium, including SPB time synchro-nization requirements.

- Execute log duties for the assigned auditorium.

- Execute Forensic Marking (FM) control operations.

- During all normal operating conditions, continuously monitor and log integrity status of all security components.

- Support suite playback enablement (authentication followed by keying) such that no more than one of each type of SE is enabled (i.e., one LD Block, one image MD, one audio MD).

- Secure Processing Block behavior and suite implementations shall permit the SM to prevent or terminate playback upon the occurrence of a suite SPB substitution or addition since the previous suite authentication and/or status query. The SMs shall respond to such a change by immediately purging all content and link encryption keys, terminating and re-establishing: a) encrypted link sessions (and reauthenticating the suite), and b) suite playability conditions (KDM prerequisites, SPB queries and key loads).

- Perform and log all the above functions under the operational (not security) control of the particular SMS designated by the exhibition operator. The use of multiple KDMs for any CPL is allowed. The SM shall honor any valid playback time window.

There are extensive provisions for logging. Despite what appear to be rather stringent security requirements, the philosophy espoused within the specification is "control lightly, audit tightly." The DCI retains the right to update and renew the security and rights management procedures. And the security and DRM specs issued by the DCI may be extensible to other media such as films distributed over the Internet.

SMPTE DRM and Broadcast Flag

DRM for television does not apply to the current NTSC system; rather, it is designed for use with digital television (DTV). The entity responsible for DTV standards is the Advanced Television Systems Committee (ATSC). The ATSC set and issues 18 standards for DTV profiles that included multiple progressive and interlaced formats and standard (SD) and high definition (HD) resolutions.

Once it became clear that programming would come to the public's televisions, content owners expressed concerns about the ability of consumers to make unlimited copies of unprotected HD bitstreams of their high-value material. Nothing in the ATSC standards would specifically inhibit such copying. As time went on and networks speeds and capacities grew, copyright holders observed the havoc that P2P file sharing caused to business models in the music industry.

They threatened to withhold their programming from terrestrial DTV unless their copyrighted content could be protected it. The response of SMPTE engineers was called 'broadcast flag.' Note that SMPTE committees also created the security and rights management system for digital cinema, so there is more than a passing resemblance between the DCI standards and the SMPTE system for television. The components of the SMPTE security and rights management system for television are the broadcast flag, encryption, MXF wrappers (containers), and rights management metadata.

Broadcast Flag

In this context, the word flag means a signal, not a national symbol made of cloth, waving in the breeze. The broadcast flag is composed of a set of status bits (or flags) placed in the bitstream of a DTV program that signals whether the material can be recorded and the presence of restrictions on recording. The restrictions are the conditions specified in CGMS, as noted in Chapter 4: Copy freely, copy once, no more copying, no copying. In addition, it did not permit copying of HD, limiting the resolution of digital copies to SD. It also prevented them from skipping commercials. Figure 5.5 shows how signals would flow through a broadcast flag-enabled CE device.

The ATSC approved the broadcast flag and the U.S. Federal Communications Commission ordered that consumer electronics implement broadcast flag recognition in their products by July 1, 2005. However, on May 6, 2005, the U.S. Court of Appeals for the D.C. Circuit struck down broadcast flag, saying that the FCC exceeded its authority by requiring CE makers to alter the design of their products.

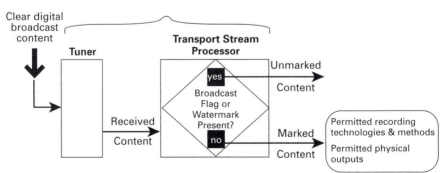

FIGURE 5.5 *Broadcast Flag Flow Diagram*

The supporters of the flag may appeal this ruling to the Supreme Court, or they may lobby Congress to change the scope of the FCC's statutory authority, or they may find a way to integrate the flag into CE devices' existing copy protection technologies. Of course, if consumers are determined to copy DTV, they will probably be able to find devices that do not incorporate broadcast flag, available in markets where there is no regulation against copying.

The broadcast flag took advantage of a copy control mechanism within the ATSC standards, called the Redistribution Control Descriptor (ATSC RC). The 8-bit RC signaled copyright assertion by the program rights holder. But it did not prescribe how CE devices would respond to the descriptor.

Broadcast flag did not prevent consumers from making copies on PVRs, D-VHS, or DVD recordable discs. Nor did it stop them from sending it over home networks. But it did call for reduced resolutions in these cases.

CATEGORY	DESCRIPTION	MAXIMUM LENGTH
Rights	Rights metadata	
Copyright	Copyright metadata	
Copyright Status	Assertion of copyright	127 bytes
Copyright Owner	Owner or license holder	127 bytes
Intellectual rights	IP rights beyond copyright	
IP Type	Human-readable IP description	32 bytes
IP Right	Human-readable description of usage rights	32 bytes
Legal personalities	Legally defined participants	
Rights Owner	Owner or license holder	127 bytes
Rights Management Authority	Rights manager	127 bytes
Interested parties	Other participants	127 bytes

TABLE 5.7 *Partial List of Security and Rights Management Metadata within SMPTE Metadata Dictionary RP210 version 2*

CATEGORY	DESCRIPTION	MAXIMUM LENGTH
IP Right options	Usage descriptions	
Maximum Number of Usages	Describes number of allowed usages or repeats	2 bytes
License options	Directions for license extension or renewal	127 bytes
Financial information	Payments, costs, income money and other financial elements	
Currencies	Description of accepted currencies	
Currency	International Standards Organization Codes for currencies and funds	4 chars
Payments and costing	Payments and cost information	
Royalty Financial Information	Royalty payments	127 bytes
Income	Income information	
Royalty Financial Information	Royalty income	127 bytes
Permitted Access	Description of permitted access to the media product	
Restrictions on Use	Type and level of any restrictions	32 bytes
Security	Description of content encryption/decryption mechanisms	
System Access	Description of permitted access to the technical system or platform	
Username (ISO 7-bit)	Domain user with system access	16 chars
Username (Unicode)	Domain user with system access	16 chars
Password (ISO 7-bit)	User password for access to the system	16 chars
Password (Unicode)	User password for access to the system	16 chars

TABLE 5.7 *(Continued)*

CATEGORY	DESCRIPTION	MAXIMUM LENGTH
Encryption	Content encryption/decryption information	
Film Encryption	Description of encryption/decryption information for film	
Scrambling Keys	Film decryption keys	
Scrambling key kind	Film decryption key type	4 chars
Scrambling key value	Film decryption key value	64 bytes
Publication Outlet	Distribution channel: Broadcast, internet	
Broadcast and Repeat Information	Business rules	
Broadcast Flags	Signals for security and rights management	
First Broadcast Flag	Signals if broadcast is first-run	1 byte
Repeat numbers	If not first-run, how many repeats?	
Current repeat number	Current repeat status	2 bytes
Participating parties	Credits	

TABLE 5.7 *(Continued)*

SMPTE Security and Rights Management for DTV

SMPTE also provided for more security and rights management information within DTV metadata, specified in the SMPTE metadata dictionary, SMPTE Metadata Dictionary RP210 version 2, as presented in Table 5.7.

As noted in Chapter 4, an additional SMPTE standard, 401-M, allows for even more security and rights management functions than are built into CGMS. Within SMPTE-compliant facilities, the ExCCI can be handled as metadata, including transport, processing, storage, and encoding and decoding.

The extended copy control information instructions in this standard are called ExCCI, shown in Table 4-8, as summarized S. Merrill Weiss.[11] Essentially, ExCCI provides for:

- Control of analog and digital outputs

- Analog protection via APS

- CGMS-A and CGMS-D

- Limited resolution of copies from HD to SD

- Copy control via CGMS-A and CGMS-D

- Prevents redistribution over the Internet

- Restrictions on generational copying

- Harmonization with European standards

- Control within home networks and multiple devices

- Specification of usage rights and restrictions, including time windows

- Possible future extensions

SMPTE DRM and VC-1

As part of its development of professional standards for DTV in the television industry, SMPTE adopted a compression standard, also called a codec. There was heated competition between two standards, AVC H.264, MPEG-4 Part 10, sometimes just called AVC for Advanced Video Coding. It was developed by members of the International Telecommunication Union Video Coding Experts Group (VCEG) and International Standards Organization MPEG. The codec results in a high quality picture while achieving a high level of compression. The other contender was Windows Media 9 codec.

There was considerable controversy within and without SMPTE when the trade group chose the Microsoft codec. Windows DRM was not part of the Media 9 codec. However, new the 64-bit version now does include a DRM Protect Utility, which allows for the addition of DRM protection to files after the encoding process, as well as providing for use of a decryption key.

---

11. Weiss, S. M. *Extended Content Control Information (ExCCI) Packet — The Studio Side of DRM.* (Powerpoint presentation, Jan. 28, 2005). Available at: http://www.hpaonline.com/files/public/ExCCI_Packet_Presentation_HPA_Tech_Retreat'05.ppt

DVD DRM and Advanced Access Control System (AACS)

The Content Protection System Architecture (CPSA) is the umbrella term for the overall framework for security and access control across the DVD family. It was developed by the "4C" entity (Intel, IBM, Matsushita, and Toshiba) in partnership with the Copy Protection Technical Working Group (CPTWG). The CPSA covers encryption, watermarking, and protection against copying via analog and digital outputs.

On pre-recorded DVDs, two bits of CGMS Copy-Control Information (CCI, see Chapter 4) are place in the header of each disc sector. Compliant DVD players and

COPY PROTECTION TECHNOLOGY	PROTECTION MECHANISM	EFFECTIVENESS
CSS	Prevents copying content to PC	Good until DeCSS
CGMS	Prevents copying to digital recorder, and analog inputs to digital camcorders and D-VHS machines	Works with about 40% of DVD players
ACP (Macrovision)	Prevents analog copying to VHS, digital recorder, analog outputs of digital camcorders, and digital VCRs	Very effective
Content Protection for Prerecorded Media (CPPM)	Protects digital audio	Does not protect "analog hole," recording via analog outputs
Content Protection for Recordable Media (CPRM)	Prevents copying of DVD to blank media	Effective but not recognized by all DVD players
High-Bandwidth Digital Content Protection (HDCP)	Protects against moving DVD content to unprotected devices by authenticating them	Effective

TABLE 5.8 *Security for Current Generation of DVD Players and Recorders*

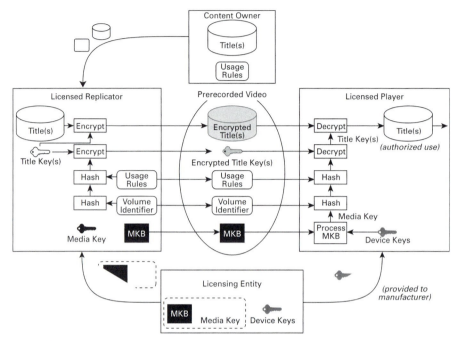

FIGURE 5.6 *Overview of AACS Encryption and Decryption (Permission from AACSLA)*

drives read and embed the data into audio and video output; compatible recorders read it to determine copyright status, including access and copying rights. The current generation of devices employs six protection mechanisms that work together to solve a range of possible methods of copying DVDs, as shown in Table 5.8.

Copy protection and rights management for DVD players and recorders was the first comprehensive copy protection system. In spite of the complexity of the system, the developers admit it won't stop well-equipped professional pirates. The entity that approves DVD protection technologies is the DVD Copy Control Association, which added layers of protection in a piecemeal fashion over several years. The group is now working on copy protection and DRM for the next generation of DVD players and recorders, two competing technologies, Blu-Ray and HD-DVD.

Next-Generation DVD Protection: Advanced Access Content System (AACS)

Eight companies participated in the development of AACS: Intel, IBM, Matsushita, Microsoft, Sony, Toshiba, Walt Disney Company, and Warner Bros. The system is copyrighted intellectual property and must be licensed from the entity formed by

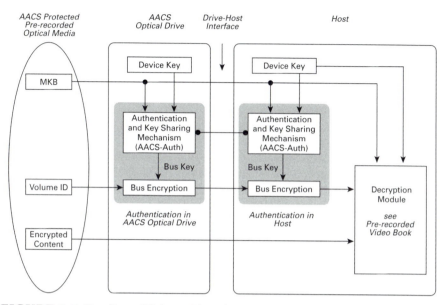

FIGURE 5.7 *Reading of Volume Identifier in a Drive-Host Configuration (Permission from AACSLA)*

the developers, the AACS Licensing Authority. The AACSLA establishes and administers licenses for the content protection system.

The developers describe the system as an "advanced, robust, and renewable method for protecting audiovisual entertainment content, including high-definition content."[12] AACS is intended to limit access to both audio and video (including high definition) content as specified by license holders. It works on both personal computer and consumer electronics platforms. It incorporates published AES encryption algorithms, a Media Key Block for key management, and other methods that prevent copying, as shown in Figure 5.6. The system is renewable, meaning that if decryption keys are compromised, they can be revoked and the system can use another uncompromised key.

To add more protection on personal computers, AACS employs a different drive authentication procedure than that used by CSS. Copying will not be permitted on drives that support only CSS. AACS. When a user wants to copy to a drive, AACS makes additional steps to read the volume identifier, located on the pre-recorded media. Figure 5.7 shows how the protection system proceeds when it encounters a personal computer environment.

---

12. Intel et al. *Advanced Access Content System (AACS): Technical Overview (informative)*. July 21, 2004, p. 1.

AACS provides for protecting content in the online environment. When users have AACS-protected blank media, they can connect to the AACS Network Download Center and record content, binding it to a particular piece of media. Another online application is called *AACS Online Enabled Content*. In this scenario, the user has obtained content but is unable to play it. By connecting online and successfully concluding a transaction for the rights, the user can acquire a license online and play the content, as permitted by the terms of the transaction. Finally, AAACS may also be applied to AACS streamed content, media delivered on-demand from the Internet.

Windows DRM

Rights management guru Bill Rosenblatt calls Windows DRM a meta DRM standard, meaning that it is used in many different situations and modified to work with different media and platforms. He notes that Microsoft is the principal user of the rights language XrML; most systems use MPEG REL. "XrML is baked into Microsoft product lines. If you want to interoperate with Microsoft DRM, one way to do that is to exchange rights specifications in XrML. Lots of players are conforming to it, and it has become a de facto standard," reports Rosenblatt.

The first implementations of Microsoft DRM systems worked only on personal computer platforms. However, the company's new DRM system, code-named Janus, works with Web-connected consumer electronics devices, mobile phones, PDAs, and networked STBs. It allows users to access and buy content over the Internet without using a personal computer. It also works with PCs, which can transfer the purchased content to the other consumer devices.

The Janus architecture calls for a separate license server from the content server, as shown in Figure 5.8. It employs encrypted digital keys to transfer licenses and policies securely between devices. It uses AES encryption with 128-bit keys, 1024-bit RSA cryptography for private key security, and SHA-1 with 1024-bit RSA encryption and AES OMAC1.[13] It requires about 194 kB of ROM for program storage and 27 kB of RAM operating overhead. In Microsoft laboratories, the DRM can run on ARM 7 and T1 55x-class digital signal processors.

On portable devices, the system uses a hybrid 56-bit DES and 64-bit RC4 algorithm, but plans call for the next generation DRM system to use AES. The current

---

13. Kiran, A. *Windows Media DRM*. Wipro, 2005. Available at:
http://www.wipro.com/insights/win_media_drm.htm.

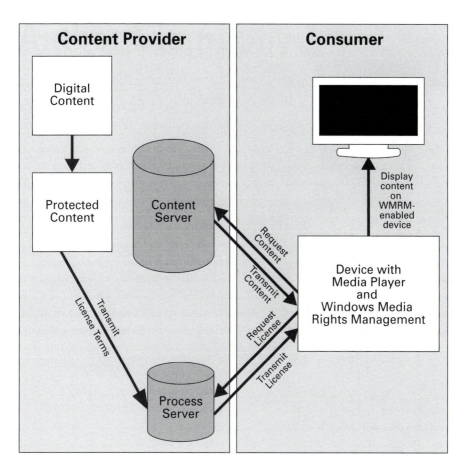

FIGURE 5.8 *Windows Media Rights Management (WMRM) System*

DRM stores the keys via a 160-bit Public Key Infrastructure (PKI). Devices connected to a network, including STBS, use 128-bit AES and 2,048-bit PKI cryptography. Finally, Microsoft's new DRM only works with content encoded in Microsoft's Advanced Systems Format (ASF), a container used primarily by its Windows Media format and codec.

Like other proprietary DRM systems, Windows DRM must be licensed from Microsoft. At launch, the initial license fee was set at $25,000 plus a negotiated per-unit royalty.[14]

---

14. Merritt, R. *Microsoft Details DRM for Consumer Devices.* May 7, 2004. Available at: http://www.digitalconnectmag.com/showArticle.jhtml?articleID=20000209.

Windows Media Rights Manager (WMRM)

The Windows Media Rights Manager (WMRM) technology is baked into Microsoft's Windows Media Player, to enable the execution of transaction-based business models for content products over the Internet. WMRM creates packages of media files that contain an encrypted media file. An encrypted license and the key are delivered separately, and a key ID locks and unlocks the package. When the packaged content is unpacked, it is saved on the receiving system in Windows Media Audio (.wma) and Windows Media Video (.wmv) formats. The file can be distributed on the Web as a download, streamed from a media server, e-mailed, or distributed on a compact disc. In this way, copy-protected files can be distributed.

WDRM operates with a typical license server architecture; licenses come to the consumer via a license clearinghouse server that may belong to Microsoft or the provider. The server holds records that define the specific rights, terms, conditions, and business rules that apply to a given piece of content and creates a WMRM license based on the information. The server fulfills its duties as instructed by the content provider.

From a consumer perspective the system can be explicit or transparent, depending on the business model of the content provider:

- Consumers download the content

- They receive a key to unlock and play the file

- WMRM brings up a Web page to carry out a transaction

- The transaction may be explicit, such as making a credit card payment, or it may occur in the background, as with an ad-supported transaction

- The content plays only in Windows Media Player, obeying the rights as specified in the license by the transaction

Licenses are flexible. They may respond to time limitations, such as start times, expiration dates and times, or a specified duration. They may be usage based, allowing a given number of plays. They will allow or prevent copying to other media and media platforms.

WDRM for Big Screen Content on Little Screens

CinemaNow (CN) lets consumers order, pay for, and stream or download movies from their website. The company adapted WDRM to operate as DRM for video-on-demand (VOD), one that meets the special needs of VOD and enables customized usage rules and pricing schemes. CN called its application PatchBay. CN wanted to have different prices that depend on how the user accesses the content. It also wanted to be able to change prices for alternate geographies that reflect the contractual agreements studios make when distributing their movies.

When a consumer chooses a movie and clicks on the screen to download it, a transaction screen comes up, telling the customer how much and how to pay by credit card. After the transaction is completed, the download link goes live. PatchBay mediates between the transaction and the license server, giving the server information about the user's request and telling it to issue a license. Of crucial importance to CN is that PatchBay collects back office user and usage data: title requests, demographics, and credit card approvals and declines.

The CN system is actually quite complex, beyond a simple link between a content server and a license server. The information about geographic territories comes from an application from Digital Envoy, NetAcuity, running on its own server. An ad manager from DoubleClick and verification and payment services come from Verisign.[15]

Microsoft Meets InterTrust

There is a certain irony that Microsoft's DRM system, which is intended to protect intellectual property was itself used by Microsoft in a way that violated the IP rights of InterTrust. In 2001, 1InterTrust sued Microsoft, saying that the software giant has violated 11 of its patents in its Windows, Office, Windows Media Player and Xbox products. In July 2003, a federal judge agreed with InterTrust and Microsoft was obliged to cough up $440 million to resolve all disputes between the two companies and to obtain a blanket license to the InterTrust DRM patent portfolio.[16]

The settlement was probably a good deal for Microsoft, since it enabled the company to move quickly to develop and promote DRM as an essential part of its long-pursued entry into the delivery of entertainment.

---

15. Iler, D. *DRM: The guardian and protector of digital media.* CED Magazine, Aril 1, 2002. Available at: http://www.cedmagazine.com/article/CA203505.html.

16. Galli, P. *Microsoft Settles with InterTrust*, April 12, 2004. Available at: http://www.pcmag.com/article2/0,1759,1566127,00.asp

InterTrust

As the legal tussle with Microsoft indicates, much of InterTrust's prominence stems largely from its holdings of patents on key DRM technologies. InterTrust counts a large number of respected companies in the entertainment and communications industries as its partners and licensees. Sony is a part owner and AOL Time Warner, Nokia, Digital World Services (a subsidiary of Bertelsmann AG), and Pace MicroTechnology are all allied with Intertrust. Service partners include Sun Microsystems, Artesia Technologies, a content management vendor, nCube, a maker of media servers that underly large deployments of streaming and on-demand services, Portal Software, a customer management and billing developer. These companies are part of what Intertrust calls the RightsAlliance.

The company's website displays a partial list of Intertrust patents relating to digital media, web services, commerce automation, and distributed trusted document management:

- Management of web services

- Authentication of software component integrity

- Credentials and driver signing

- Independent delivery of business and usage rules, enabling supply chain management, secure peer-to-peer sharing, and secure pass-along sharing in accordance with specified policies

- Media content and enterprise information management

- Automated enterprise-to-enterprise transaction handling

- Secure, automated auditing and reporting of transaction and use data for compliance records

- Portability of business and usage rules that let users loan or move content to other users and machines

- Multiple rule sets associated with different portions of content or information

- Silicon protection measures that ensure that hardware is tamper-resistance

InterTrust's second-generation platform is the Java network technology-enabled Rights|System. Its three components are packagers, servers, and clients, all running on a Sun platform. The market for the InterTrust product is large-scale content providers, including cable and satellite TV operators and Internet content providers. The DRM will work on just about any client device, including STBs, PCs, and portable and mobile devices, even phones.

If the license-holder specifies encryption,the Packager creates two files, an encrypted content file and a rights management file, called the Rights|Pack.Metadata, which describes the content and the usage rules associated with it. The files are placed in a digital "container." The container can have integrity protection or not. Subsequent containers may be linked to the first container, allowing license-holders to change or revoke the initial rules. The server transmits the encrypted content file to the content aggregator, distributor or provider for serving to the customer. The rights management file goes to a Content Rights server, a license server under another name.

Consumers purchase the content directly from the distributor's e-commerce infrastructure. After the transaction has been approved and the Rights|System is notified, the Rights|System authorizes the consumer device. Armed with the authorization, the Rights|System 100 kB firmware client can now access the encrypted content and usage rules in the Rights|Pack and consume the content based on the rules. The user can then retrieve the content according to the rules described in Rights|Pack.

There is flexibility built into the Rights|System:

- The rights may permit content to be copied to other devices

- The system can renew usage rules after the encryption of the content and the Rights|Pack without making the consumer download the content file again

- It can apply business rules based on conditions or user attributes. For example, members of a given group may receive special discounts

- Rights|System enables "pass-along" superdistribution. When people to send content to friends and the new recipients access the files, they receive instructions on how to get the rights to use it

InterTrust provides security for the Rights|System itself to protect outside interference with its processing. Of particular importance is the ability of the system to provide an audit trail of the transactions and usage that occurred. The company developed chips, the TrustChip and the Rights Chip, and works directly with manufacturers to put in security mechanisms at the silicon level for use in STBs and user devices. InterTrust employs other anti-hacking security measures as well.

InterTrust has successfully made some of its technologies part of industry standards for interoperability between DRM systems. The search for interoperability, as well as other improvements to DRM, will be covered in the next chapter.

ContentGuard

Like InterTrust, ContentGuard is a proprietary DRM system that is at the center of some DRM standards. The company is a 2000 spinoff of Xerox, now owned by Microsoft, Time Warner, and Thomson. Originally, Xerox developed and patented the rights language that became XrML, which is incorporated into the MPEG REL and the REL of the International Standards Organization (ISO) DRM system, MPEG-21, as the ISO/IEC 21000-5:2004 International Standard.

ContentGuard started out life as a technology company that would provide end-to-end DRM infrastructure but, under the lash of competition and market uncertainty, it morphed into a company that sells intellectual property and software to entities that want to build DRM systems. The company holds patents in several areas that are important to DRM system designers:

- Security and trust

- Content protection

- Rights

- Usage terms and conditions

- DRM system architecture

ContentGuard executives believe that sophisticated DRM systems must be based on an equally sophisticated REL, as shown in Figure 5.9. If a content provider wants to go beyond mere protection and to realize business models, then rights management is an essential ingredient. As CEO Michael Miron put it: "We are coming out of technology that began in 2000, that was basically a set of proprietary DRMs, where one vendor supplied an end to end solution and their aim was entirely defensive to combat piracy. And we are headed in 2005 for interoperable standards built around componentized DRM, which facilitate new business models that are more offensive and less defensive."[17]

---

17. *Faultline*, ContentGuard talks DRM future. Available at:
http://www.theregister.co.uk/2005/01/19/contentguard_drm/

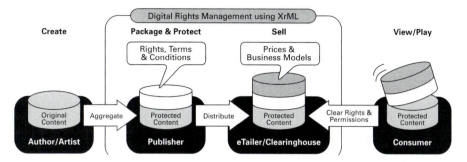

FIGURE 5.9 *DRM using XrML (Permission from Professor Heng Guo[18])*

The ContentGuard conceptual view of DRM encompasses five elements:

- A *source* that provides the content

- A *destination* that uses the content

- A *digital asset*, which is any kind of content

- A *license* that defines how the destination can use the digital asset

  - Identification of the digital asset and the destination

  - The usage rights that are granted

  - The conditions under usage rights are granted

- A *trust model* that covers all elements and devices that are involved in the process, from source to destination and usage.

For ContentGuard, trust means that the source holds the appropriate rights for issuing a license, that the license is secure and accurate, and that the destination, including devices and users, will honor the terms and conditions under which the license is granted. Finally, the means for realizing the trust model include such processes and technologies as encryption, watermarking, authorization, access control, copy protection, and other security technologies. A particular implementation may call for additional components. Many include an e-commerce infrastructure to handle the commercial transaction.

---

18. Heng G., *DRM System Architecture*, Helsinki University of Technology. Available at: www.tml.tkk.fi/Studies/ T-110.501/2001/papers/guo.heng.pdf

Protected Entertainment Rights Management (PERM)

PERM is the brainchild of the Digital Entertainment Network initiative Consortium, whose members are consumer electronics manufactures Kenwood, Onkyo, Pioneer, RCA, Sharp, Echostar, and BridgeCo. These companies recognize that successfully marketing consumer devices depends on the availability of premium content. Content owners demand that devices provide for copy protection before they release the material they own for consumption on new devices, particularly content in high definition formats.

Since manufacturers are keen to sell a new generation of devices based on consumer interest in high definition devices and they can't do it without content, they formed the DENi Consortium. The purpose of the group is to develop open standards for the sharing of digital content within home networks that support content security, copy protection, and rights management technologies. Another goal is to establish licensing procedures.

The group saw drawbacks to existing solutions as well. They are proprietary – Windows DRM, InterTrust, and ContentGuard, for example. Licensing them is expensive and adds costs to devices. Nor is there a single standard that manufacturers can follow.[19]

- The DENi Consortium set out to produce a solution that would meet a set of requirements:

- Not bound to a single license authority

- Not tied to specific device behaviors

- Would interface with existing systems

- Work with a broad array of media and media platforms, including broadcast and removable media

- Would work with IP networking

- Would offer a flexible protection model that includes both usage zones and user activities

---

19. Gildred, J. *Protected Entertainment Rights Management PERM.* Overview. 8/1/04. Available at: www3.ietf.org/proceedings/04aug/231.htm

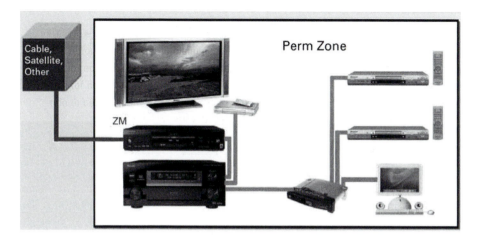

FIGURE 5.10 *Connecting Home Devices with PERM Ethernet*

There are two parts to PERM. Part 1 is an open standard protocol; Part 2 creates a mechanism for key licensing and management and product certification. The basic idea of PERM is to establish a content protection and rights management system for home networks that offers authenticated signals of usage rights. The PERM network is specified as wired 100Base-T Ethernet, making it compatible with Internet and local area networking technologies. (However, the engineers working on PERM were well-aware of wireless home networks as well.) PERM is compatible with Internet Engineering Task Force standards for authorization, credential provision, and public-key management. The DENi Consortium enhanced the Ethernet protocol to better handle audio-visual streams, as shown in Figure 5.10. The network was designed to be secure, private, and safe.[20]

It should be noted that there has been considerable movement towards making IEEE-1394 the networking standard for devices. Fourteen companies and 7 cable companies submitted the IEEE-1394 standard to the U.S. FCC to form the basis of a national plug-and-play standard between digital TVs and other devices, and is the specification for STBs, and the CEA adopted them as well. Nevertheless, in 2003, PERM was approved as a standard by the Consumer Electronics Association (CEA-2008).[21]

---

20. Unattributed, untitled document available at:
http://www1.ietf.org/proceedings_new/04nov/perm.html

21. CEA Newsline, *CEA Adopts DENi™ Standard.* September/October 2003. Available at: http://members.ce.org/publications/vision/2003/sepoct/
p29b.asp?bc=dept&department_id=3

The coalition placed PERM within the context of existing DRM technologies, including such processes as authentication (of devices, users, and services), key management, encryption, digital signatures, integrity assurance, and secure delivery. However, PERM extends these techniques into the home network.

The PERM Zone

Consider how people consume content in their homes. Many have multiple STBs, TV sets, DVD players, computers, and portable devices. PERM establishes a zone of mutually authenticating devices. Although zones are often located within a home or work space, the zone itself is not geographical. Devices in other locations may fall within a particular user zone; they are all tied together through the same secret zone key.

Within the PERM zone, devices play different roles. The device that receives the signals initially such as the STB, the DVD player, or the digital TV tuner is called the Content Source Device (CSoD). Only the CoSD generates the secrete zone key, which authenticates a content protection session, and encrypts the content protection key. The zone key generator is called the Zone Master. The downstream devices are called Content Sink Devices (CSiD).

All the keys change frequently and devices are re-authenticated periodically throughout a session. In addition to device authentication, a particular implementation may require additional levels of authentication for users, devices, or services. The content provider establishes the usage rules, called 'sharing models' within PERM, and also chooses the certification authority.

PERM is a system that supports renewability, meaning that the information devices act upon can be updated and changed. Because the devices are connected on a network, they communicate with one another. The messaging allows devices to exchange new information about usage rights and identification, renewing any previous information stored on the device. Devices and rules may also be revoked, a feature called revocability.

When content comes into the home from a satellite or cable provider, PERM anticipates that it will enter a home media gateway. The gateway either stores the content or it forwards it immediately to a display or other device. The gateway also receives keys, license, rights specifications, and usage rules. The authentication of the device includes an inspection to insure the integrity of the tamper-resistant mechanisms within the device. PERM profiles define how far protection is extended, as shown in Figure 5.11.

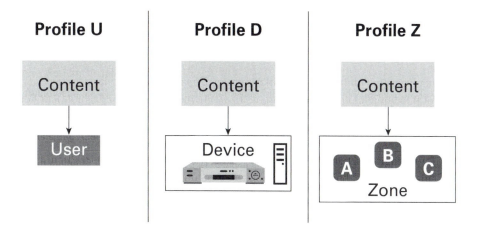

FIGURE 5.11 *PERM Profiles and Protection*

Copyleft

The information in this section comes from Wikipedia, which presents a great deal of information about Copyleft.[22] Fundamentally, it is the opposite of copyright. The Copyleft symbol is a circled reverse-c, opposite to the circled c copyright symbol; instead of "all rights reserved," Copyleft says, "all rights reversed." Richard Stallman, a pioneer computer programmer and software writer, created Copyleft and its GNU license, called the GNU General Public License (GNU GPL or GPL).

Stallman created software that a company, Symbolics, asked to use. After Symbolics extended and improved the software, it refused to allow Stallman access to the improvements. This behavior motivated Stallman to create the GNU GPL. GPL allowed a content creator to perpetually transfer rights to others, including any revisions that are made to that content.

Many important software programs carry GPL licenses, including Linux. Users distribute a GPL license along with their content. The license says that recipients can use the content without limitation, redistribute as many copies as they wish, and modify it in any way. However, the creator of the derived work agrees that the modified content will be available to others under the same GPL license. All such content must be available in a form that allows modification. Copyleft GPL licenses cannot be revoked.

22. Unattributed article. Wikipedia. Available at: http://en.wikipedia.org/wiki/Copyleft

Copyleft originally covered computer software. Some of the Copyleft provisions differ from those of open source software. Under Copyleft, downstream creators are co-creators who share in the copyright. However, they have already agreed to give up the rights and benefits that normally accompany copyright in perpetuity. By contrast, once a creator has modified open source software, the material can be copyrighted and license fees attached to its use. Licenses which are open source but not Copyleft include the BSD operating systems, the X Window system and the Apache web server. In addition, some parts of a work may be copylefted, while others are not.

There are strong and weak forms of Copyleft. Weak Copyleft licenses occur when material is copyrighted but uses copylefted material as part of its operation, usually as links to libraries, calling up a copylefted process. The copylefted material is under a strong Copyleft license; the copyrighted work that calls on it is not. The strong license is called the GNU General Public License (GPL); the weak version is called the GNU Lesser General Public License (LGPL).

Copyleft Licenses and Works of Arts

There are open-source record labels. The GNU license that applies to such works is called the GNU Free Documentation License (GFDL or FDL), since it has no reference to source code, a term that would apply to software but not other material.

Artistic content has some aspects that do not lend themselves to Copyleft. In Europe, moral rights and droit d'auteur regulate procedures for transferring the ownership of artistic works. The GFDL and other Copyleft licensing systems allow authors to attach some limitations to the use of their works. GFDL allows the artist to specify some sections that cannot be altered. They may also specify that the original artist must be credited; however, there is no guarantee this will occur.

It is likely that there will be some changes to the GPL. The Free Software Foundation controls changes to the GPL and the group has announced it will release Version 3 for public discussion. The new version will contain provisions to ward off "pirates armed with patents," which would prohibit use of GPL by companies that allege that GPL software infringes its patents.[23]

---

23. Shankland, S. *Overhaul of GPL set for public release.* CNET News., Jan 11, 2006. Available at: http://news.com.com/Overhaul+of+GPL+set+for+public+release/2100-7344-6025310.html?part=dht&tag=nl.e703

For example, there might be penalties prohibiting use of GPL software if a company files a lawsuit alleging that GPL software infringes its patents. Other changes may include limiting the use of GPL software on devices that have DRM restrictions; and clarifying rights to modified works that have not been publicly distributed; making GPL more compatible with other free software and open-source licenses.

Creative Commons

Creative Commons is a variant of Copyleft that issues licenses sometimes referred to as share-alike licenses. It allows creators of any kind of content to identify the work, specify its format, and spell out to others what they can or cannot do with the work. Creators can direct whether the work may be used commercially and whether it can be modified. They can specify attribution to the original creator. Finally, they can assert copyright and reserve the rights to exploit their work commercially.

The next chapter will examine business models for content that is copyrighted and copy protected. It also looks at content where the rights are managed.

6 DRM and Entertainment and Media Business Models

On the whole, DRM is taken to mean content protection. But that simply is not the case. Content protection and security protect copyright. Rights management defines the terms and conditions for use. In the balance between these two functions, most entertainment and media companies are overwhelmingly concerned with security and spend relatively little time thinking about rights management.

This emphasis on security is understandable but unfortunate. It has led these companies to think of their customers as hostile adversaries and to employ self-fulfilling technologies that lead their customers to behave as hostile adversaries. Security interfaces are often non existent or just terse "This material cannot be copied." And there is always the stern FBI warning when DVDs spin up. Security necessarily deals with restrictions.

But there is an opportunity for rights management interfaces to be more informative and helpful. They can be interactive. They can be colorful. They can be animated or live action, presented by famous actors and performers. In short, they can serve as an introduction to the content itself and take the same tone as the upcoming content, dramatic, comedic, adventurous, suspenseful, or informative. Rights management can focus on limits to usage, but they don't have to. In fact, they can and should focus on what customers **can do**, not what they **can't do**.

This opportunity to gift the customer is lost in the emphasis on security. Moreover, rights management is the way to implement business models in the digital environment. Through rights management, content owners and distributors can describe usage windows and allowed copying mechanisms. Most important, they provide a means to make additional offers to customers for an expansion of usage rights.

One reason rights management is not often considered as a way to facilitate and enable business models is that many industry companies do not analytically explore the entire range of models that are open to them. Often ideas for a business unit come with the business model pre-defined and it is not questioned thereafter unless the initial effort does not flourish. Or there are organizational pressures to adopt a particular model.

The next sections examine legacy and new business models in the entertainment and media industry. It describes each one and then suggests how DRM might be used in the context of the model, and how it might affect owners and distributors who are considering adopting a given model.

Business Models

Operating any business begins with a business plan, one of the most basic documents for commercial enterprises. The plan lays out the specifics of the organization, its management, products, marketing and sales opportunities, and financial arrangements and goals. Part of the business plan is a business model, which shows how the planned company's goals will be achieved if the resources and processes are applied to the model. For example, if the numbers and resource inputs that are described in the plan are then plugged into the business model, tit will show how the company's activities can result in a profitable outcome.

Executives cannot discuss actual numbers from their business plans in public. However, they can and do talk about their business model, usually referring the strategies that the company believes will lead to success. Business plans are fairly similar across industries. But business models reflect the unique customs, practices, and conditions that define of a particular industry or segment, at a particular point in time.

For decades, the business models for entertainment and media companies were relatively simple and straightforward. In the TV industry, for example, one commonly-heard advice for choosing a revenue model was: "Deliver eyeballs, get ads; deliver value, get subscriptions."

Traditional Business Models

In the old days, the business model was synonymous with the revenue model. Producing and acquiring content, marketing it, and distributing it were predetermined by existing industry and commercial customs, communications infrastructure, and technology. But today, entertainment and media businesses must create much more complex business models than they did in the past, because the environment affords a much wider range of possibilities for accomplishing operating a content-based business. The overall business model now entails specifying 4 component models:

- **Content model:** How the enterprise creates or acquires the content product

- **Distribution model:** How the enterprise transports and delivers the content to the consumer

- **Marketing model:** The persuasive methods a content provider uses to turn a potential consumer into an actual consumer

- **Revenue model:** How the enterprise gets revenue.

This chapter examines how the adoption of DRM affects the business models for companies that make, market, sell, and deliver digital content. It looks at the limits it places on traditional models and new ones that have come to prominence as the marketplace of digital media and entertainment has unfolded in the past few years. The component content, distribution, marketing, and revenue models can be combined with one another in any number of ways to generate unique business models, specifically-tailored to the particulars of content, audience, product, distribution, and transactions.

Content Models

The choice to add security and DRM to content reflects a simple reality. If the content has the potential to bring in revenue, it needs to be protected against casual copying to preserve value and rights must be managed to maximize revenue. There are two kinds of revenue potential: popular or hit status and the long tail. A business can package content that is popular for anything longer than a day or two because it almost certainly cannot be reproduced quickly and easily. The more difficult the material is to produce, the higher the asking price is likely to be.

Content with a long tail is also material that is difficult, expensive, and time-consuming to create. In addition, it usually has some other features that generate interest within narrowly-defined communities. Often consumers in these audience segments are willing to pay more later than they did when the content was initially introduced.

For companies to market either extremely popular or long-tail products, they cannot be readily downloaded over the Internet. On the other hand, there is a whole body of material that is neither popular nor of interest to specialized audience segments. Such content may exist on the Net but it has little effect on its potential for bringing in revenue because the potential was never there. Simple availability on the Net does not ensure revenue.

When companies define a content model, they start by generating ideas for content that they believe will appeal to an audience. For example, the traditional broadcast network content model was known as "least common denominator" programming. The audience included all television viewers, everyone, so the content was designed so as to exclude no one. Hence, it appealed to the widest set of interests shared by the population as a whole. Over time, the most universal interests turned out to be sex, violence, news, and music.

Print media, radio, and cable television channels also produce some generalized products but these media are more likely to cater to specialized niche audiences that are much more narrowly defined. So there are several publications for quilters and cable channels and radio stations that transmit content for Catholics and golfers. Although broadcast media create material solely for the consumer audience, the print medium is divided into consumer and industry trade segments.

Online content may appeal to a broad audience, such as Yahoo! or address a micro-niche audience, like www.itvt.com, which presents material for people interested in interactive TV. The questions surrounding just how narrow a niche should be are important, as they relate to both creating content and drawing an audience. A substantial niche requires a substantial investment; a sliver niche can be done on a shoestring.

Figuring out the boundaries of online efforts are particularly problematical because the medium is still new and there are fewer guidelines to follow. However, like the print medium, plans for online content usually call for deciding whether it will be targeted to a consumer or trade audience. Specialized content, perhaps an entire website (or channel), is created to appeal to that group. Large corporate websites can have a public area, supplemented by password-protected private areas devoted to vendors, suppliers, distributors and resellers, institutional buyers, and employees.

When a site serves the general public or consumer, it is engaged in B2C or business-to-consumer activity. When the site serves businesses, then the content reflects a B2B or business-to-business orientation. Depending on whether the activity is B2C or B2B, the content on the site is apt to be quite different. And it is likely to require a different level and kind of DRM.

Broadly, there are four kinds of online content types: information, entertainment, services, and applications. It's difficult to separate type from another, and particularly hard to distinguish services from applications. One guideline might be: Services do something for people; applications let people do something.

Services are products or free offerings like 24/7 availability, price comparisons, online ordering, online banking, customer service, gift registries, live personal shopping assistant (voice or text), and so forth. Applications are search, payment calculation, currency conversion, use of an online program to perform a task like photo or video editing, spread sheet manipulation, etc. Here again, there is some overlapping — search is an application but it provides a service. On the other hand, a live personal shopping assistant calls upon a whole array of applications to provide the service.

Applications have led to a new class of online content providers called ASPs, or application service providers. These purveyors offer their customers the ability to use software to accomplish their objectives. An ASP can provide anything from quick lookup of stock market ticker symbols to extended sessions using sophisticated enterprise resource programs (ERP) or digital video editing. The ASP market is predicted to grow substantially to a multi-billion dollar market in the next few years, although estimates vary widely because online businesses that market applications are relatively new.

Whether they appeal to consumers or businesses, there are three broad types of content models:

- **Content aggregation models:** Focuses on the content, creating or acquiring r a wide variety of materials, either exhausting a content category or spanning a range of content categories. Examples: DIRECTV, Cablevision, AOL.

- **Audience aggregation models:** Focuses on creating or acquiring content to appeal to and aggregate as many content consumers as possible. Examples: Google, Yahoo!, ABC, NBC, CBS.

- **Audience segmentation models:** Focuses on creating or acquiring content to appeal to as many content consumers as possible who fall into a particular segment. Examples: Court TV, FOX News, BET.

There are specific content models associated with each overall type of model, as shown in Table 6.1. Although a content provider can assemble content in a number of ways, certain types of content gravitate to each model. Content aggregation models are like to require payment, by the bucket or bundle, subscription or pay-per. Purveyors of this type of content are apt to need some kind of content protection and DRM.

CONTENT AGGREGATION MODELS	AUDIENCE AGGREGATION MODELS	AUDIENCE SEGMENTATION MODELS
Consumer experience	Free content	Vertical portal and destination
Bundling and bucket	TV portal	Affinity
Interface control	Horizontal portal and destination	User-created content
Screen real estate		• Interest-based community
General user-created content		
Syndication and licensing		

TABLE 6.1 *Content Models*

Audience aggregation models are like to be free or nearly so, with some kind of advertising or promotional effort providing the revenue stream. The content may not need any protection and DRM; indeed, copying and pass-along may be quite desirable. But DRM may be extremely useful for tracking and data mining, activities which may even provide an independent revenue stream.

Audience segmentation models are often well-suited by user-generated content, especially when the audience segment is composed of experts. User-generated content does not usually have rights management, but in some industries, it may need to be kept secure. However, highly engaged audience segments with high levels of disposable income may pay the most for premium content that fulfills their information or entertainment needs. High-value content will nearly always be protected and rights managed.

Content Aggregation Models

These models call for the content designers to focus on the content first. In an age when aggregations of content can be massive indeed (the MGM library, the Shoah Foundation, digital collections of newspapers and magazines) the aggregation job may prove to be quite an undertaking.

Consumer Experience Model

This model holds that all the content, taken together, must provide the consumer with a unique and pleasant experience, not just information, data, or service. The crux of this idea is that just as goods and services are products, so are experiences, and they are distinct from traditional product categories. In this view, the industrial economy was replaced by the service economy, which is now itself being replaced by the experience economy.[1]

"Make no mistake: Information isn't the foundation of the new economy. Information is not an economic offering. As John Perry Barlow likes to say, information wants to be free. Only when companies package it in a form customers will buy – informational goods, information services or informing experiences – do they create economic value," say Joseph Pine II and James H. Gilmore.[2]

Shapers of media and entertainment utilizing this approach will want to ensure that the customer will not be confused, angered, frustrated, or otherwise affected negatively by the entire process of finding, retrieving, viewing or playing, sampling, ordering, buying, and ultimately using the product or site. Designing a positive experience is not easy — research shows that at least 25% of people who have started a sales transaction on the Internet do not complete it. Since it takes many clicks to get through the process, such a result is not surprising.

Now consider the challenge for the implementation of DRM systems. The best of current systems face consumers with an administrative task. The worst of them are insulting and onerous. Now think again about the theatrical box office. It's glamorous (or at least pleasant), seductive, well-lit, information-full, polite, quick, easy, understandable. DRM designers simply must pay more attention to the consumer-facing interface with an eye towards the consumer experience.

DRM designers need to take the same care with the consumer interface that they do with other portions of the code. Here is a good example from the Internet of how concern about the user's experience translates into interface and interaction design. The website for *Caroline in the City*, produced by Eyemark Entertainment, a subsidiary of the CBS television network, is at http://www.carolineinthecity.com/. Joanne Burns, VP New Media at Design described some of the considerations that went into the site to make it easy to enjoy for site visitors: On the home page, a graphic of the main cast members and the show title are up front and center. The guest CONTINUED ▶

---

1. B. Joseph Pine, James H. Gilmore, B. Joseph Pine II. *The Experience Economy: Work Is Theatre & Every Business a Stage*, Cambridge MA: Harvard Business School Press (1999).

2. J Pine II and J H Gilmore. *Are You Experienced?* Industry Standard (April 9, 2000). Available online at:
http://thestandard.net/article/article_print/0%2C1153%2C4167%2C00.html.

CONTINUED ► has no doubt that he or she has found the website for the show. The typeface and design carry through the theme of lighthearted, romantic whimsicality that pervades the program.[3]

All the main choices are there on a page that requires no scrolling to get it all in view. The choices are clear and highlighted, with special features emphasized. The site has a very personal tone and there is an invitation to join the "Caroline Club" on the home page. The main selections are clearly stated and text that more fully explains what a click-through will bring appears when the mouse hovers over a choice. Community is encouraged by an easy-to-access message board, which adds new, self-populating content to the site all the time.

The navigation bar is positioned at the top of the page so it doesn't constrict the visual design of pages. Site subsections are readily identifiable. Frames at the left hand side always clearly indicate to visitors exactly where they are within the site, and it is easy to move from one area to another. Special promotions are also clickable from every page.

These are just the structural considerations — it does not include a discussion of the subsections or individual pages, each with its own informational, interactional, or transactional requirements. If these were added to the discussion, the requirements to provide a smooth, unified experience for visitors to the website would continue for any number of pages.

Bundling and Bucket Model

Bundling means putting many different kinds of content together into attractive packages. The content can come from different sources and reflect many different types. Bundling is common in the cable, satellite, and PC software industries, and consumers usually pay a single price for the bundled content.

Buckets usually mean large amounts of the same type of content that customers can access on a single-price, "all you can eat" basis. Monthly fees for an unlimited number of music downloads or movie downloads are good examples of content buckets. So are buckets of cellphone minutes.

---

3. J Burns. Panelist at seminar at the American Film Institute's Los Angeles campus, sponsored by the National Association of Television Programming Executives (NATPE) and Entertainment Technology Commerce (ETC), November, 2003.

Before releasing content, owners are likely to impose conditions for content protection and DRM measures. Such conditions are almost certain when they make material available to new providers using new delivery platforms, such as the Internet or broadband networks. In these situations, it is very important to make clear to consumers the conditions that attach to their transaction. Doing so in a way that does not discourage the customer poses a considerable challenge to DRM interface designers.

User-Created Content Model

The job of populating a website with content is demanding and expensive. However, many people want the opportunity to express themselves and to create material that they can share with others. Sites that post user-created material often feature it as the majority of their content. Blogger (www.blogger) is a good example.

Social networking sites are another good example. The popularity of social networking sites demonstrates the power of user-created content. Social networking websites are mainly populated by young people in their teens and twenties. Two popular sites are www.facebook.com and www.myspace.com. NewsCorp paid $580 million to buy Intermix, the parent company of MySpace.[4] In late 2005, Nielsen/NetRatings reported that MySpace ranked 15th among U.S. websites for the number of page hits, with 40 million members.

User-generated content destinations require some administration. The procedures and rules for posting material must be clear, prominently displayed, and strongly enforced, usually by paid moderators. Sites for the general public most often guard against pornography and offensive graphics and language.

Blogsites are usually only minimally monitored, and are rife with profanity and insulting language. According to the Blog Herald, which tracks the number of blogs on the Internet, there are 70 million bloggers worldwide, 36 million in the U.S.[5]

User-created material makes the most sense for the Internet, but has limited value for other media platforms. This type of content requires a great deal more tweaking in other digital television venues such as over-the-air TV, cable TV, and even broadband TV. For example, "America's Funniest Videos" employs an entire staff searching out videos, gathering them, ordering them into a rundown, and

---

4. Cover story, *The MySpace Generation*, Business Week. Dec 12, 2005. Available at: http://www.businessweek.com/magazine/content/05_50/b3963001.htm

5. The Blog Herald site is updated regularly: http://www.blogherald.com/2005/07/19/blog-count-for-july-70-million-blogs/

editing them. The producers contract with expensive talent to host the show wrap-arounds and tweenies and assembled a studio audience to give the program add the energy of a live group of viewers. (Reality-based shows, while focusing on real people, are not user-created for the most part.)

User-created content per se requires some minimal security and no DRM. Community and blogging sites usually require registration and subsequent logging in with a username and password. Interestingly, www.myspace.com requires registrants to fax or mail in a copy of some form of photo ID in order to establish a personal "room" on the site. At some point, there may well be disputes about who owns the content on such sites, although the act of creation itself establishes copyrights. Some sites may exercise copyright assertion to posted material in user agreements, which few users read. There is little question but what the data mined from registration forms and visitor tracking belongs to the site owner.

Syndication and Licensing

From the content producer's perspective, syndication and licensing are ways of bringing in revenue. From the point of view of a site operator, they are content aggregation strategies. Web syndication has not really taken off, but it seems inevitable that its day will come.

Web syndication will allow content creators to create once and publish in many venues. It will also be good news for web site owners because they won't have to manage a staff of people to create material. Instead, for reasonable licensing fees, they can populate a site with content that is geared toward their particular audience.

Another important feature that Web-based syndication would bring is automated contracting, distribution, and royalty collection. Television syndication is an expensive, time-consuming, laborious process that requires an intense negotiation over every piece of content or content bundle. Web syndication would be a much more streamlined process.

Both television and Web syndication companies aggregate content from many different providers and send it to outlets with touch points to the end user. Right now, much syndicated material is re-purposed from print, so that the columns are wordy blocks of text. More and more, we will see material especially created for the Internet with more graphics, streamed media, and page-formatted for horizontally-biased PC screens, instead of vertically-biased print media.

The owners of some syndicated material will want to protect and manage the content, particularly when the content is of high quality and value. The technical underpinnings that will allow an automated process to enable syndication XML, an all-purpose markup language that is becoming universal in multi-site, multi-company ecommerce applications. Content owners are almost certain to require robust security and DRM mechanisms before releasing their material. To express these conditions, XML will have to be supplemented by an XML-compatible REL. Another important enabling development for syndication will be standardization of protocols for exchanging content and rights information at the server-to-server level. It could be ICE, the Information and Content Exchange protocol, MXF for audio-visual material, or some other format.

Audience Aggregation Models

The content models we just looked at start with aggregating content and then looking for audiences for it. Audience aggregation models that process and begin with strategies for aggregating a particular audience or set of audiences, then assembling content that will appeal to them. Broadcast television is the most successful industry ever to use an audience aggregation model, beside which all other media pale. Cable TV, radio, and print have a very few broadly popular properties, but many more of their products serve niche audiences.

Free Service Model

The time-honored over-the-air broadcast television model was invented before people had any means of recording a TV picture. It proved to be brilliantly successful. This model has not been adopted for multichannel television service or print. But it is a popular Internet strategy, used by search engines, blog sites, social networking sites, web access, and web hosting for photography, video, and domains.

Horizontal Portal and Destination Model

A portal is a way station; a destination is a place to spend time, a "sticky" site where people stick around for awhile. Portals provide all the needed information services to send visitors on their journeys on other portions of the media platform. The early success of portals in capturing tremendous traffic on the Net set off a race by media and entertainment giants, racing to get their own branded portal. In rapid order, Disney, NBC, and Warner Bros. bought and built their way to mega-portal status.

Horizontal portals like AOL, Yahoo!, Google, Microsoft Network (MSN), and others appeal to as many people as possible. And while Google and Yahoo!

started by offering search engines to let people locate other sites, as time has gone on, they have also become destination sites in their own right, providing email services, photo, audio, and video hosting, news, local listings, shopping, and other features.

Little of the material on portals are content-protected or managed, although they often have lists and search engines that point to such material. One exception is the audio and video material that users can store on sites like Yahoo!, Google, and Ourmedia. Users may well attach a Creative Commons license to their content.

The Portal TV Model

This model transfers the idea of a portal from the Internet on the PC screen to high-speed Internet access on the TV set. Just as AOL and Microsoft Network have become popular portals through their roles as ISPs, so broadband ISPs have the option to become portals through their ability to bring subscribers through their own interface on the TV or PC screen. This group would include telephone companies, such as Verizon, which is planning to offer television services.

In cable and satellite television, observers have often noted the opportunity for electronic or interactive program guides (EPGs or IPGs) to become portals. The TV Guide channel has added shows to run in the top portion of the picture, with the guide in the bottom portion. However, EPGs and IPGs have not yet lived up to their presumed potential.

EPGs and IPGs are intellectual property that require licensing. However, for the most part, they are not the kind of content that consumers choose to copy. Good looking, well-designed free EPGs are available on the Internet, which people who build their own Personal Video Recorders (PVRs) use to provide a guide to TV offerings. Home-built PVRs are not difficult to build. They are essentially PCs with Ethernet connections so that they can draw the EPG from the Net and display it on the TV screen or receive it from a home Wi-Fi network.

Audience Segmentation Models

The Internet is the inverse of broadcast television it has an unmatched ability to reach specialized audiences and the relatively low cash outlays for production and distribution it requires make it cost-effective to do so. Interested in aviation history, aviary management, or .avi file conversion? There's bound to be a treasure of information on the Net, just waiting to be discovered. The following models all exploit this ability of Internet to attract people who are united through some common experience or interest.

Vertical Portal and Destination Model

Vertical models work with print media and the Internet. How wide is a horizontal portal and when does it become a vertical portal? The term vertical means that it is designed to appeal to a target group. Verticals may be very wide. iVillage (www.ivillage.com) is designed for women. *Cosmopolitan* aims at young women. ThirdAge (www.thirdage.com) is a site for middle-aged people. Bolt.com (www.bolt.com) targets adolescents, and the American Library Association lists dozens of sites for kids.

There are also portals that are very narrow, serving vertical interests like motor-cycles (www.bikersites.com/) and people looking for replacement pieces for their sets of china (www.jchinareplacements.com). A narrowly targeted magazine is Fire-power, dedicated to full-auto and high-capacity firearms; the circulation is about 90,000. And here's narrow: Bird-lovers who want to know all about budgerigars can always turn to www.budgerigars.co.uk//.

Affinity Model

Affinity models segment the audience by interest and try to reach as close to 100% of those in that segment. Then they formulate strategies for reaching audiences that are interested in related topics and activities and attracting that closely-related audience to their content. For example, if there is an audience for a service or channel that provides information about parenting, then probably some part of the audience is also interested in shopping for children's clothes, toys, books, day camps, and so forth. And another part of that audience might want to know about caring for newborns. Still another part of the audience will be drawn to informa-tion about home improvement or family entertainment, or bulk food purchases. And vice versa, audiences that seek content from these related sites may be enticed to consume content from the parenting site.

Affinity models are based on agreements between content providers to share access to one another's audience in the hopes of building the a larger audience than any one of them can working alone. The concept of affinity models began on the Internet and has evolved into both affinity websites and "webrings." Usually there are links at the bottom of the home page that directs the user to related compatible or complementary content, services, and products.

Affinity relationships may involve revenue. The House of Blues provides an interesting example because the company maintains an active affinity program even though it is rather difficult to pinpoint groups that might like blues music. While there may be some slight demographic skew to blues-lovers, they exist among every conceivable grouping.

HOB lets web site owners decide if they think HOB content would enrich their site and that their visitors might be interested in it. When they join the HOB affinity program, they download music and a House of Blues clickable logo. When the visitor clicks on the logo, they hear the music and have the option of clicking on a link to HOB where they can listen to more music and purchase it online. If they make a purchase, the originating site gets a percentage of the sale.

Community Model

In some ways, making community a centerpiece of a website or digital service is a particular case of user-generated content. However, all user-generated content is not community, which focuses on creating services that allow members of the group to communicate with one another. The means of communication may be an asynchronous message board, an e-mail discussion list, or a blog where participants post their comments, and then sign on later to read responses and post again. Or it might be real-time chat that lets participants conduct text-based discussions. A good example is a community website for video editors who use Sony's Vegas software, www.vegaseditors.com.

Communities can form around any sort of interest or concern, and there are thousands, perhaps hundreds of thousands of them on the Internet. In addition to being a nearly essential part of every web site that is not a merely personal home page, there are Internet news groups and discussion lists. One site that tracks discussion lists is at http://webscoutlists.com/.

Following the community model doesn't mean there is no other content. Usually the moderator/operator puts additional material believed to be of interest to the members of the group on the site. Information, services and applications, and e-commerce interactives are quite commonly found on community sites.

Community models do not typically have content that needs to be secure or managed. Nevertheless they may have an effect on the success of high value content through advertising on the website or word-of-mouth discussion. One example is the runaway success of *The Passion of the Christ,* which was a favorite topic within Christian communities.

Yahoo Groups is an interesting program. It lets people start their own email discussion lists. A look at the directory reveals thousands of groups covering just about every conceivable interest, from Assemblage Artists (903 members) to bowel-cleanse (2913 members). This portion of the site has some fairly unobtrusive advertising. For example, a click on the Assemblage Artists group brought up an ad from eBay that said it had materials for assemblage artists for sale.

A reading of the Yahoo! privacy policy suggests why this large horizontal site is willing to provide the space and processing for such groups. It not only brings people to Yahoo! who might never use its search service. More importantly, it provides a mechanism for detailed data collection that is itself a valuable resource. (See section on Marketing Models – Data Mining, below.) You can be sure that Yahoo! secures and protects that particular piece of intellectual property with great care.

Distribution Models

Just as content models are more complex than they used to be, distribution models have evolved as well. Content distribution poses some unique challenges for both transport security and DRM. Indeed, each of the three models makes different and difficult demands on the design of a DRM system.

Although distribution is concerned with bringing content from a provider to a customer, security and DRM systems enforce limits on distribution. Windowing models impose restrictions on the times and time periods for content release. Willed garden models define limits on the space where users can find and access content. And cross-platform models demand security and DRM systems that persist across platforms, networks, and providers.

Once content is developed, a distribution model lays out how it will get to consumers, in terms of media platforms and technologies. In times past, the product itself defined its distribution. Movies were shown in theaters, and later rented from video stores; songs were played on the radio, then purchased in stores that stocked vinyl record stores and later CDs; TV shows were shown on TV, and so forth.

In the digital environment, it is no longer clear how a given content vehicle will reach its consumers. A song is played on the radio, on an audio pay service over cable and satellite, on the Internet, and over a mobile phone.

Windowing Model

Windowing means to release a property in stages to different distribution mechanisms for a specific length of time, the window. In the motion picture industry, it is describes the wholesale level of film distribution. The order of the release windows is based on the revenue brought in per viewer. Domestic and increasingly international theatrical release come first because each viewer pays for a ticket, $4.50 to $12.50. Pay per view is next with a charge of $4 to $5 per household, followed by home video rental for $3 to $4.50 per night. After these follow premium cable, foreign TV, network TV, syndication packages for TV stations and basic cable channels, each of which brings in a smaller and smaller flat fee or package price.[6]

Revenue per viewer is not the only conceivable way to structure release windows. Strategies for reaching particular audiences might define them. Or media platforms. For example, one analyst proposes that film studios to create an early release window via satellite HDTV channels, a "First-Run HDTV Channel." It would feature pre-theatrical releases of movies to the 100,000 people or so around the world who have HDTV sets. Dale Cripps, who developed this idea, believes that there are about that many people who would pay $10 to be the first ones to see new films. The income would be $10 million per month, and it could provide valuable word-of-mouth to support the theatrical release right afterward. (Except for disappointing films!)[7]

Windows now extend into the digital realm, with new ones added such as DVD, video CDs, and eventually the Internet, and other networks.. And slicing and dicing can permit the distribution of snippets, portions of text, individual scenes, and single photos.

While the overall number of windows has increased, the length of windows is decreasing. And some windows are collapsing altogether. There are geography-based windows that call for a film to debut first in the U.S. and then a week or two later in Europe and Japan. More and more movie are being released on a "day and date" basis, meaning that they open on the same day in all major geographies. In addition, the time period between theatrical distribution and home video sales and then rental are ever shorter.

Piracy and casual copying are the reasons for shorter windows. Often movies are available for download on the Internet even before they debut in theaters. Studios and distributors are rushing to get content into the hands of customers before those hands get on the keyboard.

Studios need internal security to prevent leakage of content from facilities during the last stages of post-production. They need security measures like water-marking for forensic tracking of "cammed" movies and encryption and key management for DVDs. These measures will help keep movies off the Internet before they can be marketed through normal channels.

---

6. H L Vogel. Entertainment Industry Economics, 6th ed. Cambridge: Cambridge University Press, 2004.

7. D Cripps, consultant and HDTV guru. Telephone interview, November, 1999. See his web site at: http://web-star.com/hdtv/history.html.

Once standards are set for player and recording devices, studios will be able to use DRM to manage windows. They will produce DRM-enabled DVDs that will not play the movie before a given date. DRM-enabled Internet streams will have the same effect on Net-delivered movies.

Walled Garden Model

"Walled garden" is a term coined by former TeleCommunications, Inc. founder, John Malone to describe a closed network that limits subscribers' choices to a restricted range of content. Inside the garden, the subscriber can choose from a bouquet of services that are carefully selected, controlled, and often created and operated by the network providing company.

Walled gardens will work for the multichannel cable television portion of service, but it will not work for the high-speed Internet service that cable companies provide. Early Internet Service Providers like AOL and Compuserve tried to enforce a walled-garden approach to the Internet and it simply did not work. Their subscribers demanded unrestricted access to the Internet.

The day is coming when walled gardens won't work for multichannel television service either because these channels will be available via high-speed Internet service. However, operators that provide Internet service have a number of ways to preserve the walled garden or at least charge for programming that comes from beyond the walls.

They can monitor their networks and add a surcharge for audio-visual streams. They can trap the content as it comes into the headend servers and package it so that it will play only in a specialized, operator-provided player. Or they can DRM the content to track and report content usage that can provide the basis for billing.

The other main concern for walled garden operators, particularly the telephone broadband service providers getting ready to offer television services, will be to prevent users from copying content. Content owners will require them to provide content security and protection measures. And DRM can allow them to reach customers with new, unique offers for consuming the content, depending on the financial arrangements they can reach with content owners.

Cross Media/Platform Model

The cross media/platform model means distributing content across more than one medium or to more than one type of reception device in order to maximize the reach to a target audience. Consider that the same person may watch TV, listen to the radio, and surf the Internet at different times, in different locations, with varied motivations. They may also combine a broadcast medium with the Internet, the so-called "co-location" phenomenon. And they use many different devices.

Content providers and distributors have to reach consumers wherever they happen to be, on whatever devices they choose to use. Creating material for different delivery platforms, network access speeds, formats, reception devices, and consumer characteristics is another way of saying that content must be customized, tailored to address many different environments, conditions, and consumers. In the digital world, the most efficient way of thinking about a production is to create once and publish everywhere.

The target audience may be broad or narrow, but the content is tailored to the needs and desires of that group. It is created once and automated procedures convert it to needed formats for distribution across multiple media. This means that content must be flexible. It must be an exciting print vehicle, a compelling television program, a sticky Internet attraction, and an e-commerce bonanza. The cost of the content is amortized from revenues derived from all sources, across the various media where it appears.

An example of a company following the cross-media model is Martha Stewart Living Omnimedia LLC, with business ventures divided into four segments: Publishing, Television, Merchandising, and Internet/Direct Commerce. Her content creation empire and media exposure includes:

- Monthly magazine (Martha Stewart Living)

- Monthly magazine (Blueprint: Design Your Life)

Quarterly magazine (Martha Stewart Weddings)

- Half-hour program twice a day, seven days a week on Food Network cable channel that consists primarily of food-related segments from previous Martha Stewart Living television programs;

- Books written by Martha Stewart and the editors of Martha Stewart Living;

- Syndicated newspaper column, (askMartha);

- National radio show, askMartha;

- Mail-order catalog and online merchandising business (Martha By Mail);

CONTINUED ▶

CONTINUED ▶

- Internet web site that features integration of television programs, radio shows, newspaper column, and magazines, as well as seven distinct channels on the site, each devoted to a core content areas—Home, Cooking & Entertaining, etc. Each channel offers live discussion forums from 10 A.M. to 6 P.M. EST, 24-hour bulletin boards where visitors can post advice, queries, and replies, and weekly live question and answer hours with our in-house and guest experts.

- Strategic merchandising relationships with Kmart, Sherwin-Williams, Sears, Zellers, and P/Kaufmann. MSLO designs products that are then manufactured by or on behalf of strategic partners. The products designed for Kmart are sold exclusively in Kmart stores in the US. The KM stores carry Martha Stewart Everyday Home products (bed and bath products, kitchen textiles, window treatments, and bath accessories), Martha Stewart Everyday Garden products (currently patio furniture and selected garden tools, growing in early 2000 to a full line of garden tools and accessories, live plants and seeds), the Martha Stewart Everyday Baby Baby line (infant bedding) and, in late 2000, the Martha Stewart Everyday Housewares line (dinnerware, flatware, beverageware, cookware, bakeware, mirrors, picture frames, and lamps). Products designed for Kmart and Zellers are sold exclusively at their stores; products designed for other strategic partners are sold through a variety of retailers, including Sears, Canadian Tire, specialty paint stores, Jo-Ann Fabrics and Crafts, and Calico Corners stores.

Imagine designing security and DRM for Omnimedia! Delivering content to consumers and tracking their responses across multiple media and platforms is a challenge, with or without security and rights management, which add new layers of complexity. Each media platform has its own formats and standards.

This much content must be managed, and the company must have a system for handling the content assets and the metadata (including rights information) attached to them. The ability for multiple DRM systems to interpret and act on the rights metadata. For a company that creates and distributes cross-platform content, and today that will be virtually every content company, interoperability must occur both within and without the organization.

Right now, interoperability between DRM systems does not exist. And different content types going to different destinations will depend on DRM systems that match their characteristics. So for now, media companies have separate silos of content, including the metadata, security, and DRM associated with each one. The next chapter will cover the work of the Motion Picture Experts Group (MPEG) to create specifications for MPEG-21 and the industry group called Marlin to establish standards for interoperability.

Marketing Models

Marketing is the initial communication with a potential content consumer, an invitation to the party. Part of the process involves developing a value proposition that gives consumers a reason to pay attention to the content and a communication strategy for delivering the value proposition. In short, a marketing model answers the questions: What appeals does this particular content hold for a given audience segment and why should these people pay attention to it and consume it? How will they find out about it and how can the appeal be best communicated?

The core concept underlying most contemporary marketing efforts is branding. In media and entertainment, branding has achieved dominance in this field because marketers believe that the key to survival in a multi-channel environment is to build an identity, a brand name so that the content can stand out in a field of almost unlimited choices.

There are several ways to execute a content branding strategy. Broadcast networks use logos, advertising slogans ("NBC-Must See TV"), and "signature shows" (for example, Lost on ABC) to build their brand. Cable networks title their service to identify their offerings, such as Comedy Central, The Family Channel, The Game Channel, the Cartoon Network, and so forth. No matter the method, successful branding involves:

- Establishing a unique image or position in consumers' minds

- Offering a unique value proposition to the consumer

- Linking the brand with a positive emotion

The first marketing model, superdistribution, takes advantage of the fact that most people respond to invitations from people they know. It adds the power of personal social networks to marketing efforts. The second model, data mining, arms content providers with knowledge about potential customers, allowing them to tailor their messages and offers to individuals.

Superdistribution (Passalong) Model

Is it a marketing model or a distribution model? It's a marketing model **and** a distribution model. Superdistribution rests on the understanding that most people like to share their entertainment experiences with others. For example, if they download a song, they like to send it to their friends.

Superdistribution allows the free flow of content without interference from security or DRM. But it utilizes these systems to make sure that the content provider and other contributors to the content supply chain receive compensation. Say the initial purchaser downloads a song in MP3 format, then attaches it as an email to a friend. The friend receives it, plays the file, and loves the song. The second (or third or fifth) time he or she tries to play the song or to copy it to the hard drive or a portable MP3 player, a pop-up appears on the screen, directing them to an e-commerce site where they pay to license it.

If the cost is a dollar or less, there is a good chance the potential customer will become an actual customer.

The monitoring of the number of times the receiver played the song, the appearance of the pop-up, and the direction to an e-commerce infrastructure are all accomplished through persistently attached DRM metadata. The DRM software worked in the background to let the original buyer consume the song according to the terms and conditions of the transaction. Those terms included the ability to pass-along the material. The software also tracked the usage of the buyer's friend and initiated the transaction.

Superdistribution in Action: Share Music With PassAlong

Send music recommendations to friends and earn PassAlong Points when they buy the songs you suggest. Then use those points to buy more music for yourself!

Send Songs Using 1Pass
See a song you like and send a clip to a friend instantly, through email or Instant Messenger. Earn points and keep in touch at the same time.

Express Yourself With MyShowcase
Share your favorite songs with the world by creating a Showcase and earn 10 percent - in the form of PassAlong Points, good for free music - whenever anyone buys directly from your MyShowcase page.

CONTINUED ▶

CONTINUED ▶

You may make ten (10) burns of any individually purchased song to CD.

- You may store your digital music purchases on up to five (5) personal computers.

- You can transfer your digital music purchases an unlimited number of times to up to three (3) supported portable music devices.

- In the event of a legitimate hard-drive crash or other related technical issue, at our reasonable discretion, you may be provided with a reinstall.

Data Mining

Steve Milanovich of Merrill, Lynch refers to monetizing customer relations as "hunting or gathering." Reaching out for new customers is hunting; pitching existing customers for more transactions is gathering. Data mining is a valuable technique for gathering by using information about customers to create targeted value propositions to them. If a marketer knows a set of facts about a past buyer, analyzing that data in detail can provide guidance for such efforts. Sometimes additional information, such as zip code characteristics and census data can be added to the mix, giving powerful additional clues about how to approach a given customer. The more interactions a seller has had with an individual, the more targeted the approach can be.

Data mining is inherently cost-effective. Snagging a new customer on the Internet costs about $50, while making a sale to an existing customer is substantially less. However, data mining has not yet come of age yet because marketers may have too little, too much, or just the wrong information. (Too much data is confusing and useless without the knowledge of what is worth looking at.) Moreover, individuals can be unpredictable.

Over time, however, even eccentricity becomes remarkably predictable! Expect data mining techniques to become more sophisticated, increasingly guiding marketers to ask the right questions and make the relevant observations about customers' behaviors.

And as ecommerce expands, techniques that allow further inferences to be made about future buying behavior make information about consumers will become ever more important.

There are limits on the usefulness of information is the quality of the data: its freshness and accuracy. And privacy issues loom large. As of mid-2000, there were more than 300 bills in the US congress addressing what is believed by both consumers and lawmakers to be an important concern.

> The information about the Yahoo! privacy policy offers insight into how the company uses personal information:
>
> - Yahoo! collects personal information when you register with Yahoo!, when you use Yahoo! products or services, when you visit Yahoo! pages or the pages of certain Yahoo! partners, and when you enter promotions or sweepstakes. Yahoo! may combine information about you that we have with information we obtain from business partners or other companies.
>
> - When you register we ask for information such as your name, email address, birth date, gender, zip code, occupation, industry, and personal interests. For some financial products and services we may also ask for your address, Social Security number, and information about your assets. Once you register with Yahoo! and sign in to our services, you are not anonymous to us.
>
> - Yahoo! collects information about your transactions with us and with some of our business partners, including information about your use of financial products and services that we offer.
>
> - Yahoo! automatically receives and records information on our server logs from your browser, including your IP address, Yahoo! cookie information, and the page you request.
>
> - Yahoo! uses information for the following general purposes: to customize the advertising and content you see, fulfill your requests for products and services, improve our services, contact you, conduct research, and provide anonymous reporting for internal and external clients.[8]

Revenue Models

Revenue models deal with product packaging, pricing, mechanisms for receiving money (or services in the case of barter), and revenue sharing schemes. Many of the models used by traditional media carry over into the digital marketplace.

---

8. Yahoo! privacy policy is at: http://privacy.yahoo.com/privacy/us/

Not surprisingly, there are usually some unique twists when this analog to digital conversion takes place. Although revenue models in new media markets may have the same name as those used in traditional venues, they may mean quite different things. For example, pay-per models can cover smaller informational pieces than in the cable industry. And affiliation means something else altogether on the Internet than it does in the TV industry. Table 6.2 shows new media models.

CONTENT-SUPPORTED	AD-SUPPORTED	E-COMMERCE SUPPORTED	MISCELLANEOUS
Tiering	Sponsorship	Longitudinal cohort marketing	Multiple revenue streams
Subscription	Product placement	Affiliate	Consumer information sales
Pay-per (view,bit, stream, program)	CPM - Cost per thousand impressions		
Tentpole	CPC – Cost per clickthrough		
Big bite			

TABLE 6.2 *New Media Revenue Models*

Content-Supported Revenue Models

People will pay for content they want. Timeliness and time-to-market are always important, because information and entertainment products are highly perishable, like fresh flowers or lettuce. Freshness is especially critical for financial and business information, and companies and investors are sometimes willing to pay considerable sums to get it first. People like to be the first to receive entertainment but it is equally or more important for it to be, well, entertaining.

Tiering Models

Tiering is a way of pricing a range of products and services to get the maximum revenue for them. It is well-developed by multichannel TV providers, but less used in other environments. Tiering by time is charges the first tier of buyers more than subsequent tiers. Products may also be tiered by charging different amounts for content packages or bundles of programming, a preferred technique by the cable, satellite, and the computer software industries.

In the cable industry, the first tier is basic cable. The second tier is composed of "extended basic" packages, each one costing an additional monthly fee. The third tier is made up of individual premium channels; the fourth is a digital tier of bundled channels; and the highest tier is pay-per-view, charges for receiving individual programs, usually movies and sporting events. (High-speed Internet access and telephony are not considered a tier; they are services.)

Subscription Models

Tiering is frequently an adjunct to subscriptions, but not always. A subscription is a revenue scheme where the subscriber pays an agreed upon amount for a specified amount of time. In the cable world, system operators charge a monthly fee for the basic tier but perchannel/per month fees for premium channels. Ultima, a persistent world game, is a subscription site that costs $9.95 per month to play.

Online, an example of subscription combined with tiering is AOL, which charges one subscription fee for a limited number of hours online and another amount for unlimited access. CompuServe is a subsidiary of AOL and will allow unlimited access to both services for still a 3rd price. In addition, on CompuServe, other premium services may carry surcharges.

Pay Per Models

Long before the term "pay per" came into being, people paid per ticket to attend movies, plays, and performances. Then telephone companies introduced pay per minute charges for long distance and local long distance. Cable systems launched "pay per view" service, which in the case of the NBC 1984 coverage of the Olympics, was extended to mean "pay per event" or "pay per package." And the advent of videocassettes and players brought about pay per night rentals.

Pay per models are attractive to both buyers and sellers, and there are various proposals for pay per download, pay per bit, article, photo, song, and video sequence. The problem with many of these schemes is that of "micropayments," small transactions that are more expensive to meter and collect than the value of the payment. Until some form of "digital wallet" technology is standardized, it is likely to be difficult for content providers to make money on small units of information.

Tentpole Models

This idea is the opposite of "multiple revenue source" plans, where money comes into the cash register from as many directions as possible. Tentpoling is a strategy where one content product or service supports the entire business. In the TV business, it is not unknown for a single successful show to carry a production company for some length of time.

A good example of an online pioneer was the Internet soap opera, "The Spot." However, after a few months, the site was unable to support itself on the single property, and it stopped production and closed down. This experience has led some analysts to believe that while it may work in the TV industry, tentpoling is not a viable web site strategy because no single property can generate sufficient traffic for any length of time.

Big Bite Models

Big bite models are the opposite of windowing, which monetizes content by releasing it in stages to different distribution systems. "Forget windowing. It'll never work in the age of digital re-creation," cry the proponents of this model. Instead, they argue that content owners must monetize the first bytes out of the box and move on. The motto might be, Eat the apple, then toss the core, because if the product can't make a decent profit when it first rolls out, it will probably incur a loss.[19]

Content providers have to get the money while the getting is good, immediately. As soon as the product is widely available on the Net, its sales price will quickly drop to zero. Downstream money will be found money, and just about as likely. They point to the game business. It takes 18 months to 2 years to create the product and a couple of months to sell them out—or bulldoze them under.

Ad-Supported Revenue Models

Advertising is the stalwart of over the air television and a major source of revenue for basic cable and satellite channels, through thirty, twenty, fifteen, and ten second commercial spots. It is increasingly important to Internet web sites as one of several sources of revenue. Marketers can buy a place on a Web page, usually the home or landing page. These availabilities include space for banner advertisements, pop-up windows, streaming video buttons boxes (V-box), and click-on animations, logos, banners, and buttons for audio clips. Sponsoring a web site will give an advertiser access to all these forms of placement, as well.

In traditional media, audiences are sold to advertisers on a CPM (cost per thousand) impressions. On the largest Internet sites that command millions of visitors like AOL and Yahoo!, this formulation works well. However, on the majority of Internet sites, advertising rates are less certain. Even though sites deliver customers with specific demographic and psychographic profiles, and their behaviors can be monitored and recorded, measurement issues still cloud the picture.

One controversy is that of impressions versus click-throughs. Site operators want to be paid for the number of targeted consumers they bring to the site. They have no control over the effectiveness of the ad itself, so they believe site traffic is the key. Advertisers want click-throughs and sell-throughs. They'd rather pay on a per click-through basis or on sell-through as a percentage of the transaction (an e-commerce-supported model).

The measurement of streamed content is particularly difficult. Edge technologies that position servers on different networks and corporate networks that use proxy servers all make it quite difficult to get accurate data about how many people see the content.

Moreover, there discussion lists covering webcasting and streaming are filled with acrimonious accusations that content providers and their infrastructure partners exaggerate the number of people who logged on and minimize the number who failed to receive the stream through a myriad of technical difficulties.

The International Webcasting Association (www.webcasting.org) has established a committee to begin resolving these problems in a formal way. They hope to standardize reporting procedures and data formats by engaging the talents of people from companies engaged in streaming media. Only when such tools are recognized and accepted will the Internet be able to capture a substantial share of advertising budgets.

When high-speed broadband access becomes more widespread, advertising will play an important role in supporting content for it. Video and audio are much more expensive to produce than the mainly text + graphic sites that are now the norm on the Net. Broadband distribution will make content providers more dependent on commercial revenues to produce palatable material and is likely to reduce many of the irreverent, zany, flippant, obscene, snotty, thoughtful, silly elements of the rich stew that characterizes online content.

eCommerce Supported Revenue Models

One of the advantages that the Internet offers is that it is "actionable," meaning that it can be acted upon immediately. On the Net, a click and a credit card will do it. Contrast this ease of purchase with television and radio, where the viewer or listener has to drive to a store or place a phone call and execute a long series of actions to get a product. For this reason, ecommerce models are not suitable for one-way media; they apply only to interactive platforms such as the Internet and interactive TV.

One way designers conceptualize the development of web sites is "wrapping ecommerce opportunities around content." Sometimes it is relatively seamless, like on Pseudo.com shows when the Internet Jockey wears branded clothing or hawks advertisers' products.

Or they may be obnoxiously intrusive pop-up windows, consistently reported by users as the most disliked form of online advertising.

On many sites, the relationship between content and ecommerce is taken directly from the company's operations in the bricks-and-mortar world. Information on a web site may go little beyond scanning in the catalog. Other sites present a bewildering hodge-podge of specs and other data. Only in a few cases is there a carefully thought-through and executed plan to guide the visitor through an extended experience of the content and the ecommerce opportunities. Two models suggest ways e-tailers might think about their site and customers.

Longitudinal Cohort Models

This revenue model goes particularly with audience segmentation content schemes, which offer material to a specific group of consumers. It tries to anticipate the array of wants and needs members of the group have in common, to provide content that interests and supports them, and to wrap around and embed appropriate ecommerce solutions. Mariana Danilovich, CEO and president of Digital Media Incubator LLC is an articulate advocate of this perspective. "This whole game is not about the creation of great programming. It is about serving a niche demographic. Now you can't serve a niche demographic with a single property. You can be very creative but it's the whole experience, designed with the entire lifestyle of the audience in mind, allowing you to fully serve the target demographic," she advises.

A key element in this model is its longitudinal aspect. Marketers must continue to profile their consumers over time so that the content and ecommerce opportunities evolve in sync with the changing customer. The Web is still so young that this aspect of cohort marketing is only now surfacing as people in the Gen X cohort enters their 30s. E-tailers who have focused on that group must now shift their strategies from urban, fashion-conscious, entertainment-driven singles to suburban marrieds with children buying their first home and entering the substantive years of their careers.

DEN, the Digital Entertainment Network, a site aimed at Gen Y, based its operations on this model. It went belly-up because of the actions of the organizations involved in its IPO, rather than a failure of the business model DEN pioneered. MXGOnline, a site aimed at teenage girls, is another example. MoXieGirl was originally a catalog that carried fashion merchandise for adolescent females. Now it is a media company with a magazine, MXG, a web site, and a broadband streaming site, MXGtv.com. The site features articles, interviews, entertainment news, reviews, streamed audio and video, and user-supplied content, all free to users. For revenue, MXGOnline markets apparel, shoes, fashion accessories, jewelry, perfume and beauty-related products, home furnishings, and CDs through a partnership with CDNow.

iVillage.com revolves around women, Marthastewart.com around the home, and Bolt.com around Gen Y teenagers. On all these sites, it is more than a matter of just content, or just e-commerce. It is the ongoing symbiotic relationship between them as experienced by a specific cohort that can result a substantial stream of revenue over time.

Affiliate Networks

In television, an affiliate station carries the programming of a broadcast network, and gives up commercial time that the network can package with stations all over the US to sell to national advertisers. On the Internet, an ecommerce site puts together an affiliate network of other sites, distributing clickable content, logos, banners, and links. When customers click, they are taken to the e-tailer's Web storefront to make the purchase. In return, the seller shares the revenue with the referring site. These use of these kind of agreements has grown as the cost of placing banner ads on portal sites has risen.

Essentially, it's a way of reaching out to potential customers instead of waiting for them to come to an e-tailer's site. If the affiliates have content compatible with the target audience, then visitors who are looking for the type of products on offer are reasonably likely to click on the link. Just as it is with cohort marketing, compatibility is crucial. Sites that offer information about entertainment are a natural for selling books, videos, music, and tickets. Sports sites can sell event tickets and sports equipment. Personal finance dot.coms might market research on individual stocks and mutual funds.

Here is how a site might analyze the business case for establishing an affiliate network:

- 250 Affiliated Web Sites, with 1500 daily page views per site, to get 11,250,000 impressions per month;

CONTINUED ▶

CONTINUED ▶

- A 3.5% click-through rate generates 393,750 targeted, self-selected sales prospects;

- A 1% conversion rate of the prospect results in 3,937 products sold per month;

- If average purchase is $25, total sales = $98,425 per month

- Less 10-50% commission to referring web site ($9,842 - 49,212) + cost of goods sold = profit

Establishing and managing an affiliate network presumes a certain scale and sophistication of infrastructure. The e-tailer must have a product database and the means to process transactions and fulfill orders. Affiliate referrals need to be integrated into the database and tracked so payments can be calculated and distributed.

Some examples of affiliate networks is Barnes & Noble's agreement with the New York Times. Visitors to the NYT web site who are reading book reviews can click and buy it from the B&N. On Sportsline.com, the MVP shop sells team merchandise. Its affiliate program will kick back a 10% commission on sales to sites whose visitors click on a link to MVP.sportsline.com their merchandise. The pioneer of affiliate networks is still the biggest. Amazon.com has more than 230,000 affiliated sites, and it is carried on 5 of the 6 most visited sites on the Internet.

Amazon.com pays 15% commission but there is considerable variation in what different e-tailers pay. Garden.com gives a $10 referral bounty, Lending Tree Branch pays up to $12 a head. V-Store pays up to 25% commission, and CarPrices will share up to 50%.

Other Revenue Models

There are a few miscellaneous models that do not fit conveniently into the other categories. The multiple revenue stream model brings in money from any and all of the its operations. The cybermediary model is the electronic incarnation of "middlemen," performing the functions of traditional intermediaries between product manufacturers and consumers (and a few more) in the online environment. Finally, in a business environment where sales are targeted to specific consumers, there is a robust market for information about them that some sites may be able to market as a product in itself.

Multiple Revenue Stream Models

The multiple revenue stream contrasts with the tentpole model, where an enterprise is supported by the income generated by a single product or service. The value of multiple sources of revenues in media and entertainment became clear with the rise of the cable industry. Broadcasters who had always relied on money from the sale of commercial time found themselves in competition with TV programming providers that could deliver multiple channels and brought in receipts from monthly subscriptions, advertising, premium channels, pay-per-view, and now high speed Internet access and telephony. And they are thrilled with the prospect of interactive TV which would give them a piece of T-commerce as well. Like cable operators, Internet service providers and web sites almost always adopt a revenue model with multiple sources of income.

Cybermediary Models

In US commerce, there is a huge infrastructure between the makers of products and the buyers of them. A study of the US distribution and sales of high quality shirts found that the wholesale-retail chain, the intermediaries that facilitate the exchange, account for about 62% of the final price to the buyer. At the same time, many analysts have advanced the notion that networking enables a direct communication between the parties to the transaction that could eliminate these middlemen. They call this flattening of hierarchy "disintermediation."

Keep in mind that in this view, bricks-and-mortar retailers are intermediaries to the final sale, along with the more traditional definitions of middlemen in the distribution process. However, some intermediaries earn their money by performing valuable functions. They include packaging products into attractive, saleable merchandise categories; providing consumer-friendly product information; matching consumers to products; providing transactional economies of scale, and managing risks for both producers (verifying checks and credit cards) and consumers (handling returns).

Indeed, so valuable are some of these services, they have fostered "re-intermediation" by cybermediaries. So online fingers do the walking on Yahoo! and Lycos instead of through the local Yellow Pages. Car buyers can get the Blue Book value of their used car from Kelley's Blue Book online (www.kbb.com/) instead of calling their cousin Pete who works at the General Motors dealership. They can shop in online malls, multiple storefronts lodged in a single site in place of driving to the store. Internet fan clubs, discussion groups, and chat rooms exert peer influence on the products people choose to buy. eBay.com acts as a cybermediary between millions of buyers and sellers. Business to business sites provide realtime spot market and barter networks. And shopping 'bots' scour the Net, bringing back product and price comparisons.

Some cybermediaries generate revenues through commissions as well as per query charges, such as the Kelley's Blue Book site. Search and directory sites like Yahoo! and AltaVista bring in money from advertising and contractual arrangements to position some businesses high on the list of returns to users. And, of course, ecommerce through the product sales or service provision directly support many others.

Consumer Data Sale Models

In addition to the dollar amount spent by customers, there is also the data the company owns about the consumers and their behaviors. Indeed, this information about actual purchasers may well be the most valuable asset the company will ever own. It can be used as a bargaining chip to partner with others or simply sold. Depending on the depth and breadth of the data, it can also be repackaged into segments for use or sale to multiple buyers.

New Markets, New Models—New WWWorld

Many of the traditional principles and ways of doing business will change less than we might anticipate. But they are changing much more than a lot of people in business are comfortable with. And consumers are going through their own painful adjustments, even as they follow up on many new opportunities.

The next chapter will look at how media and entertainment companies are responding to a networked business environment. It will examine the transformations and trends that are appearing as connectivity becomes ubiquitous. And it will summarize some of the problems that pose a challenge to the vision of instant broadband communication anywhere, anytime, to anyone.

End Notes

This idea is articulated in a coalition-sponsored White Paper on the iXL website at: http://www.ixl.com/whitepapers/index.html.

M. J. Wolf. *The Entertainment Economy*. New York: Random House (1999):223.

J. Berst. "Secrets of Spiral Branding." *ZDNet.com* (November 13, 1998). Online article available at: http://www.zdnet.com/anchordesk/story/story_2745.html. Also, see related Powerpoint presentation at: http://www.zdnet.com/anchordesk/story/story_2745.html.

J. Berst. Op. cit.

G. Johnson. "Investors have dot-qualms on ad spending." *Los Angeles Times* (May 8, 2000): C-1,5.

B. McClellan of PricewaterhouseCoopers articulated this model in "The Future of the Entertainment and Media Industries: 2005." PricewaterhouseCoopers, 2000

E. Neufeld, et al. "Consumer Internet Economy Portal Landscape, Revenue Strategies, Five Year Projections." *Jupiter Communications Research Study* (July, 1998). For information, contact Jupiter Communications at 627 Broadway, New York, NY 10012, phone: 212-780-6060, www.jup.com.

M. Danilovich. Personal interview, Las Vegas, April, 2000.

These offers came from a website that provides information about affiliate and referral programs in March, 2000. For a current list, see: www.referit.com/main.cfm?screen=info/topten.

L. Thurman. Personal interview, Westwood, CA, October, 1999.

R. Benjamin and R. Wigand. "Electronic markets and virtual value chains on the information highway." *Sloan Management Review*. (Winter, 1995):62-72.

M. B. Sarkar, B. Butler, and C. Steinfield (1995). "Intermediaries and cybermediaries: A continuing role for mediating players in the electronic marketplace." *Journal of Computer-Mediated Communication* 1:3 (1995). Online at: http//www.ascusc.org/jcmv/vol1/issue3/sarkar.html

7 DRM Stakes and Stakeholders

So what is at stake in the struggle over copyright policy and DRM technologies? The outcome affects an impressive list of important basic issues of modern life in a democratic society: free expression and free speech, the public right of fair use, the free flow of information and the marketplace of ideas, the future of innovation in technology, and the future of key industries, including the $274 billion dollar entertainment and media industry (as shown in Figure 7.1) and the $113 billion consumer electronics industry.

What's at stake varies, depending on where the seat an actor takes at the public table. Audiences and consumers love the content entertainment and media companies produce, sell, and provide ways for people to experience it! Globally, this market brings in revenues of well over $1 trillion. According to the Consumer Electronics Association, U.S. households own 25 consumer electronics products on the average of 25, reported the 2005 CE Ownership and Market Potential study. Each U.S. household typically spends more than $1,250 per year on consumer electronics products.[1]

With this much money on the table, it is not surprising that the battles over copyright protection and DRM are fierce. Feelings can run very high indeed. For example, at one conference, an entertainment executive accused the president of a p2p software company of being "a child pornographer," contending p2p files sometimes contain such material, and a p2p supporter called entertainment executives "morons."

---

1. Consumer Electronics Association, *CE Ownership and Market Potential.* May 17, 2005. Available at: http://www.ce.org/press_room/press_release_detail.asp?id=10753

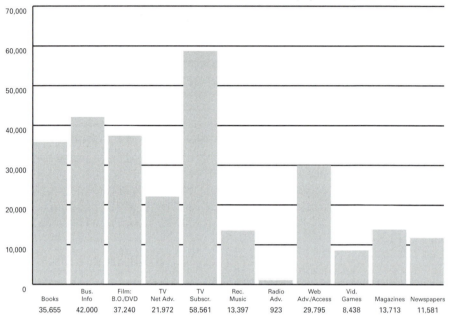

FIGURE 7.1 *Revenue from Copyright Industry Sectors, 2005 (Source of data: PricewaterhouseCoopers Outlook, 2005-2009)*

Many interests are affected by copyright and DRM policies, ranging from society as a whole to a host of companies, organizations, even governments. Four constellations of interest groups play major roles in the ongoing debates, forming content, distribution, technology, and social stakeholder clusters. All of them converge on the argument, bringing their own specific concerns, strategies, and solutions. This chapter will look at each of them, detailing their points of view and activities as the participate in these important technologically-induced changes to the commercial and social fabric of authorship, free market economics, and free expression.

Content Stakeholders

Table 7.1 summarizes the stakeholders in the content cluster of interests. Although they all take positions on copyright and DRM policies, they have different concerns and roles to play. They include the creators, the owners, the users, and the buyers of IP and content.

STAKEHOLDER	CONCERNS	ROLE IN DEBATE
THE CONTENT STAKEHOLDERS	PROTECTING AND MONETIZING CONTENT	INTERESTS TYPICALLY REPRESENTED BY TRADE ORGANIZATIONS
Content creators (writers, producers, performers)	Their ideas will be stolen at the outset If their work is posted on a p2p network, they will never be paid for their work	Occasionally participate as individuals. Content owning and distributing companies and trade organizations often claim to represent content creators' interests
Content owners (E & M companies: studios, labels, networks)	The value of their catalog will be gutted They will not be able to monetize current hits They will have to change their business models The new business models may not be so profitable Implementation of rights revocation and customer care Interoperable DRM technologies	Usually represented by trade organizations Large entertainment and media organizations may have direct political relationships
Content licensees (aggregators, product manufacturers)	They will lose the money they have invested in licenses and exclusivity contracts The value of the brand may be degraded through unauthorized alteration in creative works and characters, i.e., Lesbian Barbie	Participate through their relationships with content owners

TABLE 7.1 *Stakeholders in Copyright and DRM Policies*

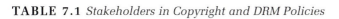

STAKEHOLDER	CONCERNS	ROLE IN DEBATE
Content buyers and consumers	They will lose rights they have had in the past: fair use, personal copying, etc. The new business models will cost them more for less. They will be inconvenienced by cumbersome DRM technologies Responsive customer care policies and systems	Represented by consumer and civil rights groups

TABLE 7.1 *(Continued)*

The interests in the content cluster are all concerned about the value of content. The creators, owners, and users all want to protect the material and to be paid as much as possible for it. Consumers don't care about security and want to pay as little as possible for it.

The power in this cluster is held by content owners and consumers. Except for a few stars, the people who create content: writers, graphic artists and illustrators, musicians, performers, programmers, and other skilled contributors of creative projects have little power. Many of the other players invoke the creators in the course of debate, but their comments are almost always merely self-serving rhetoric. Content licensees, particularly manufacturers who use branded content to market products, speak through the content owners whose material they buy.

Content Creators

Since content creators have so little power, they generally do not participate in the debate over copyright and DRM. Some stars have been recruited by content owners, mostly music labels, in public relations campaigns to influence decision-makers to pass regulations stiffening copyright protections. However, content creators are important in another way – they may be disadvantaged by draconian copyright enforcement and DRM. As a result, content creators are not heterogeneous in their opinions. Some support strict copyright enforcement and DRM, while others oppose it.

One reason for the opposition of some content creators is illustrated by the experience of DJ Danger Mouse. DJ DM is what is known as a remixer, an artist who uses samples from others' work to create what they consider new, original works. In 2004,

DJ DM self-released a musical work, The Grey Album, to critical acclaim. The work used the words of rapper Jay-Z from his album, Black Album, mixed with rhythms and chords from the Beatles' White Album. The remix became an Internet hit.

Executives of EMI, the label that owns the rights to the Beatles' sound recordings, was not entertained because DJ DM had not asked for permission the use the Beatles' music nor paid for the rights to it. EMI sent a cease-and-desist letter to Danger Mouse and the retailers who were selling it, and DJ DM pulled the music from the market rather than face a lawsuit and potential blackballing within the industry.

But DJ DM is just one example. There are a number of instances of new works of music based on samples of existing songs that have been effectively suppressed through legal action by content owners.

One website, http://www.illegal-art.org, lists 20 remixed creative works that use bits and pieces of pre-existing works:

Negativland, *U2: Special Edit Radio Mix* (5:46)
Biz Markie, *Alone Again* (2:52)
People Like Us, *Swinglargo* (5:20)
Culturcide, *They Aren't the World* (4:30)
The Evolution Control Committee, *Rocked by Rape* (4:28)
Beastie Boys, *Rock Hard* (4:53)
Dummy Run, *f.d.* (1:23)
John Oswald, *black* (2:01)
Corporal Blossom, *White Christmas* (3:19)
Tape-beatles, *Reality of Matter* (2:37)
Public Enemy, *Psycho of Greed* (3:11)
The Verve, *Bittersweet Symphony* (4:35)
Wobbly, *Clawing Your Eyes Out Down to Your Throat* (1:21)
De La Soul, *Transmitting Live from Mars* (1:07)
Buchanan and Goodman, *The Flying Saucer* (4:18)
The JAMs, *The Queen and I* (4:50)
Elastica, *Connection* (2:20)
Steinski and Mass Media, *The Motorcade Sped On* (4:26)
Invisibl, Skratch Piklz *white label edit* (5:30)
Xper.Xr, *Wu-chu-tung* (1:43)
Boone Bischoff, *Happy Birthday To You* (0:28)

As Richard Posner argued: "West Side Story borrowed from Shakespeare, who borrowed from Arthur Brooke. Paradise Lost borrowed from Genesis, as did Thomas Mann in Joseph and His Brothers. Manet borrowed from Raphael, Rembrandt, and others. If these are examples of plagiarism, then we want more plagiarism!"[2]

Content Owners

Content owners and licensees have a dilemma: They want to be able to protect content so they can sell it at a profit in the commercial marketplace, but choosing the wrong DRM technology or implementation can result in consumer rejection and lost sales.

Individually, prominent entertainment and media companies, as well as the top echelon of management that runs them, may have access to the highest levels of decision makers in the legislative and executive branches of government. However, for the most part, content owners form trade associations to represent their interests. Some of these trade groups such as the Motion Picture Association of America (MPAA), the Recording Industry Association of America (RIAA), the National Association of Broadcasters (NAB) exercise considerable political clout. They make hefty campaign donations and use their positive contributions to the U.S. international trade balance to good effect.

The MPAA and RIAA are proactive in the fight against copyright infringers. The MPAA employs its own staff of detectives. The RIAA has sued Internet service providers to get the names of users who download files from p2p services and has sued some of those users. Examples of content owners' major successes in influencing legislation include the Digital Millennium Copyright Act and the Sonny Bono Act.

Content owners also form technical groups to develop technological enforcement of copyright and barriers to piracy. One example of such an alliance is the Copy Protection Technologies Working Group, with members drawn from entertainment and media, consumer electronics, computer, and DRM vendor companies, examines DRM technologies and follows legislation and regulation activities that center on copy protection and DRM.

Content companies have a great deal to gain from DRM technologies. But, so far, they have not been willing to pay for them. There are significant costs associated with DRM, as noted by Bill Rosenblatt: [3]

---

2. Posner, R. On Plagiarism, *The Atlantic Monthly.* April, 2002.

3. Rosenblatt, B. *Paying for DRM*, paper delivered at Buma-Stemra Conference, July 4, 2003. Available at: http://www.giantstepsmts.com/paying_for_drm.htm.

- The design and development of appropriate technologies

- Development, promulgation, and acceptance of standards (whether open or de facto) that promote interoperability among different content distribution and playback components

- Design of products based on good technologies and standards

- Unit costs of playback devices or software that contain DRM technology

  There are other likely costs as well, including:

- Consumer education

- Possible consumer backlash and subsequent reduction of sales

- DRM-related consumer usability problems

- DRM-related customer care

- Constant vigilance to monitor of hacks of DRM technologies and upgrades to patch security holes

- DRM-related consumer electronics and computer performance deficits

Content owners could push some of these costs onto content distributors, by making DRM part of distribution contracts. However, distributors would simply pass the costs on to the consumer, who see no benefits from DRM, and a rise in prices could dampen consumer demand for many entertainment and media products. Perhaps the most popular current hits would be relatively unaffected, but sales of catalog and less popular titles could suffer.

Consumers

Consumers also hold considerable that they can (and do) use in several ways. The first is power of the purse, particularly when it is snapped shut. There are a number of instances that indicate DRM played a role in the failure of products; perhaps was even the main cause of failure. In the audio arena, the copy protection placed on Natalie Imbruglia's 2001 CD White Lilies Island would not play in some CD and DVD players. In another instance, a California consumer sued the makers of Charley Pride's A Tribute to Jim Reeves, which prevented buyers from converting the songs into MP3 files. The case was settled for an undisclosed amount.

Another example comes from the software arena. Intuit markets a tax preparation application called Turbo Tax. In 2002, the company DRM-protected the program and required customers to activate the program in order to use it. Consumers complained that the program made it difficult to switch computers and computer components and that the activation monitoring system used too much memory. Legitimate buyers resented being treated like thieves or potential thieves. Finally, they did not believe that Intuit would allow activation for an unlimited period of time, so that eventually, they would receive a message that would prevent them from activating the product: "We no longer support Turbo Tax 2002." Ultimately, consumer rejection of the product forced Intuit to remove the activation feature altogether.

DRM may also hinder the sale of music online. Many observers believe that a significant percentage of people want to be honest and purchase their music, and that they would do so if it were available at a reasonable price point. At the same time, there are also those who reject outright the limitations placed on their use by DRM. So while Apple's iTunes has developed a fairly permissive DRM scheme that has helped overcome this resistance, sales on the service are still only a miniscule percentage of overall downloading of music.

Distribution Stakeholders

These stakeholders move media to consumers. The least vocal of all the factions, they include wholesalers, who are the syndicators and other middlemen who aggregate and market content to exhibitors; retailers, who make up a long list of outlets that make material available to end users; network provides of all kinds; and redistributors, professional pirates and casual copiers who obtain content, make copies of it, and make it available to others, for fun and for fee. Table 7.2 summarizes their concerns and roles.

STAKEHOLDER	CONCERNS	ROLE IN DEBATE
THE DISTRIBUTION STAKEHOLDERS	VARIED; SEE INDIVIDUAL ENTRIES	EITHER DO NOT PLAY A ROLE OR DO SO THROUGH TRADE ASSOCIATIONS AND ORGANIZATIONS
Wholesale distributors (syndicators, middlemen)	Investments in contracts for content will lose revenue or fail to make money	Participate through relationships with content owners and licensees

TABLE 7.2 *Distribution Stakeholders*

STAKEHOLDER	CONCERNS	ROLE IN DEBATE
THE DISTRIBUTION STAKEHOLDERS	VARIED; SEE INDIVIDUAL ENTRIES	EITHER DO NOT PLAY A ROLE OR DO SO THROUGH TRADE ASSOCIATIONS AND ORGANIZATIONS

Retail-level Distributors (theater owners, television and radio broadcasters, website operators, video game arcade establishments, libraries, in-store and online stores)	All except theater owners and broadcasters worry about loss of sales or patronage due to consumer-unfriendly DRM
	
	Website operators: Want cheap (or free) content to attract hits to site
	• Do not want lia-bility for copyright infringement
	• Are worried about large files in an all-you-can-eat subscription environment
	• Libraries: Want to be able to loan material to library card holders and library users
	• In-store and online retailers:
	  - Customer care
	  - Ease-of-use and convenience for consumers
		Usually represented by trade organizations
		
		Large entertainment and media organizations may have direct political relationships

Networks providers: cable, satellite, telephone, and IP networks and Internet Service Providers)	Want to encourage usage by large numbers of people and heavy usage of the network • Do not want liability for incidents of copyright infringement	Participate through trade associations and organizations

TABLE 7.2 *(Continued)*

STAKEHOLDER	CONCERNS	ROLE IN DEBATE
THE DISTRIBUTION STAKEHOLDERS	VARIED; SEE INDIVIDUAL ENTRIES	EITHER DO NOT PLAY A ROLE OR DO SO THROUGH TRADE ASSOCIATIONS AND ORGANIZATIONS
Unauthorized redistributors (professional pirates, p2p services, and consumers-sharers)	Pirates: Want to minimize casual copying and use of p2p networks Casual copiers: Want free or inexpensive content with no restrictions	Pirates: Do not participate Consumers-sharers: Represented by consumer and civil rights organizations

TABLE 7.2 *(Continued)*

Like content stakeholders, distribution players vary in their concerns and their positions on the utility of DRM for their activities. Indeed, it seems strange to lump together Group W (wholesale distributor), Blockbuster (retail distributor), and the DVD seller on the street corner with his wares spread out on a blanket (pirate retailer). But they do share a common dislike of casual copying and subsequent distribution by consumers: None of them wants their potential market saturated by free or almost-free versions of the content they hope to sell. They differ with respect to DRM, however. Authorized sellers support DRM; pirates do not. At the same time, distributors face the same dilemma that content stakeholders do: that a poor choice of DRM technology or implementation could drive away people who would otherwise purchase a content product.

Content Wholesale Businesses

Traditional wholesale distributors of media, including movies, TV (syndicators), books, and music are businesses that aggregate, warehouse, and deliver media hard goods (albums, CDs, DVDs, books, film reels, videotape cassettes) to bricks-and-mortar businesses. New online wholesalers also aggregate material, but they store it on servers, and move it across networks to e-tailing websites or directly to consumers. All wholesalers typically operate on narrow profit margins. If they are fortunate, they are able to add a small percentage to the prices of a large volume of material to create a profitable business.

Wholesalers have been hit hard by the digital revolution. Some services that they offered to content producers for distribution of hard goods have been rendered obsolete by digital distribution. Negotiations between producers and wholesalers may be fierce. The markup that wholesale distributors add to the prices of content products is watched jealously by content producing companies, who would like to bring in that revenue themselves. They may be tempted to cut out the wholesaler entirely and to set up direct sales links to buyers, an option facilitated by broadband networks. Over the last decade wholesalers have proved their worth, whether it is in the hard goods domain or online, because most content producers find that handling every aspect of distribution takes their attention from their core business.

Producers and wholesalers are united in their opposition to piracy, however. The small profit margins of wholesaling mean that such businesses suffer disproportionately from widespread piracy.

Retailers and E-tailers

Purveyors of content share a common aim: they all want customers, end users of the content products. Any business that hopes to make money from the sale of content must be concerned about piracy. However, the disparity in the various types of content purveyors inevitably leads to differences in their approaches to DRM. Generally speaking, an enterprise will oppose any implementation of DRM that discourages rates of purchase and usage.

Theater owners' only concern is piracy. Their customers do not interact with DRM, so they care only that DRM combat piracy effectively. Before the sales of TV series on DVD, broadcasters wanted a bigger audience, so if their content was copied or carried on a network, it would not have mattered. But now broadcasters have a stake in the sale of hard goods and they will soon profit from cable operators' on demand service offerings of their programs. Finally, motion picture studios refuse to allow their movies to be aired by broadcast networks in high definition. All these developments have encouraged broadcasters to adopt DRM, as exemplified by the efforts to standardize an embedded "broadcast flag" in television signals.

All distributors to consumers, except theater owners and broadcasters, have tremendous worries about the loss of sales or patronage due to consumer-unfriendly DRM technologies and implementations. Each type of seller has specific issues with respect to DRM. For example, website operators want cheap (or free) content to attract people to their sites. However, they don't want too much free content because the cost of serving huge files to large numbers of visitors becomes very expensive. And if they populate their site with content uploaded by users, they do not want to assume liability for copyright infringement.

In-store and online retailers want to make sure that there is sufficient after-sale customer care. If a buyer has a bad experience with being able to access and enjoy the purchased content, the seller is likely to suffer. Key for these distributors is ease-of-use and convenience for consumers.

Libraries have similar concerns about convenience and ease of use. In addition, they need DRM technologies and implementations to allow them to loan content to their cardholders.

Network Providers

Network providers are split over their support of DRM. Cable and satellite operators make money from on-demand and pay-per-view sales, so they want content protected. They favor limiting the number of views and the length of the viewing window to protect their revenue streams. By contrast, IP network providers and Internet Service Providers (ISPs) prefer content that is not copy-protected or locked up by DRM because their revenues depend on ever-increasing traffic. In a macro economic sense, the more consumers pay for content, the less disposable income they have for network access and services and, if prices for content are high, the less content consumers will download or send across the network.

ISPs are both network providers and website operators, so they share the concerns of both types of businesses. They want inexpensive content to attract people to buying an online service and to draw users to their website. However, they do not want to assume liability for copyright infringement by their subscribers. Moreover, since ISPs have to pay for bandwidth, servers, and storage, the cost of large content files can eat up profits in an all-you-can-eat flat-fee subscription environment.

Unauthorized Redistributors (pirates and casual copiers)

In the analog world, there is an enormous distinction between professionally-executed commercial piracy and casual downloading for peer-to-peer distribution. Take a videocassette of a movie. Professional pirates have banks of VCRs patched to the playback machine. They may copy dozens of copies at a time and may even reproduce the four-color packaging to sell them as originals. By contrast, the casual analog copier hooks up a second VCR to the player and gives the copy to a friend or relative. Maybe even two or three. But how many times is someone going to shove in tapes when their pals can rent them for four or five dollars?

In the digital world, the professionals behave the same as they did in the analog world. They get one copy and copy it hundreds, thousands, hundreds of thousands, even millions of times over. They package it and often sell it on the street, although they may successfully sell it through retail outlets as well.

The casual consumer copier digitizes the film and stores it on the computer's hard drive. The person may be a suburban housewife or a high school student living in a bucolic small town who has never even received a parking ticket on his bike. The student is just being a good friend when they share the media they love. But when that individual puts the movie online, it becomes available to millions of other consumers. There are also some people who see themselves as swashbuckling Robin Hoods, providing escape for content that "wants to be free" and escapism for their online community members who want to be entertained.

In the digital world, content takes on a life of its own, independent of its original creators, packagers, marketers, distributors, and even consumers. Content is a finished product; its components are assets. But one person's content is another person's asset. With unprecedented processing power at consumer's fingertips, buyers are likely to consider the content they buy as assets(their assets, not copyrighted content) that they can turn to the uses they want, such as playing and displaying on multiple devices, making home productions...whatever.

Once the material is made available on a peer-to-peer service, any number of people can download the music, film, book, software program, or game from the host PC. Now the material is on that number of hard drives. And any number of people can download from them from those new locations. It's an exponential increase that means hundreds of thousands, even millions of copies of content can get around the world in a matter of days, even hours.

The interests of professionals are diametrically opposed to those of casual copiers. Thus, professionals detest consumer peer-to-peer downloading as much as legal owners do – p2p costs them money. The last thing professional pirates want is competition from free content. Their markets and profits are undermined by casual copying and the use of P2P networks. The professional pirate may be a criminal, linked to organized crime. They are thieves in it only for the money, profiting from content they didn't finance, create, publicize, or market.

By contrast, consumers want inexpensive or free access to content with no restrictions. They want to use content on any appropriate device. For example, a user may want to view a DVD on a DVD player attached to a TV, a computer, or a portable DVD player with its own small screen. People want to play CDs at home, in their cars, on their computers, and on portable music devices, like an iPod or a minidisc player. They want to be able to play content wherever they happen to be. For example, they want to be able to play a DVD when they are at a friend's house, not just in their own DVD player at home. Users like to share their purchased content with family, friends, and acquaintances. Some of them like to share it with the world, which is where most content owners draw an absolute line.

Users have other precious rights at stake. They have always been able to quote a paragraph from a book. But if a DVD has Macrovision protection, they cannot "quote" or use a short clip from a motion picture they have purchased in a home video. Or put :30 seconds of a song behind video footage taken at a family anniversary. Even if these are legal uses, it is illegal for consumers to circumvent the copy protection technology that keeps them from copying even a short portion of the material. In this way, the rights and technologies of content owners trump the rights of free expression of consumers and citizens.

However, from the perspective of the content owner, the digital environment erases the difference between professional piracy and casual copying. For owners, the consequences of copying are the same whether it is done by a friendly student or a professional thief: Loss of control of the content, loss of surprise, and loss of revenue – perhaps on a massive scale.

Technology Stakeholders

Digital content is irretrievably tied to technology for its creation, transport, and use. Users cannot experience it without some kind of device on which to play it. Technology stakeholders include the manufacturers of these consumer electronics devices (such as TVs, radio, DVD and CD players, iPods and minidisc players, etc.), and the makers of computers (Table 7.3).

As we have seen, DRM schemes themselves depend on some underlying technology platform such as software, hardware, usually a combination of both. Thus, there are two types of DRM-related enterprises that are stakeholders in the development of content protection and monetization technologies: DRM vendors, and DRM standardization bodies.

STAKEHOLDER	CONCERNS	ROLE IN DEBATE
THE TECHNOLOGY STAKEHOLDERS	**DRM MEANS MONEY— MAKING IT OR SPENDING IT**	**THEIR PARTICIPATION REQUIRED TO CREATE DRM AND IMPLEMENT IT**
Consumer electronics manufacturers	Don't want to add cost to their products Need content to sell their products Don't want DRM to stifle innovation Don't want to discourage consumer uses	Participate through trade associations and organizations
Computer hardware manufacturers	Do not want to add costs to their products Do not want to limit users or uses Need content to sell faster, bigger new products Don't want DRM to stifle innovation	Participate through trade organizations
DRM Developers and Vendors (Researchers, private companies)	Researchers: • Usability for consumers • Implementation of consumer rights • Reliability • Security • Interoperability Vendors: • Cost • Security • Reliability • Interoperabiity	Researchers: Participate through conferences and papers DRM Vendors: Participate through trade organizations

TABLE 7.3 *Technology Stakeholders*

STAKEHOLDER	CONCERNS	ROLE IN DEBATE
THE TECHNOLOGY STAKEHOLDERS	DRM MEANS MONEY— MAKING IT OR SPENDING IT	THEIR PARTICIPATION REQUIRED TO CREATE DRM AND IMPLEMENT IT
DRM Standards Bodies	Interoperability Rights revocation Rights languages DRM infrastructure	Participate through: • Private companies • International standards bodies • Government commit-tees and agencies • Trade organizations

TABLE 7.3 *(Continued)*

Consumer Electronics and Computer Manufacturers

Companies in these two categories do not always have the same interests, but they are similar with respect with to DRM technologies. They need high quality content to sell hardware. Indeed, it is a well-known truism within technology and network provider industries that entertainment content is a "killer app," which means that consumer enthusiasm for compelling content drives the purchase of both devices and network services.

Although technology companies are proceeding with DRM implementation, they have concerns. Their businesses depend on the rapid evolution of technology so that they can deliver newer, better, faster, higher quality products on a regular basis. They believe that DRM is a threat to technological innovation because, while the purpose of copyright was 'the promotion of science and the useful arts generally,' DRM may well be used by media and entertainment to subsidize existing inefficient channels of content delivery and to inhibit the development of more efficient mechanisms of distribution.

With such misgivings about the effects of DRM on innovation, technology companies would not implement DRM at all. They would far rather make profits on the backs of media and entertainment companies' free content, if only they could. But content-producers are aware of their power to propel sales for technology giants, and increasingly demand that manufacturers incorporate copy protection in their technologies. For example, DVD recorders, PCs, and videocassette recorders all recognize the presence of Macrovision protection on DVDs, and will not copy such protected DVDs. Similarly, as a result of the insistence of the

Recording Industry Association of America, minidiscs are protected by an early form of DRM, the Serial Copy Management System (SCMS).

The positions of manufacturers are well-documented. Computer companies generally agree with the sentiments of Craig Barrett, the chief executive officer of Intel Corporation, when he called for the adoption of DRM technologies that allow consumers the flexibility to manipulate the content as they choose. Speaking at a seminar in Tokyo, he criticized the restrictions imposed by some existing and proposed DRM systems.[4]

The Consumer Electronics Association (CEA) speaks for the makers of consumer electronics devices. One document supporting consumers home recording rights shows illustrates the position of device makers:

CEA POSITION: CEA advocates protecting intellectual property while maintaining consumers' privacy, home recording rights and ability to use lawfully acquired media for noncommercial purposes. CEA also emphasizes the need for voluntary inter-industry resolution of digital rights issues rather than government-imposed technology mandates.

BACKGROUND: Conflicts between consumers and content owners resulting from the migration to digital technology continue to generate action and controversy in the public policy arena. CEA has consistently opposed anti-consumer legislation that would have imposed significant burdens and costs on the consumer electronics and information technology industries, while setting the stage for a revival of fair use principals in legislative and regulatory proceedings.[5]

An important note sounded in this position paper is the mention of costs. DRM costs money. No one is anxious to pay for it, even those companies that would most benefit from it, the content producers. Consumer electronics product marketplaces are usually very competitive, so product makers are reluctant to add costs to each unit. These costs could be very high given the lack of standardization and interoperability between the various DRM schemes and technologies.

4. Williams, Martyn. *Intel's Barrett calls for more flexible DRM system*, The Standard, February 24, 2004. Available at:
http://www.thestandard.com/article.php?story=20040224173710416&mode=print

5. CEA. *Protecting Consumer Home Recording Rights*, January, 2004. Available at:
http://www.ce.org/shared_files/initiatives_attachments/268HomeRecordingRights%200104.pdf.

Both content producers and consumer electronics manufacturers have incentives for interoperability between DRM systems. By contrast, DRM vendors seek to differentiate themselves, so they have been slow to move towards making their technologies work together. Frustrated by the slow pace, consumer electronics formed a group in early 2005 to allow CE manufacturers to incorporate DRM into their devices that will work across products from all manufacturers. In short, to standardize.

The development group is named the Marlin Joint Development Association (MJDA). Members include Sony, Philips, Samsung, Matsushita/Panasonic, and Intertrust, a DRM vendor jointly owned by Sony and Philips. The Marlin initiative will be covered in the section about standardization efforts.

DRM Vendors

In the past five years, there has been considerable consolidation among DRM companies. Today, patents on DRM technology are held by a handful of companies, as shown in Table 7.4.

VENDOR	DRM PATENTS
Sony, Philips	Co-owner of Intertrust
Macrovision	DVD and Video Cassette protection
Microsoft, Time Warner, Thompson (ContentGuard)	End to end DRM system
RSA	Encryption
Digeo	DRM for cable industry
Pat-Rights Ltd.	Internet user identity, secure mobile transactions
Matsushita (Panasonic)	Digital content protection system, including key management, storage, authentication, and encryption

TABLE 7.4 *Key Patent Holding Companies*

For the past decade, many DRM vendors have one objective: to stay afloat as going concerns. Gord Larose, an expert who maintains the DRM-related website, www.info-mech.com, has compiled a list of now-defunct companies that have died or been acquired – the DRM graveyard, as shown in Table 7.5.[6]

6. Found at: http://www.info-mech.com/drm_vendor_graveyard.html

COMPANY/PRODUCT	CONTENT TYPES	REMARKS
Beeble	Various PC	BIOS based DRM; resurfaced as Ancoratech
Cinea	Movies	Acquired by Dolby Laboratories
Cryptolopes	Software	From IBM, killed in beta
Digital Owl	Documents	Dead.
Secure Digital Container	Java	Java-based DRM for mobility
eLicense	Software	Merged with ViaTech
Elisar	Web Pictures	Died Dec 2003
Greenleaf	Software, media	
Hyperlock	Software	aka BroadBridgeMedia
Infraworks	Windows Files	Died Spring 2003
Liquid Audio	Music	Acquired Philips
MediaShell	Software	Born at Queen's U in Kingston, Ontario
Modern Software	Software	
NetActive	Software, Video	1997-2002
NetQuartz	Software	1997-2003
Powerlock	CDROM Software	From now-also-defunct American Disc Corporation
Preview	Software	Some assets acquired byAladdin
Rainbow	Software, VPN	Merged with SafeNet
reciprocal	Various	Uses Windows Rights Management Services for its enterprise product, Certified Delivery.

TABLE 7.5 *The DRM Graveyard*

COMPANY/PRODUCT	CONTENT TYPES	REMARKS
Softlock	Software	
SoftWrapper	Software	
Sospita	Software, Web pages	Euro based, died sometime in 2004
Techwave	Software	
TestDrive	Software	Source of famous "quake crack" in 1990s
TTR	Software, audio	Bought by Macrovision fall 2002

TABLE 7.5 *(Continued)*

DRM Standards Bodies

There are two types of standards, de jure and de facto. De jure standards are spec-ifications that have been reviewed, approved, and promulgated by official stan-dards bodies, including the International Standards Organization, and regional standards-setting groups around the globe. Typically imported products must meet the standards set by countries that are signatories to de jure standards agreements.

In the United States, some standards are set through the government, via the National Institutes of Standards and Technology (NIST) under the Department of Commerce. In the arena of television-related matters, the Federal Communications Commission is a key player. Other standards are approved by private entities, such as the American National Standards Institute, a private national coordinating board that often acts as a third-party certifier. Professional groups may also set standards that later become promulgated by official bodies. Such groups include the Institute of Electrical and Electronics Engineering (IEEE), the Internet Engineering Task Force (IETF), the Video Electronics Standards Association (VESA), the Electronic Industry Association (EIA), and the Society of Motion Picture and Television Engineers (SMPTE).

De facto standards are set in the marketplace. Usually the market's first mover is able to achieve market dominance and creates a standard that companies following after must meet. Microsoft Windows is a good example. Software makers that hope to market their wares to the large numbers of Windows users must pay Microsoft for access to the software code that lets users install software under that operating system.

One wag commented about today's standard-setting process: "The best thing about standards is that there are so many of them." For the people who pioneered television standards after World War II, today's melee is something of a disgrace. In the 1950's there was still something of a public spirit that motivated large groups of disparate forces to get together and come to an agreement that would benefit the common good. People who work on standards committees are expected to advance their company's agenda, to establish the company's turf as part of the standard, and to forego discussion of a more general good, unless it helps accomplish the first two goals. In short, standards are just another battleground of corporate warfare, but one that has profound effects on revenue.

> Standards themselves have become revenue generators. For example, the compression scheme developed by and named after the Motion Picture Experts Group (MPEG) licenses the standard via its Licensing Authority (MPEG LA). One author wrote:
>
> > MPEG-2 has been a royalty gold mine. Each time a DVD player is sold, the pool receives $2.50 for the MPEG-2 decoder the player contains. Each time a prerecorded DVD disc is sold, the pool pockets 3 to 4 cents. These royalties are split among the patent holders in the pool, and MPEG LA takes a 10 percent cut, according to one person with knowledge of the company's business model. Tom Cruise's agent should have it this good. In 2004, 37 million DVD players were sold in the United States, and 1.5 billion DVDs were sold in North America, according to the Digital Entertainment Group, an industry association. That translates into over $15 million for MPEG LA's coffers. The pool also picks up royalties from other products and services—such as on-demand television or computer DVD drives—that use the MPEG-2 patents.[7]

Commercial Standardization Initiatives

Companies looking to provide or incorporate DRM technologies have formed many alliances and associations, some of them for very limited purposes and others to achieve grand ambitions. Over time, necessity has forced them to move towards the more grand proposals because so many standards have been created. So, for example, the current mission of the Content Protection Technologies Working Group is to review content protection technologies. The 4C entity (IBM,

---

7. Cohen, A. Diving In, IP Law & Business, February, 2005. Available at:
http://www.ipww.com/texts/0205/splash0205.html

Intel, Matsushita, and Toshiba) concentrated on secure storage; the 5C entity (4C, plus Hitachi) focused on secure transport of content between components.

The recently formed alliances must now harmonize the many standards that are involved in an end-to-end DRM system, particularly if the technology must work throughout the entire content life cycle. The new buzz word in the DRM is "interoperability," meaning that, even if it is impossible to settle on a single set of DRM standards, there must be some way to allow communication between them.

At present, there are two competing commercial standards groups, which are coming to a head over the new high-definition, high-capacity DVD players and recorders. The Blu-Ray Disc (BD) and HD-DVD are also competing to become the standard. The Coral Consortium group began in 2004 to define an interoperability framework for content services and consumer electronics devices and would permit multiple DRM schemes to co-exist. Its membership supports the Blu-Ray Disc, including Sony, Philips, Hewlett-Packard, and Matsushita. The Coral DRM is based on Intertrust's NEMO (Networked Environment for Media Orchestration), and the group announced they would make the DRM system open source so that all software and hardware companies could build products based on it. A related group, the Marlin Joint Development Association, will implement Coral software in hardware products, expected to come to market in 2006. The Coral Consortium says their technology will work with existing DRM systems including Apple Fairplay, Sony MagicGate, and Microsoft Media DRM, providing they open their systems.[8]

The Content Reference Forum is the competition. It is based on Microsoft Windows Media DRM. It is not likely to result in open source software, as it would conflict with Microsoft's strategy to establish market dominance in consumer electronics.

DRM standards will ultimately affect everyone who accesses, uses, and experiences digital entertainment and information, that is to say, just about everyone. It is probably unrealistic to expect those involved in setting standards to be more high-minded than people in other walks of life. But performing work where there is such a potential for enormous influence places a burden on standards-setters to be serious, responsible, thoughtful, and fair.

---

8. Schwerin, J. B. *The Other Shoe Drops*, 2005. Available at:
http://www.infotechresearch.com/2005/01/other-shoe-drops.html

Social Stakeholders

DRM affects society as a whole, and it also has impacts on individual components of the social sphere. Like the other stakeholder clusters we have covered earlier in this chapter, society and its institutions are at odds over how DRM should be implemented, even if it should be implemented at all (Table 7,6). Similarly, governments differ on the issues, depending on whether their countries are content producers or consumers.

For the most part, the U.S. government supports DRM. Political actors are concerned about trade and, since content and information products are one of the most important categories of the U.S. balance of payments, the well-being of the content-producing industries matters to political actors and agencies. The policy of the state is enforced by the justice system as a result of the Digital Millennium Copyright Act. The legislation was a successful lobbying effort by the content-producing industries to take copyright violation out of the civil arena and moved it to the criminal arena, invoking the full force of the law enforcement apparatus.

On the other side of the struggle over DRM are educators and the public as a whole. Educators dedicate their lives to the dissemination of information. Nevertheless, there are some interesting conflicts for educators. For example, some of them are content producers and owners themselves, and they often make substantial sacrifices to create information that they sell at less than optimal market value. Often universities share in the revenues generated by the intellectual property created by members of the professoriate, and they have an interest in protecting the income that results from this IP.

The public as a whole, which will bear the brunt of the impact of DRM, is largely unaware of the potential for some DRM implementations to limit their uses of content they have purchased and of threats to their rights, privacy and freedom of expression. College students and other users of P2P services are probably the most knowledgeable about DRM.

STAKEHOLDER	CONCERNS	ROLE IN DEBATE
THE SOCIAL STAKEHOLDERS		
Government and political Actors	Must balance the requirements of international trade, interest groups, supporters, and voters	Decision-makers

TABLE 7.6 *Social Stakeholders*

STAKEHOLDER	CONCERNS	ROLE IN DEBATE
THE SOCIAL STAKEHOLDERS		
Legal and law enforcement Communities	Legal community: Represent plaintiffs and defendants Law enforcement community: The DMCA brings consumer/ infringers under the purview of law enforcement. They will continue to enforce copyright law against professional pirates	Litigators and enforcers
Education Community	Heavy users of copyrighted material Producers and owners of content Vulnerable to lawsuits.	Participate through research, papers, conferences, and professional organizations and associations
Public at large and society as a whole	Don't want to lose traditional rights Fear infringement of free expression Fear stifling of innovation in content creation, i.e., Shakespeare's work was derivative Limits on information threaten the free flow of information Access to information is a prerequisite for an informed voting public Large-scale copyright infringement creates social norms of winking at law-breaking	May simply ignore copyright laws — as many people do now. May refuse to buy products with DRM implementations they find odious Represented in debate by consumer and civil rights groups

TABLE 7.6 *(Continued)*

Government and Political Actors

Political decision-makers are called upon to balance the many interests that have a stake in DRM. To the extent that DRM protects the revenues of content, a key economic sector, the government is likely to support DRM initiatives. However, it is also important to note that if DRM technologies were to adversely affect the bottom line so significantly as to have an impact on the balance of trade, legislators might well take action to set standards for DRM. Content owners and technology companies have long opposed such governmental action.

In the wake of the DMCA, another branch of government, the courts, have set limits on some of its provisions that were not welcome to content owners. For example, Verizon successfully fought against identifying one of the telephone company's subscribers who was believed to have violated copyright laws and releasing her name to the Recording Industry Association of America (RIAA) who intended to serve her with a subpoena. Verizon argued that the DMCA provision did not apply to files residing on a subscriber's computer, only to those files on its own servers. After a series of ruling s and appeals, the D.C. Circuit Court agreed with Verizon and the subpoena was quashed.[9]

Legal and Law Enforcement Communities

Litigation over copyright may prove to be a lucrative legal specialty, rather than the obscure area it has always been. The DMCA forces everyone to seek legal advice: is a given use of material allowed or forbidden? Is it fair use or not? What are the circumstances under which it may be used? In that sense, perhaps DRM will be helpful in pre-defining uses and cases. In any case, the lawyers are already lined up on either and both sides of all the copyright and DRM issues, and the legion is more likely to set up shop than disappear.

At the same time, the law enforcement community is re-aligning to defend the nation's balance of trade against those who would tilt it against media and entertainment companies through camming, counterfeiting, downloading, and emailing. The DMCA brings consumer/ infringers under the purview of law enforcement and they say they will rise to the occasion to bring both professional pirates and overly generous adolescence to copyright justice.

Local law enforcement is most often involved in arresting street vendors who sell DVDs in highly visible locations. Studios prompt the occasional sweep, but for

---

9. Electronic Frontier Foundation. *R.I.A.A. v. Verizon Case Archive.* Available at http://www.eff.org/legal/cases/RIAA_v_Verizon/

the most part, vendors sell their wares in relative freedom. The effort to arrest large-scale counterfeiters and casual users falls to the Federal Bureau of Investigation, under the U.S. Justice Department.

"It is a high priority now for the FBI," said Frank Harrill of the FBI in a 2004 telephonic interview. "It is a large component of FBI's crime enforcement agenda...cybercrime is the number three priority...counterterrorism, counterintelligence, and cybercrime. We have an entire US attorney's section dedicated to enforcement with a specially trained cyber and intellectual property office within the US Attorney's departments.

Each case is situation specific, studio. A case may involve everything from undercover operations to interviews. The work may be sophisticated or just take old fashioned shoe leather. The facts of the case determine what we do. We try to identify groups and organizations that engaged in a...dismantle these orgs and do so in a way that is best utilization of our resources.

"We see the broad gamut, folks for whom it is their first brush and professional camcorders. And we build a case," explained Harrill.

The federal law enforcement agency has arrested studio and post-production employees. They also go after camcorders, who typically record films within the first few days of its release by bribing theater employees. The quality of cammed copies has improved with digital video and audio, via 3-CCD cameras and hearing-assisted in-theater devices to help the hearing-impaired.

The FBI does not have access to all of the studio's security keys. "The studios analyze the keys and they can often take it to a particular reel and theater that was the source of compromise. That security is becoming more and more common with placement of unique identifiers and watermarks embedded in every theatrical release. It enhances the ability of law enforcement to move in on a particular suspect," said Harrill.

The Educational Community

Educators are heavy users of copyrighted material, providing reading lists and sometimes article collections to their students. Their work is public and their institutions large, so they are vulnerable to lawsuits. Interestingly, they are also producers and owners of content that they create through their research papers, reports, and books. Educators participate in the debate over DRM through their own writings, professional organizations and associations, and through conferences designed to examine copyright issues.

Educational uses of content are allowed under the provisions of fair use of the U.S. Constitution, as interpreted by the Copyright Act of 1976:

Sec. 107. Limitations on exclusive rights: Fair use
Notwithstanding the provisions of sections 106 and 106A, the fair use of a copyrighted work, including such use by reproduction in copies or phonorecords or by any other means specified by that section, for purposes such as criticism, comment, news reporting, teaching (including multiple copies for classroom use), scholarship, or research, is not an infringement of copyright. In determining whether the use made of a work in any particular case is a fair use the factors to be considered shall include -

1. the purpose and character of the use, including whether such use is of a commercial nature or is for nonprofit educational purposes;

2. the nature of the copyrighted work;

3. the amount and substantiality of the portion used in relation to the copyrighted work as a whole; and

4. the effect of the use upon the potential market for or value of the copyrighted work. The fact that a work is unpublished shall not itself bar a finding of fair use if such finding is made upon consideration of all the above factors.

Violation of copyright is of such concern to educators that there have been several efforts to codify the appropriate conditions under which they may invoke fair use. Two such guidelines are the 1978 CONTU Guidelines on Photocopying Under Interlibrary Loan Arrangements and the Agreement on Guidelines for Classroom Copying in Not-for-profit Educational Institutions with Respect to Books and Periodicals, called the "Classroom Guidelines."[10]

There are objections to the Classroom Guidelines, the most important of which is that the standards they uphold are not well-related to the statute. More recent efforts to implement the statute itself have been undertaken by the Copyright Management Center shared by Indiana and Purdue Universities. The Fair Use checklist is shown in Figure 7.2.[11]

10. Lee, Daniel. *Fair Use and Guidelines.* Available at:
http://www.ala.org/Template.cfm?Section=copyrightarticle&Template=/ContentManagement/ContentDisplay.cfm&ContentID=26700

11. Indiana and Purdue Universities. *The Fair Use Checklist.* Available at: http://www.copyright.iupui.edu/checklist.pdf

CHECKLIST FOR FAIR USE

Please complete and retain a copy of this form in connection with each possible "fair use" of a copyrighted work for your project

Name:_____   Date:_____   Project:_____

Institution:_____   Prepared by:_____

PURPOSE

Favoring Fair Use	*Opposing Fair Use*
❑ Teaching (including multiple copies for classroom use)	❑ Commercial activity
❑ Research	❑ Profiting from the use
❑ Scholarship	❑ Entertainment
❑ Nonprofit Educational Institution	❑ Bad-faith behavior
❑ Criticism	❑ Denying credit to original author
❑ Comment	
❑ News reporting	
❑ Transformative or Productive use (changes the work for new utility)	
❑ Restricted access (to students or other appropriate group)	
❑ Parody	

NATURE

Favoring Fair Use	*Opposing Fair Use*
❑ Published work	❑ Unpublished work
❑ Factual or nonfiction based	❑ Highly creative work (art, music, novels, films, plays)
❑ Important to favored educational objectives	❑ Fiction

AMOUNT

Favoring Fair Use	*Opposing Fair Use*
❑ Small quantity	❑ Large portion or whole work used
❑ Portion used is not central or significant to entire work	❑ Portion used is central to work or "heart of the work"
❑ Amount is appropriate for favored educational purpose	

EFFECT

Favoring Fair Use	*Opposing Fair Use*
❑ User owns lawfully acquired or purchased copy of original work	❑ Could replace sale of copyrighted work
❑ One or few copies made	❑ Significantly impairs market or potential market for copyrighted work or derivative
❑ No significant effect on the market or potential market for copyrighted work	❑ Reasonably available licensing mechanism for use of the copyrighted work
❑ No similar product marketed by the copyright holder	❑ Affordable permission available for using work
❑ Lack of licensing mechanism	❑ Numerous copies made
	❑ You made it accessible on Web or in other public forum
	❑ Repeated or long-term use

This document is provided as a courtesy of the Copyright Management Center, IUPUI, 530 W. New York St., Indianapolis, IN 46202. For further information and updates please visit http://www.copyright.iupui.edu/. This document last updated March 10, 2003.

FIGURE 7.2 *The Fair Use Checklist*

An educator who seeks permission to use content may be in a difficult position, as it is easier to speak of obtaining permissions to use content than it is to actually get them. In fact, it may be difficult or impossible to locate the owners of copyrights of documents, diaries, letters, songs, photographs, and other potentially copyrighted works. When the owner is located, the fees to use the material may be exorbitant, far exceeding the ability of an educational author to pay for them, as required by most educational publishers. In one case, an art historian was denied permission to use a photograph of Picasso because the copyright holder did not agree with the author's analysis of the artist.[12]

The TEACH Act (Technology, Education and Copyright Harmonization Act of November 2, 2002) covers how copyrighted material can be used in e-learning environments, particularly where such material may be shared across networks.[13] The legislation establishes the following criteria and requirements for such use:

1. The use must be by an accredited nonprofit institution.

2. The institution must have policies regarding copyright.

3. The institute must provide information about U.S. copyright laws.

4. There must be a notice to students that course materials may be copyrighted.

5. The material must be made available only to officially enrolled students in the course for which the transmission is provided.

The Public at Large and Society as a Whole

It is difficult to characterize "the public" because copyright and DRM is a very low priority for many people who are engaged in their families, jobs, and social lives. For the most part, the public is represented in the debate by consumer and civil rights groups. However, actions speak louder than words or vague ethical pronouncements. A recent national survey conducted by the Pew Internet and American Life Project acted 1,421 adult U.S. Internet users between January 13 and February 9, 2005 about their downloading habits. The margin of error is plus or minus 3 percent for when extrapolated to all U.S. Internet users, however, the findings suggest that people want access to content that is part of popular culture:[14]

•   Nineteen percent of current music and video downloaders (about 7 million

---

12. Heins, Marjorie. *Why Copyright today threatens intellectual freedom.* December 27, 2002

13. *American Library Association. Distance Education and the TEACH Act.* Available at: http://www.ala.org/Template.cfm?Section=distanceed&Template=/ContentManagement/ContentDisplay.cfm&ContentID=25939

14. Pew Internet and American Life Project. *Music and Video Downloading Moves Beyond P2P*, 3/23/2005. Available at: http://www.pewinternet.org/PPF/r/153/report_display.asp

adults) say they have downloaded files from someone else's iPod or MP3 player.

- About 28 percent (10 million people), say they get music and video files via email and instant messages (IM).

- Nine percent have received music from another's player and email or IM.

- Forty-nine percent of all Americans and 53 percent of Internet users believe P2P operators should be deemed responsible for the pirating of music and movie files

- Eighteen percent of Americans think individual file traders should be held responsible

- Twelve percent think both companies and individuals should bear responsibility.

- Thirty-eight percent believe that government efforts would reduce file-sharing and 42 percent believe that government enforcement will not be effective. Broadband users are even more doubtful – 57 percent don't think the government can stop illegal file-sharing.

- The percentage of music downloaders who have tried paid services has grown from 24% in 2004 to 43% in our most recent survey.

- The percentage of Internet users who say they download music files has increased from 18 percent (measured in a February 2004 survey) to 22 percent in our latest survey from January 2005. Still, this number continues to rest well-below the peak level of 32 percent registered in October 2002.

- About 36 million Americans (27 percent of Internet users) download music or video files.

- About half of all Internet users have downloaded outside of traditional P2P or paid online services.

It seems clear that many people simply ignore copyright laws, and are likely to do so in the future. However wrongly, they believe that if they are able to download content, they are entitled to do so. The major consequence of a severe copyright environment is that it makes large numbers of people criminals.

Society as a whole faces important choices as the future unfolds. How important are the infringements on free expression? How desirable is creative innovation, based on existing works? How important is the free flow of information? How crucial is access to information in the fostering of an informed voting public? How critical is protecting the content-producing industries in a competitive global environment?

The answers to all these questions involve making value decisions about the kind of society people want to live in. The framers of the Constitution recognized that there was a delicate balance between the rights of the public, creators, and society as a whole. Consumer advocates believe that current copyright laws and some implementations of DRM have pushed the balance too much on the side of copyright owners, while owners believe thy need strict legislation and enforcement if they are to survive to produce more creative works and bring them to market.

8 Living with DRM

A Tale of Two DRMs

Apple iTunes

The Apple iTunes Music Store as the first successful online music service. It served notice that it was possible to establish a popular online store that would begin to draw people away from P2P file sharing.

The philosophy of the iTunes Music store can be summarized as: Don't annoy customers any more than necessary. Make it very easy to take desired, legal actions and difficult to take the illegal or undesired actions.

Provide a service that lets consumers find, sample, purchase, and download songs from as large a library as possible. Let people download individual songs

Sony Root Kit

No one knew until Mark Russinovich posted a blog, describing a surprising discovery on his own computer: a root kit.[3]

> *Last week when I was testing the latest version of RootkitRevealer (RKR) I ran a scan on one of my systems and was shocked to see evidence of a root kit. Root kits are cloaking technologies that hide files, Registry keys, and other system objects from diagnostic and security software, and they are usually employed by malware attempting to keep their implementation hidden*

as well as whole albums. Keep prices reasonable. Do not charge subscription fees.

The iTunes store conferred generous usage rights. It allowed burning songs to first generation CDs an unlimited number of times, copying to an unlimited number of iPods, and playing the songs on up to three PCs.

Initially, users penetrated the protocol that iTunes used to allow sharing across three PCs and figured out how to stream the files to the Internet. Apple quickly closed that loophole.

As the number of catalogs has increased on the service, iTunes' rights polices have become increasingly restrictive. In version 4.5, they limited the number of times a playlist could be burned from 10 to 7 times. In version 4.6, the company removed compatibility with Hymn 0.6.1, to discourage file sharing by creating a trace mechanism back to the sharer. In version 4.7, iTunes removed iPod download functionality. Version 4.71 removed JHymn 0.6.3 compatibility and limited the number of people per day who could access iTunes shared music files.

Not surprisingly, there are new challenges to iTunes DRM. Famed hacker Jon Lech Johanson, who also created DeCSS, released programs called Pymusique and then SharpMusique that strip the DRM from iTunes songs.

On January 11, an article noted that the newest iTunes release included a Mini-Store pane that, when present, sends

After extensive detective work, Russinovich discovered that Sony's root kit was called Extended Copy Protection (XCP) and came from a UK company called First4Internet. He also checked the end-user license agreement (EULA), which had no reference to the Sony's putting CPU-using software on users' computers. But there was worse to come:

> The entire experience was frustrating and irritating. Not only had Sony put software on my system that uses techniques commonly used by malware to mask its presence, the software is poorly written and provides no means for uninstall. Worse, most users that stumble across the cloaked files with a RKR scan will cripple their computer if they attempt the obvious step of deleting the cloaked files. While I believe in the media industry's right to use copy protection mechanisms to prevent illegal copying, I don't think that we've found the right balance of fair use and copy protection, yet. This is a clear case of Sony taking DRM too far.

There was an enormous outcry, covered fully in the mainstream media – not just geek publications. Soon, another computer expert found more hidden software called MediaMax that spied on users.

Microsoft announced that Sony's root kit exposed Windows users to security risks. MS released a security update to identify and remove the software.

back information to Apple about the songs that users play and what songs they have purchased.[1]

A day later, iTunes posted instructions explaining how the data-sending feature could be turned off.

Although this action is a blot on iTunes and users registered considerable disappointment, the service has generally played to rave reviews. Its catalog, ease of use, and perceived and fair prices and usage rights have all garnered iTunes praise.

As of July 18, 2005, users had downloaded 500[2] million songs from iTunes.

Sony initially defended its use of the root kit and lied about how it operated. Sony also lied, saying that it did not spy on users. But 12 days after Russinovich's post, the company announced it would stop using the root kit software and stop shipment of root-kit carrying CDs.

In an embarrassing side note, it appears that Sony violated the copyrights of the original developers of the copy protection software, which had been licensed under a Lesser General Public License.

Consumers and officials in several states filed suit against Sony. In December, the 21 suits were consolidated into a single class action suit. On December 29, the company caved and settled the class action suit. Sony agreed to provide uninstall software, to recall all XCP-enabled CDs and to allow users to returned them to download 3 albums for free or receive $7.50. Users whose computers may have been damaged by the root kit are free to sue Sony.

Final approval of the agreement is expected in May of 2006. In the meantime, many users are calling for a boycott of Sony products.

1. Boing Boing, *iTunes update spies on your listening and sends it to Apple?* Jan 11, 2006. Available at: http://www.boingboing.net/2006/01/11/itunes_update_spies_.html

2. MacCentre. *500 million iTunes downloads.* Jul 18 2006. Available at: http://mac.sillydog.org/archives/000761.php

3. M Russinovich, *Mark's Sysinternals Blog: Sony, Rootkits and Digital Rights Management Gone Too Far*, Oct 31, 2005. Available at: http://www.sysinternals.com/blog/2005/11/more-on-sony-dangerous-decloaking.html

The preceding tale is a cautionary one. Even a highly success service like iTunes, with its history of good relationships with customers can raise their ire by taking a misstep with DRM. Most of the iTunes users who are blogging about the incident blame the labels, but concede that Apple has wronged users by not informing them that the company was keeping data on them.

It reveals that DRM is still quite controversial, even among people who do not know much about it in a formal way. Hell hath no fury like consumers who encounter evidence of what they consider an invasion of their privacy or when they feel they are being treated unfairly.

Trust

David Maher of InterTrust wrote about how companies can achieve a relationship of trust between themselves sand consumers.[4] He says that trust involves who determines policy and who and what are trusted to do what. They must also define policies and rules, which include what the consumer can do with the content, the conditions under which they can do them, and the consequences of doing them. Finally, there must be a mechanism for people to ask what they are entitled to do and the conditions for doing so (such as additional payment).

Not everyone agrees what "trust" means. The Trusted Computer Group (TCG), previously known as the Trusted Computing Platform Alliance (TCPA) before it re-launched, "is incorporated as a not-for-profit industry standards organization focused on developing, defining, and promoting open standards for trusted computing that will benefit users. The organization's structure has been designed to enable broad participation, efficient management, and widespread adoption of the organization's specifications. This includes:

- Membership is open to a wide range of for-profit corporations, non-profit corporations, and other enterprises supportive of TCG's goals, with clearly defined benefits at different levels of membership

- Reasonable and non-discriminatory (RAND) patent licensing policy between Members

- Board, Committee, and Work Group structure with supermajority voting

---

4. D Maher, Chapter 12: *A Trusted Third Party in Digital Rights Management*, Technical, Business, and Legal Dimensions of Protecting Children from Pornography on the Internet: Proceedings of a Workshop. National Academies Press, 2002. Chapter available at: http://books.nap.edu/html/protecting_children/ch12.html

- Marketing programs and a future logo program[5]

Expert computer users have a different view of the TCG. They characterize it as an alliance of Microsoft, Intel, IBM, HP and AMD and other vendors who define trustworthy as secure from the point of view of software vendors and the content industry. But from the perspective of the consumer or user, it makes their devices far less trustworthy, even treacherous.[6]

"In effect, the TCG specification will transfer the ultimate control of your PC from you to whoever wrote the software it happens to be running. (Yes, even more so than at present.)," says Ross Anderson's FAQ on trusted computing. He describes trusted computing (TC) as a computing platform that does not let users change application software. In addition, applications can communicate with one another and with the software authors. It would allow applications vendors to scan personal computers, to delete unlicensed software remotely, to prevent trusted applications from using data from unlicensed applications or to make them unreadable, and to enforce the registration of software and other content.

Consumer organizations agree that one aspect of trust is letting people know about any DRM attached to a piece of content. This action is often referred to as "transparency." There is general agreement that the notices consumers should receive include:

- Are copy protection and DRM systems are used?

- What contractual usage conditions does the DRM enforce;

- What are the effects? (Can the consumer copy, forward, preview the content?) What are the risks of taking any of these actions?

- Are personal data transmitted and/or kept?

- Who is responsible for the copy protection and DRM? How does the user contact that party?[7]

All this information must be conveyed in some way to consumers and must be stated in a straightforward and easy to understand manner. In addition, Maher notes that in order for there to be a relationship of trust between media purveyors

---

5. Information taken from organization's website:
https://www.trustedcomputinggroup.org/about/

6. R Anderson, *'Trusted Computing' Frequently Asked Questions, Ver. 1.1*, Aug 2003. Available at: http://www.cl.cam.ac.uk/~rja14/tcpa-faq.html

7. N Helberger, *State-of-the-art report*. Dec 2004; http://www.indicare.org/soareport

and consumers, customers must agree to the terms, conditions, and business rules that are enforced by DRM. Therefore, a company that puts DRM on content has to do it in a fair and accurate manner.

Consider the case of the Coldplay CD, X&Y, released by Capitol Records with Macrovision DRM. The outside of the CD tells consumers that the disc is copy-protected, but buyers do not know what kind of DRM it has until after they have opened the package.[8] Further, a notice to consumers informs them that they cannot return the disc because of the DRM; they can only return it for material defects.

The DRM on the Coldplay is draconian. A partial list of restrictions includes:

- Does not play in some CD players, CD-recordable or rewritable hard drives, DVD players, game consoles (Playstation, Xbox)

- Cannot be copied for play in car CD players

- Cannot be copied to mp3 format

- Cannot be played or copied on Macintosh PCs

Just one day after the terms of the agreement appeared on the Internet, the company agreed to accept returns. In addition, there were reports that users had succeeded in finding a way to defeat the restrictions. One blogger captured the flavor of consumer response:

> *What a stupid rule, I think I'll just revert to recording using a mic just to stick it to them. Haha, I bet you they'll soon say 'You are not allowed to play music on CD players with speakers so no one can record it with a mic, but this is for your enjoyment only!' You could run a cable right into your soundcard for a pretty good recording of it too. I've already seen it on a couple torrent sites. Dumbasses, you can't stop a pirate, everyone knows that! "*

In addition, customers need to know about any audits. Many DRM systems track transaction outcomes and subsequent usage of the DRM'd content. Content providers may need proof of payment and the system may match actual usage against the usage the customer has paid for. In both of these cases, the content owner is tracking consumers and maintaining an audit trail of their activities in a manner that maintains links to their specific identity.

---

8. M Bosworth, *Coldplay Can't Play: Band's New CD Comes with Onerous Limitations,* January 4, 2006. Available at: http://www.consumeraffairs.com/ news04/2006/01/coldplay.html

Privacy

Few topics arouse as much consumer indignation and anger as threats to their privacy. So it is no surprise that tracking and audit trails that identify individuals inevitably bump up against protections of people's privacy. Yet content distributors insist that they cannot manage rights without being able to track content usage. Content providers must identify what they are doing to customers and give them a way to opt-out, even if it means losing the sale. Failure to provide reasonable notification will result in strong pushback from consumers and, ultimately, is likely to result in unwanted legislating, mandating such notice.

One idea for protecting privacy is to simply request permission as a condition of purchasing a license. A suggestion for designing DRM systems that do not reveal personal identity is to separate individual identity from hardware and account identity. This separation could occur at the license clearinghouse so that usage information would identify the devices used to play the content or the number of the account.[9]

Customer Care

In addition to being careful about informing consumers about precisely what they are paying for, entertainment and media companies may need to establish customer care units. Satellite operators typically offer good customer service. Cable systems are notorious for providing poor customer care but they have invested heavily in it in the past few years. Some new content providers such as broadband networks and Internet services will offer customer care operations that will handle installation and service problems:

Now that broadband networks and Internet video services are gearing up to distribute television, they are putting together operations that will deal with installation and service problems.

- Vongo, a new Internet movie delivery service from Starz Entertainment Group, will offer Web help and resources, online chat, and around-the-clock telephone-based customer care.

---

9. P Tyrvainen. *Concepts and a Design for Fair Use and Privacy in DRM*, D-Lib Magazine, 11:2, Feb 2005. Available at: http://www.dlib.org/dlib/february05/tyrvainen/02tyrvainen.html

- Sling Media, maker of the Slingbox that puts TV programming on computer screens, has contracted with a call center operator to respond to technical support and installation issues.

- U.S. Digital Television (USDT), a wireless digital pay TV service, will deliver 30 channels in several markets. The company is financed by six U.S. broadcasting companies (including Fox Television Stations) who have invested $25.8 million. USDT created a toll-free number customer-care infrastructure that uses both outsourced and internal agents.

Movie studios, DVD makers and distributors, and record labels have never needed to have elaborate customer care departments. But it is clear that if they are going to distribute media that require a complex license and come with substantial technological infrastructure, they are going to need to offer extensive customer service. Customer care doesn't come cheap.

Accenture consultants R. Wollan and P. Nunes believe that executives have only a vague idea of their customers' revenue potential.[10] Worse, they understand even less about the true costs of serving them. Infrastructure and service costs are increasing faster than company revenues. Although executives understand the scope and complexity of what they need to change, they can't effectively put new strategies in place to drive significant, sustainable benefits.

IBM Business Transformation Outsourcing reports that customer costs are rising but companies should invest in the programs anyway. Customers increasingly expect efficient, high-quality service. Also, there is an unrecognized and unexploited potential increasing revenues by using customer care interactions as opportunities for selling, turning a cost center into a profit center.[11]

DRM State of the Art

What can DRM do? What can't it do? These are questions of a still-evolving technology that can be inferred from the technologies and systems that have been invented and productized.

---

10. R Wollan, P Nunes. *Toward a Customer Meritocracy*. Available at: http: //www.accenture.com/Global/Research_and_Insights/By_Subject/Customer_Relationship_Mgmt/Toward Meritocracy.htm

11. IBM Business Transformation Outsourcing, *Channeling and rechanneling care:The strategic economics of process outsourcing*. Available at: http://pdf2html.spawncamp.net/view.php

Copy protection and DRM systems can:

- Make the initial stripping of copying and rights information (and restrictions) impossible for the average person and difficult for experts

- Utilize digital watermarks and fingerprints to identify content and some metadata

- Incorporate metadata schemes and RELs that manage access to content, based on identity, account, or device, type of device, proximity or communication with other devices, time, geography, network, number of uses, number of copies, payment status, and other variables and conditions

- Disable playback and display devices, in part or in toto.

  Copy protection and DRM systems cannot:

- Prevent copying and file-sharing for any substantial length of time

- Incorporate fair use

- Replicate entirely and exactly the terms of legal contracts

- Make content profitable

- Interoperate with one another

- Work over home networks

- Ensure that artists (or any other participant in the supply chain) get paid the royalties they are entitled to.

Future Directions for DRM

Perhaps some DRM systems in the future will accomplish tasks they cannot now carry out. Indeed, the difficulty of the work has not yet daunted the proponents and developers of DRM systems. Three areas are currently under active development: renewability, interoperability, and operation with home networks.

Renewability

Renewability is a property of a DRM system that lets the DRM system administration entity renew information stored in all parts of the system, particularly the user device. It is useful for both content providers and consumers.

For providers, renewability means that they can make new marketing offers and content enters new parts of its lifecycle. When it is combined with tamper-resistant technologies, it allows the provider to prevent the device from playing the content as a remote action. For consumers, it means that they can receive new offers and that their provider can reset their system if the DRM part of it fails to function properly.

Interoperability

Interoperability between DRM systems is also a major issue. Interoperability means that one system can receive, read, interpret, and act on the copy protection and rights management information that comes from the system of another vendor.

There is mixed support for interoperability. Vendors have little interest in it because each one of them hopes to gain "gorilla" status, dominating the DRM market. Proprietary standards preserve competitive advantage (and disadvantage) in the vendor field.

However, content owners will probably not buy any end-to-end DRM system until such interoperability is assured. They do not want to have to buy into multiple systems. And they are afraid that if consumers are unable to traverse the DRM landscape easily, they will reject DRM'd products and systems.

There are signs of consumer unrest. iTunes AAC format won't play on many portable mp3 players. Windows WMA format won't play on iPods or some portable mp3 players. Customers become easily frustrated with such challenges to portability. Moreover, proprietary formats and DRM standards may tie them to a particular content provider that is unlikely to have all the content they seek.

There is always some possibility that consumer dissatisfaction will precipitate legislation, particularly in Europe. Laws could take the form of regulating standards, functions, or consumer notifications. No one, except consumers, wants to see regulation, so vendors would do well to implement measures that do not overly agitate customers: using reasonable copy protection and DRM schemes and reaching the necessary agreements to make DRM systems interoperable. However, no one is predicting that such cooperation will occur.

Industry Interoperability Initiatives: Coral and Marlin

There have been two industry initiatives to establish interoperability between DRM systems, the Coral Consortium and Marlin. InterTrust has played a major role in both efforts. InterTrust proposed use of its Networked Environment for Media

Orchestration (NEMO) technology to the Coral consortium. After that group disbanded, it was succeeded by Marlin. Again, InterTrust wants it to incorporate NEMO and another technology, Octopus, a kit for building DRM engines.

Coral Consortium

The Coral Consortium was the first major alliance of companies to address the problem of interoperability between DRM systems. The founding companies included computer makers, consumer electronics manufacturers, content providers and one DRM vendor: Hewlett-Packard, Matsushita Electric Industrial, Philips Electronics, Samsung Electronics, Sony and Twentieth Century Fox, and InterTrust Technologies.[12] By June of 2005, there were 30 member companies when Comcast joined the group. However, key players Apple. Microsoft, and Nokia never joined because they each had their own plan to dominate the DRM'd content space.

Coral proposed to address interoperability between different content formats, devices, and distribution services. Its aim was to create the conditions for a uniform consumer experience, while meeting the DRM requirements of content owners and distributors. The group planned to publish specifications for interfaces and core services that would promote interoperability.

Since NEMO is also likely to be a part of the successor organization, Marlin, it is important to understand what it does. NEMO securely links servers and other information processors to communicate dynamically in what it defines as an interoperability layer. A translation language enables the communication so that one DRM system does not need to "know" the inner workings of any other system with which it was exchanging information. (Previously, designs for interoperability called for universal standards or a two-way interconnection of DRM systems through agreements between individual companies.)

The Coral Consortium now has about 40 members. It plans to release a final specification in June of 2006. Following the release of specs, the group will establish compliance tests for DRM systems.[13]

---

12. J Borland. *Tech powers seek antipiracy accord.* CNET News, Oct 3, 2004. Available at: Staff Writer, CNET News.com. Available at:
http://news.com/Tech+powers+seek+antipiracy+accord/2100-1025_3-5394347.html

13. S Chin, R Merritt. *CES preview: Getting the boxes to interplay.* EETimes. Jan 2, 2006. Available at:
http://www.eetimes.com/news/latest/consumer/showArticle.jhtml?articleID=175800122

Marlin

In early 2005, the same companies that were members of the Coral Coalition formed the Marlin Joint Development Association, or Marlin JDA to work on an alternative approach to Coral. The consortium added an interoperability to translate between multiple systems. By contrast, Marlin will develop a common core of building blocks that designers can put together to create a customized overall system that relies on common elements. If content providers DRM their products in a compatible way, it will allow consumer electronics manufacturers to use a single toolkit for recognizing, reading, and acting on copy protection and rights management information.

Marlin will be XML-based. The idea is that while translation of other systems rights expressions is possible, common components are more efficient. Marlin products, which will come to market in 2006, will be aware of Coral software, so they will interoperate with the Coral framework.

Marlin is a community source project, meaning that each of the members of Marlin will contribute technology to it.[14] The Marlin JDA plans to establish a licensing authority and offer specifications on a reasonable and non-discriminatory basis. It will operate a compliance program to will also ensure that devices and media meet Marlin specifications.

InterTrust is contributing NEMO (Networked Environment for Media Orchestration), a reference technology for DRM services that was the basis of Coral. It is also bringing Octopus to the table – a ready-to-assemble toolkit for building DRM engines. It is an open specification that lets adopters choose among basic building blocks for protecting content, expressing usage rules, and tying protection and rights management to their content. They also select the cryptography, operating system, software vendor, implementation, and business model that they want to use in their DRM system. Octopus can be used by providers of all sizes; it scales from small technologies like smart cards to large content providing enterprises.

Marlin JDA authenticates users rather than devices, so that people can experience their content using any device by any manufacturer. There are two difficulties to this approach. The definition of ownership is an issue: What happens when a person sells or loans a device to another? Another problem is privacy. As noted in an earlier section, it is difficult to establish user identity without maintaining records that tie users to their purchases, usage of content, and perhaps other data, the totality of which may raise concerns about threats to personal privacy.

---

14. B Rosenblatt. *InterTrust and CE Makers Collaborate on Interoperable DRM Development.* DRM Watch, Jan 20, 2005. Available at: drmwatch.com/standards/article.php/3461921

To deal with privacy issues, Marlin will use Liberty Alliance's concept of a "federated identity." It is an identity infrastructure where no single entity owns or controls all of the information about an individual, so that different pieces are scattered in different databases. In essence, this is a scheme for separating personal identity from usage information and, perhaps, transactional information.

Bill Rosenblatt reports that Marlin is also a competitive response to Microsoft. "Marlin is an attempt to do for portable consumer devices what the Open Mobile Alliance is doing specifically for mobile phones: develop a multi-vendor interoperable standard that will compete with Microsoft and either force it to interoperate or shut it out," he says.[15]

Home Networks

Home networks is another rat's nest of standards – as well as the unsightly cables that adorn nearly everyone's media center and computer desk. There is a confusing maze of open and proprietary standards for telephones, cable and satellite STBs, and power lines, and wireline Ethernet and wireless Wi-Fi, any of which may provide the infrastructure for a home network. None of them are configured automatically, so non-geeks need not apply.

Consider the experience of Russell Beattie:

First is iTunes. I use my computer to buy a new song or rip it from CD. I can then send it to my living room using the Airport Express, or I can sync it to my iPod via a cable. Great. Can I record a song from radio automatically? Nope. Can I view an iTunes video on my TV? Not without syncing it to the iPod, carrying it to the television and plugging in the extra RCA cables. Can I get new music on my iPod without using a computer? Nope, you need to run the iTunes software to manage your music.

Next is TiVo. I can record programs from my TV to watch later. I can use TiVo To Go to transfer those videos to watch on my PC. I will be able in the near future to transfer those videos to my iPod or my PSP. Great. Can I watch streaming media on my TiVo? No. Can I buy new movies on my TiVo? No. Can I watch movies - either home movies or purchased - that are on my PC on my TiVo? No. Can I stream Tivo recordings over the Internet to my phone or laptop? No. Tivo is basically a one way street right now, except for audio podcasts and Rocketboom, with no commercial video at all, and no streaming.

15. Ibid.

Next is the Media Center PC. I have one under my desk right now. Can I manage video? Yeah. Can I buy movies, yeah. Can I watch it from my Living Room, yeah - with my XBox 360 as a Media Extender (a very, very, very LOUD Media Extender). But can I view my iTunes video from living room? No. Can I record programs like my TiVo: NO. Now wait a second, isn't that what Media Centers are supposed to do? Sure - but I don't have a cable card, and even if I did, I have Comcast digital cable, so it wouldn't work, and even if I had analog cable, the wire comes in on the opposite side of the house from where my computer is. So No, my Media Center PC doesn't record live video. My TiVo doesn't need a cable card - it just passes the video through it using coax or RCA cables - why does the Media Center need a dedicated cable port? I have no idea, but it does. I saw a bunch of CES announcements about "Cable Card" compatible Media Centers, but is Comcast and other cable companies on board with that? What sort of DRM is involved? I don't know, but it doesn't look good.[16]

The Digital Living Network Alliance DLNA has a huge number of member companies that includes most prominent computer makers, software companies, consumer electronics manufacturers, and content producers. The goal of the DLNA is to promote a seamless home network where all devices and applications will interoperate. The group will deliver design guideline and component technologies, a certification program to ensure compliance, and a logo program to announce compliance to consumers.

The first set of guidelines, the *DLNA Home Networked Device Interoperability Guidelines v1.0* "focus mainly on interoperability among networked CE devices and home PCs for media applications involving imaging, audio and video."[17] The DLNA approach calls for a several building blocks that include:[18]

• Transparent connectivity between devices inside the home, with networking at the link layer, with layer 2 bridging and layer 3 routing

• Framework for device discovery, configuration, and control

• Interoperable media formats and streaming protocols

---

16. R Beattie. *Home Media Thoughts*. Blog posted on Jan 12, 206. Available at: http://www.russellbeattie.com/notebook/1008747.html

17. Quoted from DLNA FAQ. Available at: http://www.dlna.org/about/faq/

18. DLNA White Paper, *Overview and Vision*. DLNA, Jun 2004. Available at: http://www.dlna.org/about/DLNA_Overview.pdf

- Framework for interoperable media management and control: Allows users to organize, browse, search, and select media items

- Compatible quality of service mechanisms

- Compatible authentication and authorization mechanisms for users and devices

DLNA will use Internet Protocol standards for networking. Device and service discovery and control will occur through the Universal Plug and Play (UPnP) Device Control Protocol Framework (DCP Framework), Version 1. This protocol defines devices as media servers and media renderers and the services they provide: directories of content, content transfer protocols, transport services, and rendering control (brightness, volume, etc.)

DLNA uses proximity as the mechanism for determining which devices to include in the home network. Sometimes the home network, in its totality, is referred to as a "domain." There are some critiques of proximity-based domains, in that they do not necessarily reflect the realities of modern life, such as vacation homes, vehicles, and multi-home households. Imagine not being able to play the latest Harry Potter movie when a child of divorce goes from the home of one parent to the home of the other on the weekend! This can be the stuff of a major meltdown. A few designs address this weakness by using Internet-based connectivity for device licensing to provision multi-location user domains.

Business Life with DRM

Consumers have to live with DRM , so do content providers and all the other participants in the content supply and value chain. The responsibility for choosing a DRM system usually falls on the content owner, license holder, or distributor. How do they decide which DRM they should have?

Answering that question depends on why DRM is being used at all. If the company is looking for DRM to manage and control internal documents, files, and communications, the choice will differ from that of a content owner who wants to distribute a video over the Internet to paying customers. A major studio will need a different solution than a small production company or a single video producer. A music label with dozens of artists has more complex requirements than a garage band.

The characteristic they all have in control is the fear of loss of control over their digital IP.

Whether it is company secrets, a new song, or an exciting documentary about extreme sports, losing control of owned material can result in lost revenue, opportunities, even reputation. And in the networked world, digits are released into the wild and may never be domesticated again.

DRM offers the promise of establishing control. Perhaps it will never bring back the lost digits, but it holds out the hope of preventing further losses.

Within and between enterprises, digital rights management (DRM) can provide the means to control and track the distribution and post-receipt activity of sensitive documents and media. And in some cases, it probably can.

Consultant Joshua Duhl proposes several categories that companies consider when they are evaluating DRM systems:[19]

- **Operational control:** The extent to which the organization needs or wants to have control over the system will point to in-house or outsourced DRM. Further investigation will reveal the cost, time, and resources required by each choice.

- **Strength of the DRM system:** The kind of encryption, key management, authentication and authorization handling, renewability, tamper-resistance, scalability, and architecture – all these together determine the overall strength of the DRM system.

- **Flexibility:** The ability of the DRM to protect content and manage rights across across platforms, media types, and formats – from large-screen TVs to mobile phones, and all the devices in between, and from digital cinema to DVDs. This kind of extensibility implies that the DRM works with different applications, operating systems, codecs, and business models.

- **Compatibility:** DRM functions within a media ecosystem of servers, portals, databases, content libraries, back office systems, authorization and directory systems, communications systems, and transactional and financial systems. DRM must be compatible across a variety of delivery networks, and comply with multiple standards. It must also integrate with the organization's existing infrastructure, so integration costs must be considered.

- **Business criteria:** Choosing a DRM system requires a close examination of the vendor to determine the level of trust the adopter is willing to delegate. In addition, the traditional bottom-line criteria apply, such as initial cost,

---

19. J Duhl. *Evaluating DRM*, Jul 2003. Available at:
http://www.kmworld.com/Articles/ReadArticle.aspx?ArticleID=9488

implementation costs, and maintenance costs. And a thorough ROI analysis is in order. Perhaps the most important question is: How much is the company willing to spend to achieve a given level of content protection? Set the level...determine its cost.

- **Impact on the user:** Many of the issues raised in this chapter come into play. Such concerns as transparency, ease of use, convenience, portability, enforcement mechanisms and procedures, and means of distribution and renewability.

Business Life without DRM

Critics of DRM point to important failings of such systems. They do not deliver lower prices, in spite of the fact that electronic deliver lowers distribution costs substantially. Moreover, while the ability of DRM systems to implement flexible business models exists, it is far from realized. In actuality, DRM is used to distribute content that is far less useful to consumers, permits fewer uses with less flexibility, and often costs more than non-protected content. Moreover, some implementations of DRM deprive consumers of exercising their rights, such as fair use and the right to make personal copies.

The greatest promise of DRM to content owners has not come true either. Any song, any popular motion picture, any image, all can be found on the Internet or on the street corner, for sale by counterfeiters. So far, the evidence shows that DRM has failed in every instance. Mark Cuban, the ultimate hyphenate, media entrepreneur-motion picture producer-Mavericks owner, was asked at an iHollywood Forum event: "What you see as the trend in DRM? What do you see as the way to go?" Answered Cuban: "For me, none. No DRM."

Moderator: Don't you worry about your content?

Cuban: I own millions of dollars in content, so believe me, I have a greater interest than anybody in making money from it. Now, if I license content, I work with producers and respect their wishes. But if I originate it, if you buy a copy of *World Report* from us, I say, 'make a copy and give it to a friend.' Now if I see you selling them on eBay, I'll take a needle and stick it in your fingers. The good news is, I can find you on eBay. I can find you if you are duplicating copies and selling them. The equivalent for digital rights management would be for all of us to walk into a store and empty our pockets and put rock-covered gloves on our hands so we can't potentially steal something. For our content, I don't see it as a risk. And for people who license stuff from us, I've made it a requirement that they **not** copy protect it.

Mark Cuban is not alone. A number of people in the media and information industry have found that DRM is unworkable, unprofitable, or just undesirable. For example, a footnote to David Maher's article, cited in an earlier section of this chapter, reported the following comments:

> *Robin Raskin said the cost of the system would exceed the costs of the music or television show that one tried to protect. She gave the example of a publisher dealing with authors' contracts. In looking at DRM, he decided it was cheaper in the short term (the next 2 years) to pay all the authors more money than to implement a rights management system, the costs of which, for a big publishing company, would be astronomical. Herb Lin said representatives of the adult online industry told the committee that they have problems with people copying their content and redistributing it without paying. He said it seemed doubtful that any single provider could afford to implement a DRM system...*

Probably the most well-known critique of DRM is often referred to as "Cory Doctorow's Rant," a speech delivered at the Microsoft Research Group in Redmond, Washington on June 17, 2004.[20] The gist of the rant was:

> *Here's what I'm here to convince you of: 1. That DRM systems don't work 2. That DRM systems are bad for society 3. That DRM systems are bad for business 4. That DRM systems are bad for artists 5. That DRM is a bad business move for Microsoft."*

You can read the full text of the speech on dozens of websites. Check it out. Judge for yourself.

Jim Griffin, former director of the technology group at Geffen says not to worry about DRM and trusted computing efforts because they're already doomed.[21] He believes that some kind of flat-fee, blanket license model will ultimately prevail, when it becomes clear to content owners that the costs of DRM are higher than the potential profits. A blanket license is one like ASCAP and BMI use for radio stations, where stations pay a fee and the amount is divided up among copyright holders, based on airplay. There are a variety of such proposals, but all of them have in common that they propose aggregating money from many users, providing

20. An Internet search will show this talk is available on many sites. I found it at: http://craphound.com/msftdrm.txt

21. A Orlowski, *Flat fee pricing an escape route for RIAA, MPAA.* The Register, Feb 11, 2004. Available at: http://www.theregister.co.uk/2004/02/11/why_wireless_will_end_piracy/

a mechanism for dividing it among copyright owners, and allowing the unrestricted flow of content.

What about the promises made by vendors of DRM to content owners? Answers Griffin: "When I was 14, I told girls I loved them to sleep with them, too. It was a fiction...We see [Steve] Jobs and [Bill] Gates making promises to the content industry that they have no intention of keeping. It's the promise you make to move forward. The content owner wants to hear it. If we're honest we'd say to the content owners, 'we're not going to succeed from what we can tell. The cars we build are more powerful than the brakes we build, and we won't control it. The ways to make it friction-free are more powerful than the friction we build. The audience sees no value in friction. They don't pay for it.' "

Even as renowned an expert on DRM as Bill Rosenblatt has his moments of doubt. At the end of 2005, he wrote: "CD copy protection may well be a problem with no realistic solution that balances consumers' concerns with those of antipiracy; the first step towards that determination is for music companies to put people capable of making sound judgments on this point into positions of power, giving them the time and resources to do proper analyses, and abiding by the outcomes."[22]

22. B Rosenblatt, *2005 Year in Review: DRM Technologies*, DRM Watch, Dec 23, 2005. Available at: http://www.drmwatch.com/drmtech/article.php/3573381

Index